The Story of the Regiments

Frederick Watson

Alpha Editions

This edition published in 2024

ISBN : 9789362990808

Design and Setting By
Alpha Editions
www.alphaedis.com
Email - info@alphaedis.com

As per information held with us this book is in Public Domain.
This book is a reproduction of an important historical work. Alpha Editions uses the best technology to reproduce historical work in the same manner it was first published to preserve its original nature. Any marks or number seen are left intentionally to preserve its true form.

Contents

PREFACE .... - 1 -

CHAPTER I THE FORMATION OF THE
BLACK WATCH .... - 3 -

CHAPTER II FLANDERS AND
FONTENOY (1745) .... - 7 -

CHAPTER III THE BLACK WATCH AT
TICONDEROGA (1758) .... - 13 -

CHAPTER IV WITH WOLFE AND
FRASER'S HIGHLANDERS AT QUEBEC
(1759) .... - 19 -

CHAPTER V RED INDIAN AND
HIGHLANDER (1760-1767) .... - 23 -

CHAPTER VI THE AMERICAN WAR OF
INDEPENDENCE (1775-1782). .... - 29 -

CHAPTER VII WITH THE HIGHLAND
LIGHT INFANTRY TO SERINGAPATAM
(1799) .... - 35 -

CHAPTER VIII HOW THE BLACK
WATCH WON THE RED HACKLE
(1795) .... - 40 -

CHAPTER IX WITH ABERCROMBY IN
EGYPT (1801) .... - 44 -

CHAPTER X THE RETREAT ON CORUNNA (1808-1809) ....- 49 -

CHAPTER XI WITH THE CAMERONS IN THE PENINSULAR (1810-1814) ....- 56 -

CHAPTER XII THE GORDONS AT QUATRE BRAS (June 16, 1815) ....- 64 -

CHAPTER XIII WITH WELLINGTON AT WATERLOO (June 18, 1815) ....- 70 -

CHAPTER XIV THE HIGHLAND BRIGADE AT THE BATTLE OF ALMA (September 20, 1854) ....- 76 -

CHAPTER XV THE 'THIN RED LINE' AT BALACLAVA (October 25, 1854) ....- 81 -

CHAPTER XVI WITH HAVELOCK TO LUCKNOW ....- 85 -

CHAPTER XVII WITH SIR COLIN CAMPBELL AND THE SUTHERLANDS TO LUCKNOW ....- 94 -

CHAPTER XVIII WOLSELEY AND THE BLACK WATCH IN ASHANTI (1873-1874) ....- 106 -

CHAPTER XIX WITH ROBERTS AND THE SEAFORTHS TO AFGHANISTAN (1878-1880) ....- 111 -

CHAPTER XX MAJUBA HILL (1881) ....- 122 -

CHAPTER XXI WITH THE HIGHLAND BRIGADE AT TEL-EL-KEBIR (1882) ....- 127 -

CHAPTER XXII FROM EL-TEB TO
OMDURMAN (1884-1898) ....- 131 -

CHAPTER XXIII CHITRAL AND THE
GORDONS AT DARGAI (1895-1898) ....- 141 -

CHAPTER XXIV FROM THE
BEGINNING OF THE BOER WAR TO
THE BATTLE OF MODDER RIVER
(1899) ....- 145 -

CHAPTER XXV WITH THE HIGHLAND
BRIGADE AT MAGERSFONTEIN
(December 11, 1899) ....- 153 -

CHAPTER XXVI PAARDEBERG AND
LADYSMITH ....- 158 -

CHAPTER XXVII WITH SIR IAN
HAMILTON TO PRETORIA (1900) ....- 165 -

CHAPTER XXVIII THE GREATEST
WAR (1914-) ....- 171 -

PREFACE

It is a perplexing thing when the making of history is often terrible, sometimes tragic, but hardly ever tedious, that the reading of history should be considered uniformly grey. In compiling the present book I shrank from the word 'History'—I altered it to 'Story.' It is the same thing, but it does not sound so depressing.

The Story of the Highland Regiments is not merely a narrative of regimental gallantry—it is also the story of our Empire for nearly two hundred years, the story of strange lands and peoples, of heroism and endurance, of the open sea and the frontier. It is even more than that—it is the story of self-sacrifice, of courage, of patriotism.

Long ago, when my father related to me how, as a little boy, he had watched the Highlanders march into Edinburgh after the Crimean War, I determined to secure a book that would tell me, in simple words, without any dates whatever, about the 'Thin Red Line' at Balaclava, the relief of Lucknow, and the charge of the Greys. It was just because no such book existed that I was encouraged to write a narrative history that would cover, no matter how slightly, the entire period.

Whatever may be the faults of this book there are pictures, and there are not many dates. I have also, where I could, allowed the actual combatants or eye-witnesses to tell their story in their own way, and on occasions I have inserted verses that have either won popularity or deserve to do so.

It is also my hope that, despite the simplicity of treatment, this story of the campaigns in which the Highland regiments took their part, will interest not only young people, but, for the sentiment of all things Scottish, their elders too.

In some chapters minor campaigns may appear to receive an undue attention, and greater wars, such as the Peninsular, to be treated in outline. The reason for this is obvious. This record must follow in the footsteps of the Highland regiments, and the greater the campaign the less accentuated are individual achievements. For this reason, too, I have not attempted to treat the present War in any detail, for no detail is so far to hand, and in the vast forces raised since August 1914 the Highland regiments have passed into armies, and cannot be treated as single battalions. But already one thing calls for no chronicler. Never since those old days when the clans first fought beneath the British flag has the imperishable star of the Highland regiments—whether of the Old Army or the New, Colonial or Territorial—gleamed more steadily throughout the long night of War. In answer to the last and greatest summons of the Fiery Cross, the tramp of marching feet came sounding from the farthest outposts of the Empire.

Of the books that have provided me with much of my working material I must acknowledge as the basis of this volume Browne's History of the Highlands, vol. iv., Cromb's The Highland Brigade, Archibald Forbes' The Black Watch, the various regimental records, and for their respective campaigns—Maclean's Highlanders in America, Napier's War in the Peninsular, Dr. Fitchett's Wellington's Men and The Tale of the Great Mutiny, and Sir Arthur Conan Doyle's The Great Boer War. For the chapter on Afghanistan I have drawn upon Miss Brooke-Hunt's Biography of Lord Roberts, and for the last chapter I have to thank the proprietors of the Scotsman for permission to quote some extracts from their files. I should also like to express my indebtedness to many other writers, whose books I have named where possible in the text.

There are those whose personal assistance has saved me much labour. In particular are my thanks due to my wife, who has collected much material and revised the proof sheets.

FREDERICK WATSON.

September 1915.

CHAPTER I
THE FORMATION OF THE BLACK WATCH

Let the ancient hills of Scotland

Hear once more the battle-song

Swell within their glens and valleys

As the clansmen march along!

The Highland Regiments have always enjoyed a world-wide popularity quite apart from the quality of their achievements. This popularity is due to the appeal of imagination and romance. The spectacle of a Highland regiment, its pipes playing, and the kilts swinging file by file, recalls the old days when the clans rose for the Stuarts. The Highland dress is not only linked for all time with Lucknow, Balaclava, and Quatre Bras, but, stepping farther backward, with Culloden, Killiecrankie, and Glencoe. People unacquainted with uniforms find a difficulty in recognising certain English line regiments whose records are the glory of our military history. But the Highlander, beyond his distinctive regiment, carries in the memories aroused a passport to popular favour.

Fortunately the Highland Regiments have earned by more than glamour the admiration of Britain. In campaigns extending over the last hundred and fifty odd years the Highlanders have borne their share of the fighting, and whenever the call has come have proved themselves 'second to none.'

It was in the eighteenth century that the Jacobites rose for the last time against the King of England, and whatever the rights or wrongs of the rebellion, the loyalty and bravery of the clans will for ever remain undimmed by time. Loyalty may make mistakes, but it is none the less noble for that, and when the '45 was over it was the sons of the men who died for Prince Charlie who were ready to fight for King George.

It is most important to understand, no matter how simply, the broad characteristics of the clan system, an established order of things that, in mid-eighteenth century times, the Government considered most dangerous to the peace of England. Their reason for thinking so is not hard to seek. Instead of a peaceful, pastoral country, the Highlands were an armed camp. In the twentieth century, when strong active men are needed so badly, such an organisation would have been of the greatest value; then it was rightly regarded as a menace both to the Lowlands and to the English throne.

The clan was composed of a large or sometimes comparatively small number of people bearing the same name, and sworn to obey the Chief, whose word was absolute, and whose greatest ambition was the number of swords he could summon to his side.

The Highlander took little interest in tilling or reaping. He left that chiefly to the women. His bearing and instincts were those of a gentleman, while his ruling desire was to engage in fighting. He was proud, indolent, but faithful to the death. The chiefs, who dreaded the loss of their power more than anything else, and were not so blind as to believe that progress could be indefinitely defied, rose for the cause of the Stuarts with the gambler's hope that the old days might remain a little longer.

Every one knows how the clans rallied to the standard of Prince Charlie, of their march into England, and of their defeat by the Duke of Cumberland, who was the Prince's cousin.

The battle of Culloden was to seal the doom of the clan system, and to prepare the way for the history of the Highland Regiments. It was Pitt who 'sought for merit' in the wild mountains of Scotland, and no finer recruiting ground could have been discovered. The Highlander was distinguished for his loyalty, his bravery, and his conservatism. War and hunting were his employment, but underneath his fiery temperament lay a deep vein of self-sacrifice and poetry. That none of those poor people gave up their Prince for gold is wonderful enough. That they never forgot him is more precious than all the treasures in the world.

The love of the Celt for the place of his birth provided one of the most tragic periods in our history. Emigration, ruin, and the end of the clan system inspired some of the most beautiful and moving songs in our language. The point, therefore, that must be emphasised at the moment is the poetic temperament of the Gael, his love of romance, of old tales, of old times, of bravery, of loyalty, and of leading an active life.

It was just through this love of adventure that cattle-raiding continued during the first half of the eighteenth century, and that is why people on the border line paid 'blackmail.' In modern life one of the most valuable resolves to make is never, under any circumstances, to pay blackmail; never, that is, to allow freedom of action or will to pass into the hands of another person. Payment of blackmail once, invariably means payment for always. But in the Highlands there was no such ignominy attached to the word. Blackmail carried with it protection from theft, not shelter from disgrace. It was paid in much the same way as a citizen pays the Government taxes to provide policemen to guard his house. From the year 1725 onwards law-abiding people in the Highlands congratulated themselves, in all good faith, upon the excellent work that certain newly raised companies of

Government militia were doing in keeping the district quiet. These companies were called the 'Black Watch,' partly because of their dark tartan, partly owing to the nature of their duties.

A Highland Chief

Let us see what kind of corps this was. With the hope that some display of authority would quell the simmering spirit of revolt in the Highlands, the Government, at the suggestion of an ardent Hanoverian, decided in the year 1725 to raise a local force officered by Highland gentry. It was an insignificant body at first, but from time to time further companies were added, until in the year 1740 it was embodied under the number of the 43rd, to be changed some years later to the 42nd. In this fashion, and simply as a vigilance corps, the 'Black Watch,' a regiment that has carved its name upon the tablets of history and romance, came to be formed.

It may seem strange that the marauding habits of the clansmen should have come so admirably beneath the discipline of the army. The secret is not far to seek. The qualities that bound the clansmen to the chief were simply transferred to the new regime. No finer, simpler, more powerful tribute to these qualities could be found than in the words of General Stewart of Garth, written a century ago, but not without force at the present time:

"In forming his military character, the Highlander was not more favoured by nature than by the social system under which he lived. Nursed in poverty, he acquired a hardiness which enabled him to sustain severe privations. As the simplicity of his life gave vigour to his body, so it fortified his mind. Possessing a frame and constitution thus hardened, he was taught to consider courage as the most honourable virtue, cowardice the most disgraceful failing; to venerate and obey his chief, and to devote himself for his native country and clan, and thus prepared to be a soldier he was ready wherever honour and duty called him. With such principles, and regarding any disgrace he might bring on his clan and district as the most cruel misfortune, the Highland private soldier had a peculiar motive to exertion. The common soldier of many other countries has scarcely any other stimulus to the performance of his duty than the fear of chastisement, or the habit of mechanical obedience to command, produced by the discipline by which he has been trained.... The German soldier considers himself as part of the military machine, and duly marked out in the orders of the day. He moves onward to his destination with a well-trained pace, and with his phlegmatic indifference to the result as a labourer who works for his daily hire. The courage of the French soldier is supported in the hour of trial by his high notions of the point of honour, but this display of spirit is not always steady: neither French nor German is confident in himself if an enemy gain his flank or rear. A Highland soldier faces his enemy whether in front, rear, or flank, and if he has confidence in his commander it may be predicted with certainty that he will be victorious, or die on the ground which he maintains."[1]

After the '45, when the last dream of the marauders was for ever shattered, the Highlands, possessing such unequalled military qualities of physique and imagination, were to prove a magnificent recruiting ground for the British Army. Not only the Black Watch but many other regiments were raised for the Government, and the military spirit was, by the genius of Pitt, guided into legitimate and honourable warfare.

THE BATTLE HONOURS OF THE BLACK WATCH (ROYAL HIGHLANDERS)

Guadeloupe, 1759; Martinique, 1762; Havannah; North America, 1763-1764; Mysore, Mangalore, Seringapatam, Corunna, Busaco, Fuentes de Oñoro, Pyrenees, Nivelle, Nive, Orthez, Toulouse, Peninsula, Waterloo; South Africa, 1846-1847, 1851-1853; Alma, Sevastopol, Lucknow, Ashanti; Egypt, 1882-1884; Tel-el-Kebir; Nile, 1884-1885; Kirbekan; South Africa, 1899-1902; Paardeberg.

CHAPTER II
FLANDERS AND FONTENOY
(1745)

Hail, gallant regiment! Freiceadan Dubh,

Whenever Albion needs thine aid

'Aye ready!' for whatever foe

Shall dare to meet the black brigade!

Witness disastrous Fontenoy;

When all seemed lost, who brought us through?

Who saved defeat? secured retreat?

And bore the brunt?—The Forty-Two.

Dugald Dhu.

On the head of Frederick (the Great) is all the blood which was shed in a war which raged during many years, and in every quarter of the globe—the blood of the column of Fontenoy, the blood of the brave mountaineers who were slaughtered at Culloden. The evils produced by his wickedness were felt in lands where the name of Prussia was unknown; and in order that he might rob a neighbour whom he had promised to defend, black men fought on the coast of Coromandel, and red men scalped each other by the great lakes of North America.—Macaulay.

Flanders was not altogether unknown in the historic sense to the men of the North, and the 'cockpit of Europe,' as it has been named for its successive tragedies of war, has been fated to become too often the Scottish soldier's grave. Campaign after campaign has raged across its fertile country-side, leaving in its trail desolation and despair.

It is outside the story of the Highland Regiments to discuss the political situation at the time when the Stuart cause was for ever crushed. What must not be overlooked, however, is that the French appeared more interested in the Jacobite Rebellion than could be attributed entirely to friendly feelings towards Prince Charles. No more ominous sign of how the wind really blew could be cited than the way in which Louis XV., King of France, hustled the unhappy young man out of the country in his hour of failure. The reason for his attitude was simple enough—the Highland trouble was but an incident in the European situation, no more than a pawn in the great game of war. After many years of unbroken peace and prosperity, the fall of Walpole made way for the ambitions of the Earl of Chatham, whom we have already quoted as Pitt the Elder. Pitt was naturally proud of the newly coined name of 'patriot,' and during his time of office, which opened with the 'War of Jenkins's Ear' and closed with the disastrous rebellion of the American colonies, there was hardly a breathing-space of peace.

The time inevitably arises when a great and vigorous country must expand or perish. England had set her heart on expansion, and at this period there was ample space in the world for the formation of colonies. The only rival was France, and a very brave and dangerous rival she was to prove. For the next half-century the struggle for supremacy was fated to carry bloodshed into many corners of the world.

In the War of the Austrian Succession, England assisted Maria Theresa to defend her throne against the forces of France, Bavaria, and Prussia, while from this time the rivalry with France became increasingly fierce, both in Europe and America. The conflict resolved itself into a prolonged struggle on land and sea, with the main seat of operations in India and Canada. The curtain went down on the long drama at Waterloo.

At this period we were at war with Prussia, whereas sixty odd years later Wellington awaited the timely advance of Blücher. Again another hundred years and the British forces were to approach the same fateful field, but this time allied with their old enemies the French.

We are faced, therefore, by the history of nearly fifty years of the building of the British Empire, and the corresponding downfall of France in America and India.

At this time we possessed twelve colonies along the American coast, including the township of New York. The colonists in this district were a simple, industrious people, principally descendants of those early Puritans who had sailed across the Atlantic in the Mayflower. They lived in constant dread of the Red Indians, but in no less dread of the French, whose own colonies were in close proximity, while beyond the Great Lakes was French Canada.

There were very many more English colonists than Frenchmen, but the latter possessed the advantage of closer intimacy with the Indians, who proved a powerful and active ally and a cruel and revengeful enemy.

We shall therefore follow the fortunes of the Highlanders through the long struggle with France, first on the Continent and in America, leaving the position in India for a later chapter.

There must be few, if any, to whom the name of Flanders does not instantly recall in all its tragic significance the heroism of Belgium.

How often will the old familiar lines, asking the old unanswered question, recur throughout the coming chapters.

"And everybody praised the Duke

Who such a fight did win."

"But what good came of it at last?"

Quoth little Peterkin.

"Why, that I cannot tell," said he;

"But 'twas a famous victory."

It is well for us to keep that unhappy country before our minds, for we shall return from time to time to the conflicts that have thundered themselves into the great silence.

In 1743-44 the Black Watch embarked for the Continent, and in May 1745, after some two years' service with Marshal Wade, the 42nd assembled with the Allied Army under the command of the Duke of Cumberland. The force consisted of British, Hanoverians, Dutch, and Austrians. The French army was commanded by the famous Marshal Saxe, the scene of battle being in the neighbourhood of Fontenoy. The Duke of Cumberland, who was ever an impetuous and courageous though not very skilful leader, opened the engagement, and for a considerable time pressed the French, hurling them out of their entrenchments at the point of the bayonet, while the Highlanders wielded their claymores with remarkable effect. In this, their first taste of disciplined warfare the eyes of Europe were upon them.

The point at which the Highlanders and Guards were launched was speedily taken, but things went less happily elsewhere. The cavalry under General Campbell suffered a reverse—the Dutch and Austrians reeled back before the French fire—the fortunes of the day were dependent upon the British.

Presently came the dramatic and magnificent advance of the British infantry with the Black Watch upon the extreme right. With measured tread and set faces they came on. Their ranks were ploughed and broken with shot, but re-forming in silence they drew ever nearer to the French.

It was then that Lord Charles Hay of the 1st Guards turned to the men beside him crying, "Men of the King's Company, these are the French Guards, and I hope you are going to beat them to-day."

He was not disappointed. Not for the first time, nor for the last, the English Guards hurled back the pick of the Continental soldiers in confusion.

Saxe, dreading a reverse, ordered his horse, and, supported by a man on either side because of his bodily weakness, rode forward to lead up the veteran troops of France, knowing well the inspiration that his presence would bring. And at that moment the British artillery slackened its fire, thus giving an opportunity to the famous Irish Brigade to win or lose the cause of France.

The Irish Brigade was composed of men for the most part of good family, who had left the country of their birth to follow King James into exile. They were magnificent troops, inflamed by a deadly hatred of England, and always ready to avenge the wrongs that they believed they had suffered at English hands. Their advance was practically invincible, and before very long they took ample revenge for the severe drubbing they had received at Dettingen two years before. With shouts of 'Remember Limerick!' they broke like an angry sea upon the English flank, which stood stubbornly until retreat was seen to be inevitable. Soon the French cavalry were pouring down upon the English withdrawal, and at that critical situation the hour of the Black Watch dawned. It was due to the bravery of the Highland regiment that the English forces were not driven into irretrievable confusion. Captain John Munro of the 43rd has written of the day's work: "We got within musket shot of their batteries, when we received three full fires of their batteries and small arms, which killed us forty men and one ensign. Here we were obliged to skulk behind houses and hedges for about an hour and a half, waiting for the Dutch, who, when they came up, behaved but so and so. Our regiment being in some disorder, I wanted to draw them up in rear of the Dutch, which their general would scarce allow of; but at last I did it, and marched them again to the front. In half an hour after the Dutch gave way, and Sir Robert Munro thought proper we should retire; for we had then the whole batteries from the enemy's ground playing upon us, and three thousand foot ready to fall upon us. We retired; but before we had marched thirty yards, we had orders to return to the attack, which we did; and in about ten minutes after had orders to march directly with all expedition, to assist the Hanoverians.... The British behaved well; we (the Highlanders) were told by his royal highness that we did our duty well.

"By two of the clock we all retreated; and we were ordered to cover the retreat as the only regiment that could be kept to their duty, and in this affair we lost sixty more; but the Duke made so friendly and favourable a speech to us, that if we had been ordered to attack their lines afresh, I dare say our poor fellows would have done it."[2]

So much for the Highlanders. But what did the French think of them? "It must be owned," says one, "that our forces were thrice obliged to give way, and nothing but the good conduct and extreme calmness of Marshal Saxe could have brought them to the charge the last time, which was about two o'clock, when the Allies in their turn gave way. Our victory may be said to be complete; but it cannot be denied, that, as the Allies behaved extremely well, more especially the English, so they made a soldier like retreat which was much favoured by an adjacent wood. The British behaved well, and could be exceeded in ardour by none but our officers, who animated the troops by their example, when the Highland furies rushed in upon us with more violence than ever did a sea driven by a tempest."

One can appreciate how much the French were impressed by the Highlanders by the exploit of one of the Black Watch who killed nine Frenchmen with his claymore, and was only prevented from continuing by the loss of his arm.

But half the success was due to the discretion of Sir Robert Munro, of Fowlis, who allowed his Highlanders to engage in their own way, a method of fighting that greatly upset the enemy. He "ordered the whole regiment to clap to the ground on receiving the French fire, and instantly after its discharge they sprang up, and coming close to the enemy poured in shot upon them to the certain destruction of multitudes, then retreating, drew up again, and attacked a second time in the same manner. These attacks they repeated several times the same day, to the surprise of the whole army. Sir Robert was everywhere with his regiment notwithstanding his great corpulency, and, when in the trenches, he was hauled out by the legs and arms by his own men; and it is observed that when he commanded the whole regiment to clap to the ground, he himself alone, with the colours behind him, stood upright, receiving the whole fire of the enemy, and this because although he could easily lie down, his great bulk would not suffer him to rise so quickly."

The prospect of invasion has been so very critical within our own recollection that it is interesting to recall that, after the campaign in Flanders, the Black Watch returned to England, and in view of the contemplated descent of the French upon the coast, was stationed along the cliffs of Kent.

The dispersal of the Jacobite forces at Culloden left the Duke of Cumberland free to return to the Continent, where he stationed his army to cover Bergen-op-Zoom and Maestricht, while Saxe encamped between Mechlin and Louvain.

The Highland regiment, however, saw very little fighting during this campaign, and was shortly withdrawn to England. In 1749 the Black Watch assumed the world-famed regimental number of the 42nd.

CHAPTER III
THE BLACK WATCH AT TICONDEROGA
(1758)

There fell a war in a woody place,

Lay far across the sea,

A war of the march in the mirk midnight

And the shot from behind the tree,

The shaven head and the painted face,

The silent foot in the wood,

In a land of a strange, outlandish tongue

That was hard to be understood.

R. L. STEVENSON.

The rivalry between our nation and the French died down upon the Continent, but burst into flame in North America, and it is to that wild and unknown country—for so it was in the year 1756—that we must follow the Black Watch.

The Expeditionary Force was under the command of a singularly incompetent General named Sir James Abercrombie, and landed at New York after many weary weeks' journey. The appearance of the Highlanders created a tremendous sensation, particularly amongst the Red Indians, who displayed the keenest interest in their dress, and were ready to accept them as brothers-in-arms. It must also be recalled that many Highlanders had emigrated during the years succeeding 1745, so one can take it for granted that the Black Watch were warmly received by their kinsfolk in the New World.

The French forces were commanded by the gallant Marquis de Montcalm, who in 1756, acting with his usual promptitude, had captured Fort Ontario, a success clouded over by the ill-treatment of the British soldiers by the Red Indians. In 1757 the only incident worthy of note was the fall of Fort William Henry.

So far our enemies had succeeded, and the Government, irritated by this unsatisfactory state of affairs, fitted out a further naval and military force of some fifteen thousand men.

The British force in America was divided into three expeditions. We shall deal briefly with each in turn. But for fear that hard facts may obscure the romantic setting, it will be just as well to sketch the features of the country in which these undertakings played their part. It had all the wonder of a virgin land. It was there that—

Soldiers and priests in the grim bivouac—

A handful dreaming in the wilderness—

In fancy reached Quebec and Tadousac

And told of great exploits, of long duresse,

Of Fort St. Louis' graves, of sore distress,

Of France's venture in the southern land.[3]

Vast lakes and rivers, mountains and cañons, not unlike to the glens the Highlanders had left in Scotland, confronted them. In the deep stillness of the woods wild animals slipped into the darkness, and savages were a sleepless menace. In the dead of a summer night the long-drawn cry of an Indian brave would chill the blood of some straggling soldier, or from the thicket would fly the arrows of death. It was a country where one force could not hope to keep in touch with another nor guard its lines of communication: an army was swallowed up in a wilderness of forests and rivers. In such circumstances each man carried his life and the lives of his comrades in his hands, for defeat meant annihilation or capture, and it would be better to fall into the hands of the French than to be tracked down by their ruthless allies the Indians. "Here were no English woodlands, no stretches of pale green turf, no vistas opening beneath flattened boughs, with blue distant hills, and perhaps a group of antlers topping the bracken. The wild life of these forests crawled among thickets or lurked in sinister shadows. No bird poured out its heart in them; no lark soared out of them, breasting heaven. At rare intervals a note fell on the ear—the scream of hawk or eagle, the bitter cackling laugh of blue jay or woodpecker, the loon's ghostly cry—solitary notes, and unhappy, as though wrung by pain out of the choking silence; or away on the hillside a grouse began drumming, or a duck went whirring down the long waterway until the sound sank and was overtaken by the river's slow murmur.

"When night had hushed down these noises, the forest would be silent for an hour or two, and then awake more horribly with the howling of wolves."[4]

We now come to one of those episodes of reckless bravery that have immortalised the Highland regiments—an engagement that was to ring throughout England, bringing a new renown to the Black Watch. It is associated with a place bearing the strange and musical name of Ticonderoga—'the meeting of the waters.' Many years before our story the famous Frenchman Champlain had nearly suffered defeat in that dreaded country of the Iroquois. Many years had passed since then, and now Ticonderoga was held by the French. How difficult a place it was to storm will be gathered from the following description:

"Fort Ticonderoga stands on a tongue of land between Lake Champlain and Lake George, and is surrounded on three sides by water; part of the fourth side is protected by a morass, the remaining part was strongly fortified with high entrenchments, supported and flanked by three batteries, and the whole front of that part which was accessible was intersected by deep traverses, and blocked up with felled trees, with their branches turned outwards, forming together a most formidable defence."

It was rendered not less hazardous because Abercrombie did not take the trouble to employ ordinary precautions. He could have stormed the place with artillery, attacked it on the flank, or cut Montcalm's line of communications. He did none of these things. In other words, he trusted to the bravery of his soldiers to achieve what was practically impossible. Embarking his troops on Lake George, he made his way down the still and placid lake, landing without opposition. The very silence was ominous.

In the meantime Montcalm was straining every nerve to prepare for the coming struggle. With him were a comparatively large force of French and several hundred Canadians, while a further reinforcement was hourly expected. On the report that the defences of Ticonderoga were still unfinished, Abercrombie decided upon an instant attack. The English attacking force, composed of the Grenadiers with the Highlanders in reserve, advanced heroically to the assault, only to discover that the entrenchments were far stronger than had been anticipated. Montcalm waited until the English were within a close distance of the garrison before giving the order to fire. The British were mown down in hundreds. Again and again they charged, to fall in heaps at the foot of the stockades. Even now Abercrombie would not give up the insane attack. So far the Black Watch had taken no part, but the time soon came when they could restrain their impatience no longer, and, gripping their broadswords and Lochaber axes, they broke into a charge. Madly they rushed at the stockade, only to find, like their comrades, that it was practically unscalable. They were dauntless in their despair. By scrambling upon each other's shoulders a few managed to enter the enclosure and were instantly killed by the French. After a forlorn struggle, in which the Black Watch lost some 300 men killed with over 300 wounded, Abercrombie resolved to retire. He had attempted to take a position impregnable without a bombardment. Well might the

French commander remark: "Had I to besiege Ticonderoga, I would ask for but six mortars and two pieces of artillery." Abercrombie had the artillery, but did not trouble to bring it up.

"The affair at Fontenoy," says Lieutenant Grant of the Black Watch, "was nothing to it: I saw both. We laboured under insurmountable difficulties. The enemy's breastwork was about nine or ten feet high, upon the top of which they had plenty of wall pieces fixed, and which was well lined on the inside with small arms. But the difficult access to their lines was what gave them a fatal advantage over us. They took care to cut down monstrous large oak trees which covered all the ground from the foot of their breastwork about the distance of a cannon-shot every way in their front. This not only broke our ranks, and made it impossible for us to keep our order, but put it entirely out of our power to advance till we cut our way through. I have seen men behave with courage and resolution before now, but so much determined bravery can hardly be equalled in any part of the history of ancient Rome. Even those that were mortally wounded cried aloud to their companions not to mind or lose a thought upon them, but to follow their officers, and to mind the honour of their country. Nay, their ardour was such, that it was difficult to bring them off. They paid dearly for their intrepidity. The remains of the regiment had the honour to cover the retreat of the army, and brought off the wounded as we did at Fontenoy. When shall we have so fine a regiment again?"

The Black Watch at Ticonderoga

On Independence Day 1906, in the Carnegie Public Library at Ticonderoga, a tablet was unveiled commemorating the gallantry and the severe casualties of the Black Watch in July 1758, a calamity comparable to that of Magersfontein in 1899.

Here, as throughout our story, was displayed a reckless bravery under trying conditions, an uncomplaining heroism under fire, a simple pride in the honour of the regiment.

"With a mixture of esteem, and grief, and envy," says an officer, "I consider the great loss and immortal glory acquired by the Scots Highlanders in the late bloody affair. Impatient for orders they rushed forward to the entrenchments, which many of them actually mounted. They appeared like lions breaking from their chains. Their intrepidity was rather animated than damped by seeing their comrades fall on every side."

It was following this gallant exploit the news came that for past valuable services the regiment was to be called 'the Royal Highland Regiment of Foot.' After Ticonderoga it was doubly worthy of such recognition.

The second expedition—that against Louisburg, in which Fraser's Highlanders served—sailed from Halifax on May 28, 1758, and after a stormy passage effected a landing under General Wolfe.

The town surrendered after a considerable bombardment, great gallantry being shown by the Highlanders engaged.

The third expedition, against Fort Duquesne, was under the command of Brigadier-General John Forbes. The British force, amongst whom were Montgomery's Highlanders, were confronted by almost impenetrable country, but that did not prove so great a danger as the foolhardiness that led the commander to belittle the strength of the enemy. It was rumoured that the French garrison was limited to 800 men, largely composed of Indians. A party of Highlanders, under Major James Grant, and a company of Virginians marched cheerfully ahead to reconnoitre. The honest strains of the bagpipes warned the enemy for miles around that the Highlanders were approaching. Instant preparation being made for their arrival, they walked into an ambuscade. A fierce fire from the dense undergrowth raked their closed ranks unmercifully. Major Grant, who appears to have taken no precautions whatever, was captured, while the ranks of the Highlanders were decimated. A retreat, humiliating though it was, was the only course, and this reverse so disheartening that the British commander determined to abandon any further advance. It fell to George Washington, at this time a young man of twenty-six, accompanied by Provincials, and a detachment of Highlanders, to retrieve the failure of the former expedition. His march was a notable one. It was in dead of winter, and the hills were white with snow. Defeat, as always in that country, spelt ruin and death, but the little force pressed onwards, determined to succeed, and to regain the prestige of the British arms. Nearer and nearer they came to the enemy. Suddenly, one evening, a sullen glow of firelight shot up into the sky. The disheartened garrison had set fire to Fort Duquesne, and taken flight upon the Ohio. This was hardly a satisfactory conclusion for the British force, already short of provisions, but amidst the smouldering ashes Washington planted the flag of England, naming the place Pittsburg, after the Prime Minister.

The time had at last dawned for a decisive movement. Abercrombie had been succeeded by General Amherst, who planned a second assault upon Ticonderoga. To General Wolfe was allotted the almost impossible task of storming Quebec. General Prideaux was to advance against the French position near the Falls of Niagara.

General Amherst, with whom were the Black Watch, secured an easy triumph in taking possession of Ticonderoga, already deserted by the French, and thus obtained a naval security upon the lakes.

The expedition of General Wolfe deserves a separate chapter.

CHAPTER IV
WITH WOLFE AND FRASER'S HIGHLANDERS AT QUEBEC
(1759)

Quebec, the grey old city on the hill,

Lies with a golden glory on her head,

Dreaming throughout this hour so fair, so still,

Of other days and all her mighty dead.

The white doves perch upon the cannons grim,

The flowers bloom where once did run a tide

Of crimson, when the moon was pale and dim

Above the battle-field so grim and wide.

Methinks within her wakes a mighty glow

Of pride, of tenderness—her stirring past—

The strife, the valour, of the long ago

Feels at her heart-strings. Strong, and tall, and vast,

She lies, touched with the sunset's golden grace,

A wondrous softness on her grey old face.

B. BISHOP.

Time plays strange tricks with the affairs of men, and it is not without significance to recall that the conqueror of Quebec was in the year 1746 engaged in crushing the defeated Highlanders after Culloden. More than that his hatred for the Jacobites was very genuine, though his dislike was tempered with mercy. It was for that human quality that the Highlanders bore him no grudge, and won for the name of Wolfe the victor of Quebec.

Wolfe was born in Kent in 1727. In 1743 he fought at Dettingen, and in 1745-6 in the Highlands. He was a most able and determined leader, with an odd and not inspiring presence. In Fort Amity Sir Arthur Quiller-Couch's hero remarks: "'What like is he?' says you; 'just a sandy-haired slip of a man,' says I, 'with a cocked nose, but I love him, Jack, for he knows his business.'"

In that sentence lies the whole secret of successful generalship. The troops who stormed Quebec had an implicit confidence in their leader.

General Wolfe embarked with his forces at Sandy Hook on May 8, 1759, and, after putting in at Louisburg, entered the St. Lawrence and disembarked off the Isle of Orleans in preparation for the formidable task before him.

The outposts of Canada were fast falling into British hands, but the key to ultimate supremacy was Quebec, and Wolfe had only 8000 men to take it. For a long time he besieged the place, knowing that to engage upon an open assault would be a piece of madness; and in those days artillery was not sufficiently powerful to reduce a position of such strength. The city of Quebec was also heavily fortified and entrenched. But as time went on more active measures were necessary. Days were speeding into weeks, winter was drawing nigh, and the British ships were likely enough to be held up or destroyed in the freezing of the St. Lawrence. Disease was weakening the army even more than shot, and in the end Wolfe himself was overcome by sickness. The expedition promised to be an utter failure.

In the first attack upon the fortress Wolfe was driven back with a loss of 400 men. Well might he become dispirited and long for the day when Amherst, now that Niagara had surrendered, would come marching to his aid. But Amherst did not come, while all the time the situation grew more critical. Not only was there a strongly entrenched enemy in Quebec, but from every wood shots were fired at the British, and every night rang with false alarms to wear down their strength and courage.

At last Wolfe, weak with fever, but burning with the greater fire of patriotism, resolved to wait no longer. It came to his knowledge that up the cliff side of the fortress there was a narrow pathway leading to a plateau upon the Plains of Abraham. Should he contrive to capture such a commanding position the enemy could be met upon fair terms. The situation is aptly expressed in the jingle:

Quebec was once a Frenchman's town, but twenty years ago,

King George the Second sent a man called General Wolfe, you know,

To clamber up a precipice and look into Quebec,

As you'd look down a hatchway when standing on the deck.[5]

Upon the 5th and 6th of September he embarked his forces and planned to take the French by surprise. It was a very dark night, and no moon shining, when Wolfe's force, including Fraser's Highlanders, took to their boats, and soon, in absolute silence, the transports were gliding like ghosts over the water.

Wolfe, spent with sickness, sat amongst his officers, and it is recorded that as the boats reached the cliff up which they hoped to find the way to victory, he repeated to himself some verses from 'An Elegy in a Country Churchyard,' remarking, "I would rather have written that poem than take Quebec."

By a simple ruse the boats arrived at the shore. They were challenged by a sentry, but a Highland officer replied with more resource than truthfulness that they were French. For the moment the danger was negotiated, and soon they were at the foot of a precipitous cliff which rose some 200 feet sheer above them. Landing in absolute silence, the Highlanders began to move up its front, hoisting and pulling each other from foot to foot, and ledge to ledge, clinging to roots and trees with bleeding hands and knees—but always nearing the top. The few French pickets, nodding in the darkness above, saw the danger that had crept out of the night too late. They were speedily overcome and silenced, and at dawn of day some 4000 British troops were drawn up upon the Plains of Abraham. Well might Montcalm say, "They have at last got to the weak side of this miserable garrison; we must give battle and crush them before midday." Quebec was, in that admission, already half won.

The forces of Montcalm, composed of French soldiers, Canadians, and Indians, advanced with reckless daring against the British lines, and the bravery of the French leader must ever command our respect and admiration. He led five largely undisciplined battalions against the veterans of the British Army.

Wolfe, ever in the forefront of the fight, was almost immediately hit, but it took a third shot to send him to the ground. In the meantime Montcalm had hurled his forces at the British troops, himself cheering them on, and taking no heed of his wounds, as brave and gallant a leader as Wolfe himself.

But the British regulars met the broken lines of the enemy as they met the charging clansmen at Culloden. They reserved their fire until the French were a bare forty yards distant, and in a few minutes the victory was already won, for "the Highlanders, taking to their broadswords, fell in among them with irresistible impetuosity, and drove them back with great slaughter." At the moment that Wolfe led his men to the decisive charge he fell upon the field of victory.

"Support me," he said to one of his staff; "let not my brave fellows see me drop."

"They run, they run," cried the officer.

"Who run?" asked Wolfe, scarce able to speak.

"The French give way everywhere."

"What! Do they run already? Now, God be praised, I die happy."

In the meantime, Montcalm, also mortally wounded, was carried back to the fortress, where panic had seized the French garrison. It was rumoured that the General was killed.

"So much the better for me," he sighed when he heard of it; "I shall not live to see the surrender of Quebec."

With his death passed away the ascendancy of France in Canada.

In the siege of Quebec Fraser's Highlanders took a gallant and important share. They were amongst the troops who landed upon Wolfe's Cove, as it was afterwards called, and won the Heights of Abraham, and when the French attack was broken, the regiment pursued the fugitives to the very gates of the town into which they were shortly to march.

In the following April when the French, under De Levi, advanced against Quebec, Fraser's Highlanders, under the command of General Murray, were forced to retire into the city after a severe action. Later on Lord Murray achieved a junction with General Amherst, whose arrival had been so exceedingly tardy.

Ticonderoga, which covered the frontiers of New York, was now in British hands, together with Niagara. Quebec was conquered; the only place of strength remaining was Montreal. Upon this township, therefore, the forces of General Munro and General Amherst were concentrated. The Governor, perceiving that resistance was futile, surrendered, and in this peaceful fashion concluded the campaign that added Canada to the British Empire.

In the summer of 1908 extensive celebrations were held in Canada to commemorate the taking of Quebec, and the foundation of Britain's power in the Far West just a hundred and fifty years before. Field-Marshal Lord Roberts was sent over to represent Great Britain, being accorded a magnificent reception from the Canadians, whose loyalty to the Empire has always made them her generous supporters whenever the call has come.

CHAPTER V
RED INDIAN AND HIGHLANDER
(1760-1767)

When the summer harvest was gathered in,

And the sheaf of the gleaner grew white and thin,

And the ploughshare was in its furrow left,

Where the stubble land had been lately cleft,

An Indian hunter, with unstrung bow,

Looked down where the valley lay stretched below.

LONGFELLOW.

We come now to a phase of our story that chiefly concerns two intrepid regiments, whose services were so valuable to the Government—namely, Fraser's and Montgomery's Highlanders. The Black Watch was not the only regiment raised during the middle of the eighteenth century. In answer to the appeal of the Government the clansmen followed the lead of their chiefs and enrolled themselves in several battalions, which saw service in America during the war with France, the trouble with the Red Indians, and later against the colonists. Amongst these regiments the best known was Montgomery's Highlanders (founded in 1757), which, as we have noted, suffered a reverse under Major Grant at Fort Duquesne, and were also associated with the Black Watch under Amherst.

Fraser's Highlanders, later to be enrolled in the Seaforths, were raised as the 78th Regiment in 1757, and the 71st Regiment in 1775, by the son of Simon, Lord Lovat, the Jacobite rebel. They served at the investment of Louisburg and at Quebec. The 71st Regiment took part in the American War of Independence.

Many other regiments were formed from time to time and either disbanded or absorbed. It was not until the latter part of the eighteenth century that the Highland regiments as we know them to-day, apart of course from the Black Watch, came to be formed.

Perhaps the hardest, most dangerous, and most thrilling task that was undertaken by the Highlanders at this period was the forlorn expedition of Montgomery against the Cherokee Indians.

There have been no savages who ever possessed in their cruelty and in their superhuman cunning so great a fascination in story as the Red Indians. Always behind the tools of their trade—the call of an owl, the silent arrow by moonlight, the war dance, the feathers and the paint—there lurked the glamour of the unknown.

Whether as the godlike figures of Fenimore Cooper, or the dreaded Redskins of Manville Fenn and Ballantyne, they have secured for themselves a kind of grim immortality. Other times may bring other tales, stories of submarines and aeroplanes, and the ingenious contrivances that have robbed war of what romance it may once have claimed, but never again will there be the same thrill that the simple snap of a twig in a breathless night could so painfully awaken.

We have noticed how favourably impressed the Indians had been with their first introduction to the Highlander. Like the Sikh and the Gurkha of India, like the Kaffir in Africa, and to some extent the Arab of the East, warlike peoples have always felt some link with the Highlander. But the Red Indian was to suffer some practical experiences of an activity and capacity for taking cover almost equal to his own. The Highlander at this time was skilled by centuries of marauding in the art of concealment, and in taking advantage of rough country. He was long-sighted, keen of hearing, and accustomed to move by night. There is a vivid scene in Stevenson's Kidnapped where Allan Breck and David Balfour, bound for the sanctuary of Cluny Macpherson's cave, heard but a rustle in the heather, and in a flash a clansman was at the throat of each of them.

The Highlander was no amateur in war.

In 1760 Colonel Montgomery led his regiment against the Cherokee Indians, who had become an increasing menace to the settlers. It was an undertaking as full of peril as the bravest soldier could have desired. "What may be Montgomery's fate in the Cherokee country," wrote one accustomed to the Indian, "I cannot so readily determine. It seems he has made a prosperous beginning, having penetrated into the heart of the country, and he is now advancing his troops in high health and spirits to the relief of Fort Loudon. But let him be wary. He has a crafty, subtle enemy to deal with, that may give him most trouble when he least expects it."

No truer words could have been passed upon the character of Indian fighting.

When the Highlanders approached the Cherokee town Etchowee they entered a ravine densely wooded, at the foot of which ran a sluggish river. Suddenly the war-whoop resounded from every side, while the dark figures of the Redskins were seen flitting from tree to tree, firing from every quarter. Numbers of the soldiers fell in the first attack, unfortunately several of the wounded being lost in the impenetrable thicket, only to fall into the hands of the Indians.

The Highlanders charged the enemy, driving them up the sides of the ravine, but won no definite advantage. The Indians always preferred guerilla warfare to close conflict, knowing that the farther they enticed the invader into the wilds of their country the less chance would there be that he would win back to safety. Every one is familiar with the cruelty that the Red Indians practised upon their prisoners, and those unfortunate Highlanders who in this instance were carried away by the Cherokees fared exceedingly badly. The following story, as related by General Stewart, will give an idea not only of the treatment accorded to captives, but also of the extreme credulity of the Indians at this time.

"Several soldiers ... fell into the hands of the Indians, being taken in an ambush. Allan Macpherson, one of these soldiers, witnessing the miserable fate of several of his fellow-prisoners, who had been tortured to death by the Indians, and seeing them preparing to commence the same operation upon himself, made signs he had something to communicate. An interpreter was brought. Macpherson told them, that provided his life was spared for a few minutes, he would communicate the secret of an extraordinary medicine, which, if applied to the skin, would cause it to resist the strongest blow of a tomahawk or sword, and that, if they would allow him to go to the woods with a guard, to collect the proper plants for this medicine, he would prepare it, and allow the experiment to be tried on his own neck by the strongest and most expert warrior among them. This story easily gained upon the superstitious credulity of the Indians, and the request of the Highlander was instantly complied with. Being sent into the woods, he soon returned with such plants as he chose to pick up. Having boiled these herbs, he rubbed his neck with their juice, and laying his head upon a log of wood, desired the strongest man among them to strike at his neck with his tomahawk, when he would find he could not make the smallest impression. An Indian, levelling a blow with all his might, cut with such force, that the head flew off at a distance of several yards. The Indians were fixed in amazement at their own credulity, and the address with which the prisoner had escaped the lingering death prepared for him; but instead of being enraged at this escape of their victim, they were so pleased with his ingenuity that they refrained from inflicting further cruelties on the remaining prisoners."

After this affray Colonel Montgomery had no desire for a further acquaintance with the Indians. Employing the simple device of lighting camp-fires, he retreated post-haste before the ruse was suspected, making his way back to Fort George, and from thence to New York, remarking, when warned that he was leaving the unfortunate settlers to the mercies of the victorious Cherokee, that "he could not help the people's fears." Whether such an action and such a statement was prudent, or merely timorous, is not for us to say, but to the deserted Fort Loudon it was little better than a death-warrant. Besieged by the triumphant Indians, reduced to starvation point, and with the sure knowledge that further resistance only forestalled a humiliating surrender, the garrison came to terms with the enemy. What these terms amounted to does not greatly matter, for hardly had the unfortunate soldiers evacuated, and begun their retreat, than the Cherokees fell upon them, slaughtering a large number without mercy.

In 1764 the Black Watch and a detachment of Montgomery's Highlanders set out for the relief of Fort Pitt, at that time besieged by Indians. The expedition was composed of about a thousand men, and was commanded by Colonel Henry Boquet. The whole country was swarming with the enemy, and the British force was compelled to advance through a narrow pass winding between precipitous hills. Many a time had Rob Roy and his Macgregors ambushed their pursuers in a similar spot. In those times, before long-range rifles, artillery, and aeroplanes, such places frequently proved a death-trap to an invading force, particularly soldiers unaccustomed to rough country and unable to get to close quarters with an agile enemy like the Red Indian.

One can picture the Highlanders, ill at ease, cautiously feeling their way up the silent gorge, their pack-horses stumbling along the narrow track, a strong body of the Black Watch ahead, and every man awaiting from one moment to another the attack that never came, while each step towards the centre of the defile magnified the prospect of annihilation. Suddenly, out of the stillness hummed a flight of arrows, while the dreaded Indian war-whoop echoed and re-echoed from every side. Unlike other savages, as the Zulu impi at Rorke's Drift, or the Dervishes at Omdurman, the Red Indian preferred to kill by stealth, and in those times the ways of the Redskins were not so familiar to the white men as they became in the course of the terrible struggle which was eventually to sweep the Indian off the continent of America. On this occasion, although the Indians had inferior weapons, they possessed enormous superiority in numbers. They were also familiar with every foot of the country.

It fell to the Black Watch to drive them out of their position. This the Highlanders accomplished soon enough, and by their agility put the enemy to flight, but the attack was renewed and again renewed. The thickly wooded hill-side rang with the yells of thousands of braves—on every side they rose from amongst the rocks and undergrowth. The 42nd charged them with fixed bayonets, but they might as well have charged the wind.

The Indians melted away before them, only to reassemble in another quarter, intent on causing a panic, dividing the British forces, stampeding the pack-horses, and keeping up the action until darkness drew on. Near at hand was a favourable plateau, and here the commanding officer decided to form his camp until the dawn. Through the brief summer night they awaited the assault, but as the expected rarely occurred in Indian warfare, none came. The Indians, confident that lack of water would necessitate an advance and the gradual destruction of the white men, contented themselves with false alarms and all those other time-honoured modes of wearing down the nerves and strength. It is also probable that they were none too ready to encounter more closely the strange men in tartan who played a game hardly less cunning than their own. At the same time it was important for the British to advance, for in their camp were many wounded, who could not hope to keep up with the main body, and who could under no circumstances be left to the fiendish tortures of the Indians.

Boquet was a man of resolute will. The following morning he feigned a retreat, when, with confident recklessness, the Indians rushed headlong upon his little force. Suddenly, out of the dense thicket, two companies of Highlanders appeared upon their flank. At the same time the main body advanced, and in an instant what had seemed to promise a severe disaster was turned into an overwhelming success. The British lost nearly a quarter of their number, but reached Fort Pitt without further danger, where the Black Watch passed the winter.

In the same year they set out on an expedition against the Ohio Indians, and once more the remarkable endurance and activity of the Highlanders was put to the test, with the result that, during an advance through almost impenetrable forests, there was not a single casualty through fatigue.

The war between England and France had concluded on February 10, 1763, with the Treaty of Paris. This Treaty deprived the French of rich territories both in North America and eastward of the Mississippi, but the conquest was in itself little better than a menace to the future peace of England. It was Vergennes, the French Ambassador at Constantinople, who wisely remarked at the time: "England will soon repent of having removed the only check that could keep her colonies in awe. They stand no longer in need of her protection. She will call to them to contribute towards supporting the burden they have helped to bring on her, and they will answer by striking off all dependence."

In a time when we have witnessed the noble patriotism and loyal support of our colonies, such a statement may well appear unduly pessimistic, or even absurd. But unfortunately at this period the spirit of Empire was clouded over by arrogance and insularity. People far away in England were not sufficiently in touch with the new world of America to treat the colonists with tolerance or sympathy. England had squandered much money and many lives in the war with France, and was not prepared to come to an understanding with the settlers, for whose safety it had carried out the campaign. In another chapter we shall see how humiliating the consequences of the War of Independence proved, and the part that the Highlanders took in the struggle.

CHAPTER VI
THE AMERICAN WAR OF INDEPENDENCE (1775-1782).

Thy spirit, Independence, let me share,

Lord of the lion-heart and eagle-eye,

Thy steps I follow with my bosom bare,

Nor heed the storm that howls along the sky.

SMOLLETT.

In the earlier chapters we have dealt with the actions in which the Black Watch, Fraser's, and Montgomery's Highlanders were engaged. It is now time that mention was made of the other Highland regiments that were formed about this period, and that were, to some extent, recruited from the troops disbanded shortly before the American War of Independence. It would take too long and be too confusing to enter into any detail concerning the various false starts that many Highland regiments made. The actual date of their respective foundations will be found in the list of regimental battle honours, or in the chapters devoted on occasions to the exploit of a particular battalion.

The various Highland regiments that were raised after the Black Watch were largely the outcome of personal enterprise. The chief of the Macleods, for instance, raised the battalion that afterwards became the 1st Highland Light Infantry. The principal cities in Scotland each contributed towards a regiment, and the great families of Seaforth, Gordon, Argyll, and Macdonald did much in the time succeeding and preceding the American War to foster the military spirit. The regiment created by the Earl of Seaforth ultimately became the 1st Seaforth Highlanders.

There is, I think, only one particular point to note before we continue this narrative. In times of major warfare, such as in the great campaigning of the Napoleonic wars, the Crimea, and South Africa, several Highland regiments, not necessarily all, were banded together under the control of a commander, and called the Highland Brigade. A brigade may consist of three or four or more battalions, each battalion roughly a thousand odd men, and naturally comes into severe fighting.

In the Crimea the Highland Brigade was composed of three regiments, the Black Watch, the Camerons, and the 93rd Sutherlands. It was commanded by the famous Sir Colin Campbell. In the Indian Mutiny no regular brigade was formed. In the Egyptian war in 1882 the Highland Brigade was under the command of Sir Archibald Alison, and included the Black Watch, the Highland Light Infantry, the Gordons, and the Camerons. In the Boer War of 1889-1902 the Highland Brigade was under the command of General Wauchope, and included the 2nd Battalion of the Black Watch, the 2nd Seaforth Highlanders, the 1st Argyll and Sutherlands, and the 1st Highland Light Infantry. It was these four regiments that met with the severe reverse at Magersfontein.

At the time when the American War of Independence broke out George III. was upon the throne. He was an Englishman born and bred, and, after the earlier Georges, that in itself made a great appeal to the imagination of the English people. He was a man possessed of a great sincerity and a greater obstinacy, who lived as much as possible amongst his tenants in the country or within his own domestic circle. He evidenced, in brief, most of the virtues with many of the weaknesses of the English character. Though he displayed to a large degree the genial spirit that made men call him 'Farmer George,' there was also rather too much John Bull in his personality. His were the virtues of an honest, determined, rather stupid Englishman. It might be said that such a nature as this, particularly in the riotous eighteenth century, could achieve nothing but good. Unfortunately he not only ruled his family so harshly that they all turned out extremely badly, but he also tried to carry out the same attitude towards America. He scolded the colonists as though they were naughty children, and the colonists, many of whom had no acquaintance with England, and whose forebears had left the mother-country for the very good reason that they were happier out of it, met this intolerance with a bold and determined front. They naturally resented the autocratic demands of the Government; they could not tolerate the attitude of the English officers, while although they had outgrown Jacobite sympathies, they cherished no loyalty to a Hanoverian king.

In 1761 the Importation Act was passed, an attempt to enforce payment of duty, in consequence of which English ships went far to ruin trade with the West Indies. The end of the French and Indian wars had brought with it a great increase to the National Debt, and it seemed only fair to the Government that, as the conflict had been undertaken principally to guard the interests of the settlers, the cost should be shared by them. To this the colonists retorted that they too had fought, and that Canada was ample compensation to the British for any loss of capital.

In 1765 the Stamp Act was passed, ordering that all documents of every description must be printed on paper purchased from the Government.

On October 1, 1768, seven hundred soldiers marched into Boston and attempted to overawe the residents. To use a familiar catch-phrase, 'the Government was asking for trouble.' But the colonists still displayed great patience, and though disaffection simmered, it was not until 1773 that any sign of rebellion was visible. It was then that fifty men, dressed up as Red Indians, flung a cargo of tea into Boston Harbour, and on March 31, 1774, the port was ordered to be closed by the Government. Once started, deeds followed fast upon words, while incident hurried upon incident. Little things acquire an indescribable importance at such times, just as a spark will blow up a magazine. Finally, on July 4, 1776, the Declaration of Independence was signed, and the war commenced.

In England the effect of the Declaration was provocative of hardly more alarm than the outbreak of war in South Africa in 1899. In both cases it was exceedingly difficult to estimate the power of the enemy, and hard to believe he could resist a disciplined army. Take, for instance, a typical blusterer of the period. Major James Grant stated in the House of Commons that he knew the Americans very well, and was certain they would not fight,—"that they were not soldiers, and never could be made so, being naturally pusillanimous and incapable of discipline; that a very slight force would be more than sufficient for their complete reduction; and he fortified his statement by repeating their peculiar expressions and ridiculing their religious enthusiasm, manners, and ways of living, greatly to the entertainment of the House."[6]

Pitt replied in memorable words. "The spirit," he said, "which resists your taxation in America is the same that formerly opposed loans, benevolences, and ship-money in England.... This glorious spirit of Whiggism animates three millions in America, who prefer poverty with liberty to gilded chains and sordid affluence, and who will die in defence of their rights as freemen."

Throughout England there was the bitterest resentment against the war, with the widest sympathy for the Americans. Many officers handed in their papers, and meetings were held to express the indignation that such a step should have been forced upon a loyal and long-suffering people. Only Scotland, Tory at home and abroad, supported the king against America, while, with pathetic loyalty, the Highlanders, some of whom had fought for Prince Charlie against George II., risked their lives and lost their homes in America for the cause of George III.

The Black Watch and Fraser's Highlanders sailed from Greenock on April 14, 1776, and disembarked at Staten, where the main body was stationed. Here the Highlanders were drilled in a new form of warfare, to enable them to overcome the resistance of the colonists. Broad-swords and pistols were laid aside, and greater reliance was placed upon marksmanship. After some preliminary fighting at Long Island the Americans, under Washington, secured a masterly retreat. In the month following the British troops took possession of the heights commanding New York. So far England had swept everything before her.

During the cessation that followed this engagement Washington devoted every moment to strengthening his forces. The American troops were no more trained than the Boers in South Africa, but like the latter they could claim in their favour a thorough knowledge of the country with practised marksmanship, derived from years of fighting with the Indians. Their hatred for the English, which burned deeper day by day, was in no degree cooled when they saw amongst the English troops both German mercenaries and Redskins. It is difficult for us to realise how bitterly the Americans abhorred the very sight of an Indian, while on the other hand, an unwritten page in history is the strange alliance that bound many Royalists to their merciless allies, and the brutal instincts such a fellowship aroused in some of the Highlanders, particularly those of the older, wilder generation, the scourings of the '45. On one occasion, for instance, a Highlander with the honest name of Donald M'Donald, led a party of Redskins against a block-house called Shell's Bush. After the siege, which most fortunately ended in favour of the settler, it was discovered that "M'Donald wore a silver-mounted tomahawk, which was taken from him by Shell. It was marked by thirty scalp-notches, showing that few Indians could have been more industrious than himself in gathering that description of military trophies."[7]

It is also worth mentioning, for few histories have dealt with this point, that the unfortunate Highlanders who had settled in America in the years succeeding Culloden, and who, in their loyalty to the throne, fought against the American settlers, were eventually left in the lurch at the conclusion of hostilities, and forced to trek into Canada. Amongst these hapless people who lost their homes were Flora Macdonald and her husband. Her family divided and her future in jeopardy, she set sail again for Scotland, and there she died at the end of the eighteenth century, in the land where she had befriended Prince Charlie.

The capture of Fort Washington by General Howe was an important achievement, in which the Highland regiment played an honourable part. The Fort was well stationed upon the summit of a high plateau, as difficult of access upon at least one side as, let us say, the flank of Edinburgh or Stirling Castles. But where difficulties are so obvious, caution should always be exercised the more. We have seen how the heights of Quebec were scaled simply by challenging the apparently impossible. In much the same manner the Highlanders cleared the precipice beneath Fort Washington, and last, but certainly not least of them, Major Murray, whose stoutness and valour can only be compared to that of Sir Robert Munro at Fontenoy, was carried to the summit.

"This hill," says an authority, "was so perpendicular that the ball which wounded Lieutenant Macleod entered the posterior part of his neck, ran down on the middle of his ribs, and lodged in the lower part of his back. One of the pipers who began to play when he reached the point of a rock on the summit, was immediately shot, and tumbled from one piece of rock to another till he reached the bottom. Major Murray, being a large corpulent man, could not attempt this steep ascent without assistance. The soldiers, eager to get to the point of their duty, scrambled up, forgetting the situation of Major Murray, when he, in a melancholy, supplicating tone cried, 'Oh, soldiers, will you leave me?' A party leaped down instantly, and brought him up, supporting him from one ledge to another until they got him to the top"—a spectacle not without humour.

The Americans, flying before the Black Watch, were brought face to face with the Hessians, and were compelled to lay down their arms. It is unquestionable that half the success of a victory lies in the manner that the pursuit is carried out, and unfortunately General Howe, instead of pressing hard upon the demoralised Americans, was content to go into winter quarters, thus permitting Washington to employ the succeeding weeks in strengthening his army. The time lost was never recovered. On January 22 the Hessians at Trenton were completely surprised and defeated. It had been touch-and-go for the Americans. Defeat at that moment would have ended the war. Immediately the whole situation was changed, and the future grew dark for the British arms.

Shortly after, the Highlanders in their turn were nearly overcome by a sudden attack while they were seeking some rest after long night-watching. A force of 2000 Americans attempted to rush and take them by surprise. Happily for the Black Watch their outposts were resolved to die rather than retreat, and the delay saved the situation.

About the middle of June General Howe perceiving that Washington was strongly entrenched at Middlebrook, resolved to change the theatre of war. When it is difficult to take a position there are two actions that are open to a commander—one is to mask it, as we have seen fortresses masked in the German War, and the other is simply to go elsewhere. The British forces marched away and sailed for Elk Ferry, from thence advancing on Philadelphia. Washington, hurriedly abandoning Middlebrook, pushed across country to oppose the crossing of the English at Brandy Wine River. Now the fording of a river under the shield of heavy battery fire is no light matter, but in those days, when the protection of artillery was not so adequate as it is to-day, it could only be carried with a terrible loss of life. Instead of a frontal attack Cornwallis determined to carry out a flanking movement upon the American position, so, marching up-stream, he forded the river without opposition and drove back General Sullivan. This enabled General Knyphausen to cross with his division, and at the falling of night the Americans were in retreat. Washington was beaten. On the 26th, Philadelphia fell into the hands of the British. Then followed the greatest blow of the war, and the decisive moment was come. General Burgoyne, marching victorious from Canada to co-operate with General Howe at Saratoga Springs, met with a disaster the importance of which can be estimated by the memorable words of Lord Mahon.

"Even of those great conflicts, in which hundreds of thousands have been engaged and tens of thousands have fallen, none has been more fruitful of results than this surrender of thirty-five hundred fighting men at Saratoga. It not merely changed the relations of England and the feelings of Europe towards these insurgent colonists, but it has modified, for all times to come, the connexion between every colony and every parent state."

With General Burgoyne was General Simon Fraser, a Highlander of great distinction, who had served on the Continent, in the expedition against Louisburg, and with Wolfe at Quebec, where he was the officer who, deceiving the French sentry, enabled the Highlanders to land unsuspected. It is difficult to say whether the defeat at Saratoga Springs could have been averted, but it is probable that the despatches summoning Howe miscarried. Undoubtedly Burgoyne made a blunder in forcing Fraser to retreat when he was driving the troops of Colonel Morgan back. However that may be, what followed was dismal enough. Burgoyne took up his last position on the Heights of Saratoga, holding on till famine made further resistance impossible.

Saratoga was the turning-point of the war. France no longer hesitated, but threw in her lot with America. The whole character of the struggle was changed, and its wider issues lie outside our story. In 1780 the Black Watch took part in the siege of Charlestown, which surrendered on May 12. In the further history of the 42nd in America there is little more that is worth recording. The capitulation of Cornwallis (with whom were Fraser's Highlanders) at Yorktown in 1781 practically ended hostilities.

In the American War of Independence there was little honour or glory for the British name or the Highland regiments. Where the cause is unworthy of a great nation success can carry with it nothing but dishonour.

CHAPTER VII
WITH THE HIGHLAND LIGHT INFANTRY TO SERINGAPATAM
(1799)

What marks the frontier line?

Thou man of India say!

Is it the Himalayas sheer,

The rocks and valleys of Cashmere,

Or Indus as she seeks the south

From Attoch to the five-fold mouth?

'Not that! Not that!'

Then answer me, I pray!

What marks the frontier line?

Sir A. Conan Doyle.

The Highland Light Infantry is the only Highland regiment wearing the trews or tartan trousers. Other regiments of the Highland Brigade have discarded the kilt at one time or another—the Argyll Highlanders at the commencement of the last century, the Gordons at one period, and the Black Watch in Ashanti. The H.L.I. was raised as the 71st Foot in 1777, and was known at one time as Macleod's Highlanders, when they were a kilted regiment. The second battalion was raised in 1787. The first battalion wore the kilt from 1777 to 1809, and the second battalion (the 74th Foot) until 1847.

The H.L.I. have the proud distinction of more battle honours than any other Highland regiment. Few regiments indeed have such a distinguished roll of honours, or have seen such varied service. It is surrounding their badge 'The Elephant,' and their honours of 'Mysore,' 'Hindoostan,' and 'Seringapatam' that the present chapter on the Indian campaign of 1799 is written.

In an earlier chapter an attempt has been made to give some idea of the vast extent of the struggle between England and France during the latter half of the eighteenth century, a struggle that was to reach its zenith at the battle of Waterloo in 1815.

The French had long been a power in India, though at the foundation of our East India Company they were not by any means established. For one thing, the British were on more friendly terms with the Indian Princes, while the French were kept very busy fighting not only the Dutch but the English as well. The Dutch, in those days a great naval power, beat the French time and again, and it was not until the latter founded Pondicherry that they were able to lay any assured basis of prosperity.

The whole system on which the English power was maintained in India was a very indifferent one. The English possessions were guided and controlled by the East India Company—a commercial body whose chief aim, naturally enough, was to make the best possible profit out of India, leaving international questions to look after themselves. It was with the name of Clive that the first vision of the Indian Empire was seen upon the horizon of time.

It is not within the scope of our story to devote any space to the great career of Clive, save only to remind the reader of Arcot, of the Black Hole of Calcutta, and of Plassey.

In 1786, the year after Warren Hastings' return to England, Cornwallis was sent to India as Governor-General and Commander-in-Chief. He was not in any way attached to the East India Company, and in this way a new era commenced.

Cornwallis was soon compelled to enter into war with Tippoo Sahib, and at first the 'Tiger of Mysore' made things very difficult for him. For a time, however, peace was patched up, and Lord Wellesley, the brother of the future Duke of Wellington, succeeded as Governor-General.

As we shall see elsewhere, Napoleon had set his heart on the conquest of Egypt, with a view to depriving England of her colonies. After Egypt, he had every hope of conquering India, and for this reason Tippoo was a very promising personage with whom to make a secret treaty against the English. Although the French supremacy was a thing of the past, yet many native princes retained French officers to drill their troops, and their influence was not unlike the control that the Germans exercised over the Turks in 1915. When Lord Wellesley arrived, he found himself faced by treacherous Indian rulers, French intrigue, and rebellious natives.

In 1799 war again broke out with Tippoo, when Colonel Arthur Wellesley, the future 'Iron Duke,' was one of the British commanders. The Highlanders under Wellesley took an active part in defeating the Indian troops in every engagement, until at last Tippoo was surrounded in his capital Seringapatam.

Some idea of the service of the H.L.I. in India from 1780 onwards until 1806 may be gauged by the fact that no less than five names—Carnatic, Sholinghur, Mysore, Hindoostan, and Seringapatam—were added to the regimental colours.

In the Mysore campaign the 71st H.L.I. took part in all the important battles leading up to the heroic storming of Seringapatam.

Colonel Wellesley, as stated above, discovered that Tippoo Sahib was at the heart of a new French intrigue, and decided that the time had come for action. With this end in view he despatched an army numbering 43,000 men to break his power for ever, and take his stronghold by storm.

But so much time was spent in clearing the ground covering the approaches to the fortress, that on April 14, 1799, it was seen that unless the supplies of the army were to give out the place must be carried at all costs. It was no easy matter. Seringapatam lay between two branches of the river Cavery, while to its front were entrenchments, and behind these the artillery and fortifications of the city itself.

Trench warfare is so familiar to-day that there will be no difficulty in understanding the initial steps in the battle. After some days devoted to undermining the enemy's trenches—the Highlanders, under Wellesley, rushed the position, driving the Indians into Seringapatam.

Following upon that success the British guns settled down to make a breach in the walls of the city, but by the 2nd of May, when that was accomplished, the supplies of the army had run very low and as Mr. Fortescue has written, "so desperate was the situation that the General fully resolved, if necessary, to throw his entire army into the breach, since success was positively necessary to its existence."

But the prospect of carrying the breach by assault was sufficient to unnerve the finest troops. There was first a rush over one hundred yards to the river, which must be forded. On the opposite bank of the river was a wall, while between the wall and the breach lay an open ditch some sixty yards in breadth. It was an obstacle-race with death.

Two parties were allotted for the business. With Major-General Baird in one party went the H.L.I. and the 2nd Battalion of the Black Watch.

It was agreed that the enemy would least expect such a dangerous and exhausting assault in the height of the heat. In the darkness of the preceding night the storming party marched into the trenches, where they remained throughout the morning of the following day until the moment arrived. "Men," called Major-General Baird, "are you all ready?"

Ready they had been for twelve hours.

"Then forward, my lads."

Like a pack of hounds they tore across the open space to the river, and instantly the enemy opened fire. Through the Cavery they splashed, over the wall they poured, across the ditch, then like an angry river, between the ragged walls of the breach. Within six minutes the British flag was hoisted upon the outer wall of Seringapatam.

The rushing of the inner rampart headed by Captain Goodall followed.

In the meantime Dunlop's column had fought to a standstill when Lieutenant Farquhar of the 74th Highlanders rallied the Grenadiers, falling in his hour of triumph.

The slaughter of the enemy was enormous. Caught between two fires, and thrown into confusion they surrendered all further hope of resistance. By the magnificent gallantry of the H.L.I. in particular the victory was won.

The Highland Light Infantry at Seringapatam

The end of Tippoo Sahib was tragic if only for its obscurity. The British troops, fighting their way through the city, shot a wounded officer supported amidst some native soldiery. It was Tippoo Sahib, who, fearing capture above everything, and fearing death not at all, was killed in a last effort at resistance. He fell unknown beneath the bodies of his followers, while all the time the fight in the streets raged on. When the last round was fired, 10,000 of the enemy had fallen.

All India rejoiced over this exploit of the British arms, bringing the end of an evil dynasty. But peace had not yet dawned for India.

The death of Tippoo had taken place so suddenly that an inspection of his correspondence revealed the fact that he was not the only one desirous of expelling the English. There were communications from the Nawab of the Carnatic, and very shortly afterwards that province was added to the Madras Presidency with another battle honour to the colours of the H.L.I.

We must now turn to the Mahrattas of Central India. The first Mahratta war had been fought in the time of Warren Hastings. The second Mahratta war was conducted by Arthur Wellesley. After some marching back and forth the British, with whom were the H.L.I. under General Wellesley, met the Indian army at Assaye, on the 23rd of September 1803. In this engagement the Highlanders, and in particular the Seaforths and H.L.I., who were both granted the 'Elephant' as a special badge, won particular notice. In the course of this action, the Highlanders with their comrades managed to defeat a force of ten times their size. The conflict dragged on, however, a battle against French Sepoy troops was fought in Hindoostan, till finally the French Sepoys were utterly dispersed at Laswari. This practically concluded the work of the H.L.I. in India, and in 1806 they were in action at the Cape of Good Hope.

THE BATTLE HONOURS OF THE HIGHLAND LIGHT INFANTRY

Carnatic, Sholinghur, Mysore, Hindoostan, Seringapatam; Cape of Good Hope, 1806; Rolica, Vimiera, Corunna, Busaco, Fuentes de Oñoro, Ciudad Rodrigo, Badajoz, Albuera, Salamanca, Vittoria, Pyrenees, Nivelle, Nive, Orthez, Toulouse, Peninsula, Waterloo; South Africa, 1851-1853; Sevastopol, Central India; Egypt, 1882; Tel-el-Kebir; South Africa, 1899-1902; Modder River.

CHAPTER VIII
HOW THE BLACK WATCH WON THE RED HACKLE
(1795)

The sun rises bright in France

And fair sets he,

But he has lost the blithe blink he had

In my ain countrie.

Oh, gladness comes to many,

But sorrow comes to me,

As I look o'er the wide ocean

To my ain countrie.

Old Highland Air.

It may appear that our last chapter, telling of an action in 1799, has fallen out of place, but there are sufficient reasons why it should come where it does. The trouble with Tippoo Sahib commenced very much sooner, only reaching its climax at Seringapatam, while being at best but an echo of the battle thunder in Europe.

We are now entering upon the first actions in what was to prove a long and terrible war in Europe. For long England had fought France in America and India. From now until 1815 the conflict was to rage ever fiercer nearer home, to break out in Flanders, to spread to Egypt, to drench the Peninsula in blood, and finally to return to the tragic plains of Belgium.

It is important to understand the reasons for this new development.

In the annals of history the French Revolution, that wild outbreak against oppression, stands alone. Coming so swiftly, sweeping from anarchy to anarchy, from one excess to another, passing from bloodshed to bloodshed, from civil war to international strife, from democracy to tyranny, it stunned Europe into a stricken silence. Things were happening which had never happened before. Not only in France, but in many other countries the voice of the people was heard in no uncertain way, while even in Scotland, that country of old causes, a poet, Robert Burns by name, was voicing an altogether new sentiment. The future was as dark and ominous then as it was on that fateful August night in 1914, when, like wind hastening across a dark stretch of country, the word was passed that England was at war with Germany.

Against the dark background of the French Revolution the conflict between England and France had sunk into nothingness. Many are the tales that depict the tragic story of the Reign of Terror, perhaps the most frightful explosion of human anarchy in the history of the world. Innumerable are the instances of heroism, courage, and sacrifice, that have lit up that gloomy period. Were it not for actions so noble and bravery so deathless such a story would be better left untold. Later on, when we come to an equally tragic episode in the outbreak of the Indian Mutiny, it will be seen how cruelty and death called forth as an inspiration to Englishmen throughout eternity the greater and more enduring qualities of self-sacrifice and patriotism. It was that spirit, however tarnished, of tradition that carried the French nobility with unbroken composure to the guillotine. It was this same tradition—but by no means tarnished—that burned like a bright flame in the hearts of Lawrence and John Nicholson. The horrors of war are in themselves of little account when the years have passed. The thing that matters is the spirit with which they are met and conquered.

In the troubles of the French people England desired to take no share unless she was compelled to guard her own interests. The time came soon enough. Passing from arrogance to arrogance, the National Assembly of France at last issued a proclamation offering to assist any nation in Europe against its rulers—or, as it was pleased to call them, its oppressors. Upon that declaration of anarchy the kings and emperors prepared for war. In 1792 the French, defeating the Austrians and Russians in Belgium, swarmed over the frontiers, and the invasion of Holland was planned. But just as England went to war with Germany to avenge the violation of Belgium, so she was prepared to sustain the independence of Holland. So, on February 1st, 1793, war was declared.

To return to the nearer issues of our regimental story, the Black Watch embarked for Flanders in 1793, joined the army under the Duke of York at Menin, and marched to the relief of Nieuport. Some time elapsed before they saw service, but in 1794, having returned in the meantime to England, they landed at Ostend at a somewhat critical moment. The approach of the French forces, coupled with the uncertain attitude of Prussia, placed the division of the Duke of York, then stationed at Malines, at a disadvantage. Lord Moira, who was in command of the Highlanders, determined, if possible, to unite his forces with those of the Duke. The troops were accordingly formed up in the sand-dunes in marching order and advanced towards Ostaker and Alost. While they were stationed there, out of the night, like Uhlans entering Brussels, came 400 French cavalry, whom the

Highlanders very naturally mistook for their allies the Hessians. The enemy, trotting through the streets reached the marketplace, but when one of them made an attempt to sabre a Highlander on the way, the trick was discovered. The enraged soldier drawing his bayonet, attacked the horseman. The alarm was given, and the enemy were driven out by the Dragoons. Shortly after, when Lord Moira had been succeeded by Lieutenant-General Ralph Abercromby, the British were beleaguered in Nimeguen. It was deemed politic to evacuate this town, and the Highlanders, with the other troops, began one of the most terrible retreats in our history. So piercing was the cold, although it was only the beginning of November, that the enemy crossed the Waal on the ice, pushing back the English army behind the Leck. The French had taken Tuil, and a few days later General Dundas, with the aid of the Black Watch, drove the enemy back again over the Waal. Again the French advanced, and it fell to the Highlanders as at Fontenoy to cover the British rear. Retreat they must for fear of being outflanked. To make matters worse the swift advance of the French cavalry drove the Light Dragoons backward, resulting in the loss of two guns.

It was at that critical moment that General Dundas appealed to the Black Watch to recover what the Dragoons had lost. Without hesitation, but fired by the honour laid upon them, the Highlanders charged headlong at the French cavalry who fell into disorder. The artillery horses had already fallen, but undismayed the 42nd pulled the precious guns home again.

It was a swift, minor incident, but at the moment when the British army was in the heart of a hostile and frost-bound country it stood out of the dreary story like a splash of gold upon a grey sky. Never have the Black Watch refused the call, and very seldom have they failed.

It is recorded by Archibald Forbes in his admirable History of the Black Watch that on the rescue of the guns General Dundas addressed the Highlanders saying, "Forty-second, the 11th Dragoons shall never wear the red plume on their helmets any more, and I hope the 42nd will carry it so long as they are the Black Watch." It was this red plume or "hackle" that the gallant 42nd have worn on their feather bonnets to this day, and on June 4, 1795, upon the King's birthday, it was first distributed.

This was to prove the only bright episode in the retreat on Bremen. The numbers of the enemy increased daily, the British were not only in danger of defeat, but were in imminent peril of starvation, were also ill equipped for a campaign in the depths of winter, and throughout the march endured the tacit hostility of the peasantry on their line of route. "Day after day," says Mr. Fortescue in his History of the British Army, "the cold steadily increased; and those of the army that woke on the morning of the 17th of

January saw about them such a sight as they never forgot. Far as the eye could reach over the whitened plain were scattered gun-limbers, waggons full of baggage, stores, or sick men, sutlers' carts, and private carriages. Beside them lay the horses, dead; here a straggler who had staggered on to the bivouack and dropped asleep in the arms of the frost; there a group of British and Germans round an empty rum-cask; here forty English Guardsmen huddled together about a plundered waggon.... Had the retreat lasted but three or four days longer, not a man would have escaped; and the catastrophe would have found a place in history side by side with the destruction of the Army of Sennacherib and with the still more terrible disaster of the retreat from Moscow."

Out of all the army, only the Highlanders endured the rigours of the weather and such awful privation with any success, losing not more than twenty-five dead.

That for the time being concluded the operations of the Highland regiments on the Continent, for in October 1795 the Government decided to launch an attack directed against the ascendancy of the French Republic in the West Indies.

CHAPTER IX
WITH ABERCROMBY IN EGYPT
(1801)

Farewell to Lochaber, farewell to my Jean,

Where heart-some wi' her I ha'e mony a day been;

For Lochaber no more, Lochaber no more,

We'll maybe return to Lochaber no more.

Those tears that I shed they are all for my dear;

And no for the dangers attending on weir;

Tho' borne on rough seas to a far distant shore,

Maybe to return to Lochaber no more.

Highland Burial March.

To return to the main centre of operations is to be confronted with the great figure of Napoleon.

The French Revolution gave birth to many things, but the greatest force that it created was that of Napoleon Bonaparte, who in his meteoric genius embodied the spirit of the age. He rose from a humble position in the army and of poor parentage in Corsica, not only to be the greatest man in France, but one of the greatest men the world has ever seen. He took into his hands the reins of power that were already slipping from the leaders of the Revolution. He organised the Revolutionary armies and led them to victory; he brought out of the smoke of the Reign of Terror a France purged and renewed. Before setting his eyes upon England itself, he determined to seize Egypt, and from there to threaten the English power in India. Apparently Pitt, although he was acquainted with the preparations that were being put forward in the harbours of France, did not fully realise what was in the wind, so Nelson was sent post-haste to the Mediterranean to reconnoitre. But Napoleon gave Nelson the slip time and again, and reached Egypt two days before the English arrived. On August 1, however, Nelson came across a line of thirteen French battleships in Aboukir Bay. The French ships were lying close to the shore while night was already falling. Nelson, having divided his fleet into two divisions, slipped down both flanks of the enemy's line, suddenly opening a double fire. His victory was complete, only two French ships and two frigates evading his pursuit.

This 'Battle of the Nile,' as it was called, shut up Napoleon in Egypt. It did more than that, it encouraged Russia, Austria, Turkey, and Naples to unite with England in the Second Coalition.

In 1799 Napoleon, who was not satisfied to remain in a helpless position in Egypt while the Allies did what they liked in Europe, set out across the desert to Palestine, and after engagements at Jaffa and Acre—where he was beaten by Sir Sydney Smith—he returned to Egypt, and evading the English ships in the Mediterranean reached France. Once there he speedily drove the Government out of power, took the control of affairs himself, with the title of First Consul, and commenced his preparations for the conquest of England. England was outwitted, and the Allies, who had been delighted to join a coalition while Napoleon was isolated in Egypt, hastened now to come to terms with France. And so England found herself faced by the masked opposition of Europe and the threatening of a French invasion. Her only hope upon land lay in the Egyptian campaign which we are now going to enter upon.

On December 21, 1800, the fleet conveying the troops sailed in two divisions for Marmorice on the coast of Greece, where the Turks, who at that time were our Allies, were to provide a reinforcement. With Abercromby were the Black Watch, the Camerons, and the Gordons. Shortly afterwards the fleet anchored in Aboukir Bay, just where Nelson had won his victory nearly three years before. Unfortunately a violent gale sprang up, making it impossible to carry out the disembarkation of the soldiers. This delay enabled the French to prepare themselves to resist the landing, and had it not been for the remarkable qualities of the commanding officer, Sir Ralph Abercromby, the troops might have been faced with overwhelming disaster. Abercromby was as able as the British Military Secretary, Dundas, was incompetent. Despite every obstacle that the futility of Dundas could place in his path, he succeeded where a catastrophe might have been judged unavoidable. The British troops were kept months upon the sea, reduced to a miserable state of health, and landed in the teeth of a strong force of the enemy, who, like the Turks in the Dardanelles, had had ample warning of the scheme of operations. Well might Abercromby, like many another British general, remark, "There are risks in a British warfare unknown in any other service."

The enemy, who outnumbered him by two to one, already held all the fortified positions with a well-disciplined and acclimatised army, supported by excellent artillery. Under these circumstances the French could hardly believe that the British would actually attempt to land. Suddenly they saw the boats conveying the soldiers heading for the shore, when without delay they opened a terrific fire from their batteries, also from the castle at Aboukir. At Marmorice Abercromby had practised his troops in the order of the attack. In the teeth of the enemy, the British troops managed to reach the beach, where they drove back the French, and, hastily assembling, began to rush the face of the hill. The enemy, utterly paralysed at the rapidity of the assault, fired without accuracy or discretion, even allowing the Black Watch to form up and send a volley into their midst.

In the meantime, while these hills were being assaulted, Major-General Moore (the future victor of Corunna) had gained possession of the country in his front, though sustaining a heavy loss. Beaten in two quarters, the enemy retired towards Alexandria, leaving the British to complete their occupation of the shore, and the landing of their stores and ammunition.

During the time devoted to this task the French had managed to reinforce, being strongly posted, when, on the morning of the 13th, the British forces advanced to the attack. At the head of the first column was the 90th Regiment with the Gordon Highlanders. Far away behind the French lines could be seen the port of Alexandria buried amidst its immemorial ruins. There was Cleopatra's Needle, fated eventually to crumble upon the banks of the Thames, Arabian mosques and minarets, and over all that strange and timeless atmosphere, of which centuries of change have never been able to rob the East. As this was the first engagement of the Gordon Highlanders, and as we learn that its ranks were, for the most part, filled with young soldiers unacclimatised to the East, it is of interest to record that it conducted itself with as much distinction as any other battalion in the British Army. "Opposed to a tremendous fire," wrote Sir R. Wilson, "and suffering severely from the French line, the regiment never receded a foot, but maintained the contest alone until the marines and the rest of the fine came up to its support."

For some reason or another the action was ineffective. Sir Ralph Abercromby was now faced with the task of reducing Alexandria, and though his force had been so far successful, the advantage had been gained at some cost. To move artillery over a sandy desert requires a large number of horses, in which respect the British were very much inferior to the French. Our sailors, always handy men, lent their assistance to the soldiers to drag the wheels out of the sand, and in this manner the British approached the entrenched position held by the French in front of the city. The position of the British army at this stage had few natural advantages beyond the sea upon the right flank, and Lake Maadieh upon the left. There were also some ruins supposed to have been the ancient Palace of the Ptolemies.

An hour before the dawn on the day of the 21st, the French troops were on the move, but the British were not taken by surprise, and awaited the enemy in absolute silence. The morning was very dark and cloudy. Coming across the sand the tramp of the enemy was almost deadened. The French attack was made simultaneously upon the ruins, the redoubt, and the wing, held by the Black Watch, but was utterly repulsed. Falling back, the enemy sent forward another column with a six-pounder, and so stealthily did they advance that they were between the left of the Black Watch and the right of the Guards before they were seen. Colonel Stewart, who was in command of the Highlanders, acted with promptitude, manœuvring the 42nd so cleverly that the enemy was caught between two fires. The desperate Frenchmen rushed into the ruins, where they were received by a murderous fusillade. Through this predicament the gallant but unfortunate body of 'Invincibles' were forced to surrender after a very heavy loss.

Hearing that the French were again attacking, General Abercromby rode up, shouting, "My brave Highlanders, remember your country, remember your forefathers," at which the Black Watch, raising a cheer, charged the enemy. They cheered too soon, for at that moment the French cavalry cantered forward to cover the retreat of their infantry. Immediately Colonel Stewart sent the order for the Highlanders to fall back, but for some reason or another these directions were not received, and the ragged line of the advancing Black Watch was suddenly confronted by a charge of horse. It was a time when undisciplined troops might well have broken, but the Highlanders stood firm, receiving the shock as coolly as the 93rd awaited the Russian cavalry at Balaclava. The French General, alarmed at the repulse of his troops, hurried forward a column of infantry, but this body also was beaten off by the Highlanders. A second troop of cavalry advanced to meet with no better success, and shortly afterwards General Stuart's brigade reinforced the 42nd. It was now eight o'clock in the morning and nothing decisive had occurred, although the British had more than held their own. Unfortunately their ammunition had given out, so they had to endure the unceasing cannonade of the French guns without being able to reply. The situation was enough to unman any troops. An eye-witness has recorded: "The army suffered exceedingly from their fire, particularly the Highlanders and the right of General Stuart's brigade, who were exposed without cover to its full effect, being posted on a level piece of ground, over which the cannon shot rolled after striking the ground, and carried off a file of them at every successive rebound. This was more trying to the courage and discipline of the troops than the former attacks, but the trial was supported with perfect steadiness. Not a man moved from his position, except to close up the opening made by the shot, when his right or left-hand man was struck down ... To stand in this manner with perfect firmness, exposed to a galling fire, without any object to engage the attention or occupy the mind, and without the power of making the smallest resistance, was a trial of the character of the British soldier, to which the enemy did full justice."

At last the French, thoroughly disheartened with the morning's encounter, retreated back to their position before Alexandria, and the action was over. At the same moment Sir Ralph Abercromby, being mortally wounded, retired from the field. He was carried on board the Foudroyant, where he lay for some days, dying on the morning of the 28th. As a contemporary paper wrote of him, "his life was honourable, so his death was glorious. His memory will be recorded in the annals of his country, will be sacred to every British soldier and embalmed in the memory of a grateful posterity."

The action had been a severe test of the endurance of the Highlanders, and there were many who were buried in the desert sand never to see Lochaber or the Highland glens again. Those of the Black Watch who survived the fierce engagement prided themselves upon the standard of the French Invincibles and upon the word 'Egypt' added for all time to their regimental honours. The Camerons and Gordons for conspicuous distinction also added 'The Sphinx' to their regimental colours.

The command now fell upon General Hutchinson, who remained for some time before Alexandria, but very shortly proceeded to Cairo, taking up his position four miles from that city on June 16. Opposed to him was a force of 13,000 Frenchmen. But the French commander was only too anxious to surrender, on condition that his army was sent to France with their arms, baggage, and effects. It is probable that he had received instructions that his force would prove of more service in Europe.

Only the fall of Alexandria now remained to complete the conquest of Egypt. The French, finding themselves surrounded on two sides by a British army of some 14,000 men, cut off from the sea, and unable to retire on the south, capitulated on September 2. The collapse of hostilities, as swift as it was decisive, terminated the service of the Highland regiments in Egypt.

CHAPTER X
THE RETREAT ON CORUNNA
(1808-1809)

Wail loudly, ye women, your coronach doleful,

Lament him, ye pipers, tread solemn and slow.

Old Highland Lament.

During the years that the Highland regiments were on home service many eventful things took place. By the Peace of Amiens, England had surrendered almost all her conquests to Napoleon. She had promised to give up Malta and various places in the Mediterranean; she retained no territory in Africa. In the West Indies, which had cost the British army so many lives, she owned only Trinidad. She had also relinquished the claims of the Bourbons, which she had formerly supported, and she—no matter how grudgingly—recognised the authority of the Emperor. But it was obvious to everybody that the renewal of hostilities was only a question of time. Napoleon—just as much as the Kaiser at a later date—had set his heart on the downfall of England. His spies were everywhere, his network of information was immense, and he was determined, if he could not overwhelm her in arms, to strangle her in trade. He plotted to cause trouble in India—and here again it would seem unnecessary to provide a parallel. He attempted to reconquer Egypt. It therefore seemed politic to England, since bloodshed was inevitable, to enter upon a conflict before Napoleon was supreme upon the Continent, and by refusing to leave Malta (according to the agreement of Amiens), war broke out again in May 1803.

For the next two years our country was fated to fight France single-handed, and, until the battle of Trafalgar ensured our supremacy upon the sea, there was above everything else one scheme very close to the heart of Napoleon, and that the invasion of England. An army of at least 150,000 men was assembled at Boulogne, while, for their transport many hundreds of flat-bottomed boats were built, and just as the German fleet watched every opportunity to emerge and hold, even for a short time, the Channel and the North Sea, so the ships of Napoleon rode at anchor in the French ports, ever ready to dart out should the opportunity arise. Once the control of the Channel was gained they would be able to protect the transport of soldiers to English shores. It is interesting to see what our forefathers did to counteract this danger. All along the coast they built little watch-towers—many of which can still be seen—called Martello Towers. These were manned by small parties of soldiers, and provided with artillery. The Thames was fortified, and great bodies of volunteers were enrolled for the defence of the coast. Hardly a man but was in uniform, and the thoughts of every Briton were devoted to the safety of our country. Fortunately the British Navy shut the French ships within their own ports. Cornwallis, with a portion of the English fleet, locked up a French squadron at Brest. Nelson, with another detachment, enclosed the enemy at Toulon, whilst two other English admirals kept close watch at other points of danger.

In those days, when sailing ships could ill withstand stormy weather, but when, on the other hand, the dangers of submarines and mines did not exist, the vigil was not only wearisome, but also critical; for it must be remembered that if a great storm had swept the Channel, the coast of England might in a few hours have been left open to the invader.

So the weeks passed on, and it was borne in upon Napoleon that he would never gain the cliffs of Kent. He was the last man to waste his time with vain regrets, and postponing the humiliation of England he gave the order for his troops to march into Germany. But we were far from humiliation, for on October 21, 1805, was celebrated the crushing naval victory of Trafalgar.

Too often has victory been bought with a great national loss, and just as the conquest of Quebec brought with it the pathetic end of Wolfe, the success in Egypt the loss of Sir Ralph Abercromby, Corunna the tragedy of Sir John Moore, so this glorious victory carried with it that greatest of all calamities, the death of Nelson. But Trafalgar was the last supreme event in the naval struggle between Napoleon and England; henceforth he must confine his conquests and his hopes to the army and the Continent.

In the same year as Trafalgar was fought and won, and Austria, Russia, and England were again united in a coalition, Napoleon gained the victory of Ulm, and very shortly afterwards was again triumphant at Austerlitz. Before the end of 1805 Austria, never very reliable at such times, appealed for peace. The Coalition was staggering under one blow after another. Well might Pitt, on his death-bed at the beginning of 1806, breathe out his despairing spirit with the words, "My country, how I leave my country!"

The grasp that Napoleon was laying about the kingdoms of Europe was strengthened from year to year. He made his brother Joseph King of Naples, his brother Louis ruler of Holland, and Jerome King of Westphalia. In 1807 he came to terms with the Czar of Russia, forcing him to agree, together with Portugal, Sweden, and Denmark, to a coalition against England. And in the meantime he started what has been called his Continental System—an attempt to beat England to her knees by destroying her commerce. He forbade, in other words, the importation of

English trade into any country over which he had established his control. In this way one port after another shut its doors to English ships. By this means it seemed likely that England, growing less wealthy, would be weakened, and in course of time—and he had many years of promise before him—he would finally force her to capitulate at his own terms. Unfortunately for Napoleon's schemes, a blockade is useless unless it is universal. It was therefore essential to conquer those remaining countries that were not prepared to surrender their trade with Great Britain.

Principally owing to this policy the Spanish War broke out, a war that was to add not merely to the prestige of the British arms, but to the ultimate undermining of French supremacy.

It is with the Peninsular War that we shall be immediately interested, but it is necessary, before following out its story, to realise the infinite importance that lay in its success. Times of stress have a way of providing their own remedy, and even while the British nation, mourning the death of Nelson, was thinking how dark the future looked, Arthur Wellesley, future Duke of Wellington, was waiting for the hour of his destiny to strike.

In Spain, Napoleon, having compelled the king to abdicate, had placed the power in the hands of his brother Joseph, formerly king of Naples. This arrogant action irritated the Spanish nation to the point of insurrection. England, swift to seize such a chance, despatched a fleet and an army to assist the rebels, and Wellesley, who had already made his name in India, was placed in command of the British troops.

Acting with his amazing rapidity, Napoleon hastened to Spain, pouring his victorious armies to the very outskirts of Madrid. It seemed for a moment as though the cause of Spain was already lost. There was no force strong enough to challenge Napoleon. But there was a man with the genius to outwit him. That was Sir John Moore. With him were the Black Watch, the Gordons, and the Camerons, under the command of Sir John Hope. Moore attempted to unite his forces with those of Sir David Baird, but, failing to effect this, he resolved upon the desperate expedient of threatening Napoleon's lines of communication and enticing him from his advance.

The French general Soult was near a place called Saldana, where, after some deliberation, Moore decided that it would be unwise to attack him, as he had apparently received large reinforcements. Napoleon was marching inland from Madrid with 40,000 infantry and cavalry, while other French generals with their divisions were on the move towards the north of Spain. For Moore to take the offensive would have been madness. To retreat and go on retreating was a stroke of military genius.

It must not be thought that this retreat was entirely uneventful; indeed it was lit up by some of the most daring and brilliant actions in our history. Hot upon the trail of the British rearguard came the advance guard of the French army, but on no single occasion did our soldiers suffer a reverse. And yet it was a hazardous undertaking.

Moore's army was in hourly peril. He realised only too well that "it must glide along the edge of a precipice; must cross a gulf on a rotten plank; but he also knew the martial quality of his soldiers, felt the pulsation of his own genius, and, the object being worthy the deed, he dared essay it even against Napoleon." The pursuit by Napoleon was only less wonderful than the retreat of Moore. It was the heart of winter and the hills were choked with snow, yet Napoleon drove his forces over the mountain peaks and transported 50,000 men from Madrid to Astorga in a shorter period of time than would have taken a traveller to cover the same distance. At Astorga the French Emperor halted to read despatches, new come from the French capital. Napier tells us that when he received the despatches he dismounted from his horse, and ordering a fire to be lighted, threw himself down beside it. The snow was falling and it was bitterly cold, but he remained calm and unaffected, reading words that were to send him post-haste to Paris. News had come that Austria was again in arms against France. Leaving Soult and Ney with 60,000 men, Napoleon took to horse, and, accompanied by his Imperial Guard, made off at a gallop towards the Pyrenees, and so to Paris. It was left to Soult to continue the pursuit of Moore, and learn a lesson in war from the English general. In that immortal retreat the English forces lost not one gun, nor allowed their rearguard to be routed.

At the same time we must not under-estimate the tragic character of the march, nor the superb endurance of the soldiers, especially the Highlanders. Dr. Fitchett has, in his Fights for the Flag, printed portions of the memoirs of an English soldier who took part in the Peninsular campaign, and this man—Harris by name—throws sidelights of vivid colour upon incidental experiences. "A sergeant of the 92nd Highlanders," he records, "just about this time fell dead with fatigue, and no one stopped as we passed to offer him any assistance. Night came down upon us without our having tasted food or halted, and all night long we continued this dreadful march. Men began to look into each other's faces and ask the question, 'Are we ever to be halted again?' and many of the weaker sort were now seen to stagger, make a few desperate efforts, and then fall, perhaps to rise no more. Most of us had devoured all we carried in our haversacks and endeavoured to catch up anything we could snatch from hut or cottage in our route.... 'Where are you taking us to?' the Rifleman asked his officer. 'To England,' was the answer, 'if we get there!' At that 'the men began to murmur at not being permitted to turn and stand at bay, cursing the French and swearing they would rather die ten thousand deaths with their rifles in their hands in opposition, than endure the present toil.'"

It is our purpose in this book to follow the fortunes of the Highland regiments, but that in itself would make a distorted picture if we were not prepared to remember that other regiments bore as gallant a share during the various campaigns. Amongst these regiments the Rifles took a particularly glorious part in the Peninsular, and especially in the retreat to Corunna. They were commanded by General Craufurd, of whom Harris has written: "The Rifles being always at his heels, he seemed to think them his familiars. If he stopped his horse, and halted to deliver one of his stern reprimands, you would see half a dozen lean, unshaven, shoeless, and savage Riflemen, standing for the moment leaning upon their weapons, and scowling up in his face as he scolded; and when he dashed the spurs into his reeking horse, they would throw up their rifles upon their shoulders and hobble after him again."

Few generals have ever enjoyed the confidence and respect that Moore inspired in the hearts of his men. His influence upon the officers under him was so exceptional that hardly one who came under his spell but lived to achieve distinction in the years to come.

At last Moore with his ragged army entered Corunna, and the retreat was accomplished. Now had the ships been at anchor, as they should have been, the army could have embarked without further delay, and when the French came up might have been in safety. But as there was no sign of the transports, Moore decided to fortify the town and prepare to resist an attack. On the 14th of January several transports were sighted, and immediately the sick, the cavalry, and part of the artillery were placed on board. On the 16th the situation became very critical, and an assault was imminent. The division of General Hope held the left of the British line of battle, and included, amongst others, the Gordon Highlanders, while on the right, under General Baird, were the Black Watch, and to the right again, under Sir David Baird, were the Cameron Highlanders. The enemy opened the attack, and under the direction of their artillery advanced in four columns, reserving a fifth in support. General Moore, approaching the Black Watch, cried out, "Highlanders, remember Egypt!" Visions of Alexandria sprang up in the minds of the Highlanders, and under the inspiration of such words they advanced at a run, and flung back the French at the point of the bayonet. Meanwhile Paget's counter-attack was launched.

After this spirited encounter the 42nd began to retire, discovering that their ammunition threatened to give out, at which Moore addressed them again, crying, "My brave 42nd, join your comrades; ammunition is coming, and you have your bayonets." Immediately after this a ball struck the British general, bringing him to the ground. For a time he supported himself, still regarding with an intense expression the engagement in which the Highlanders were taking so remarkable a part. Captain Hardinge leapt from his horse and came to his assistance, but observing that he was distressed about the action, reassured him that the Black Watch were advancing, upon which he was immediately cheered up.

Captain Hardinge has given an account of this event. "The violence of the shock," he wrote, "threw him off his horse on his back. Not a muscle of his face altered, nor did a sigh betray the least sensation of pain. I dismounted, and taking his hand, he pressed me forcibly, casting his eyes very anxiously towards the 42nd Regiment which was hotly engaged, and his countenance expressed satisfaction when I informed him that the regiment was advancing. Assisted by a soldier of the 42nd, he was removed a few yards behind the shelter of a wall. He consented to be taken to the rear, and was put into a blanket for that purpose.... He was borne by six soldiers of the 42nd and Guardsmen, my sash supporting him in an easy manner. I caught at the hope that I might be mistaken in my fear that the wound was mortal, and I remarked that I trusted that when the surgeon had dressed his wound he might recover. He turned his head, and looking steadfastly at the wound for a few moments, said, 'No, Hardinge, I feel that to be impossible.'"

In this sad fashion, borne by a sergeant of the Black Watch and two files of Highlanders, Sir John Moore was carried into Corunna. Throughout the journey he persisted on stopping at intervals in order to learn how the action proceeded, expressing his satisfaction when the noise of firing appeared to be dying away in the distance as an indication that the French were in retreat.

"Thus ended," writes Napier so finely, "the career of Sir John Moore, a man whose uncommon capacity was sustained by the purest virtue, and governed by a disinterested patriotism more in keeping with the primitive than the luxurious age of a great nation. His tall, graceful person, his dark searching eyes, strongly defined forehead, and singularly expressive mouth indicated a noble disposition and a refined understanding. The lofty sentiments of honour habitual to his mind, adorned by a subtle playful wit, gave him in conversation an ascendancy that he always preserved by the decisive vigour of his actions. He maintained the right with a vehemence bordering upon fierceness, and every important transaction in which he was engaged increased his reputation for talent, and confirmed his character as a stern enemy to vice, a steadfast friend to merit, a just and faithful servant of his country. The honest loved him, the dishonest feared him; for while he lived he scorned and spurned the base, who, with characteristic propriety, spurned at him when he was dead."

After this melancholy event there was nothing further to prevent the army embarking in their transports and sailing for England. One division, in which the Black Watch was included, landed at Portsmouth, and the other at Plymouth.

Throughout the campaign the Highland regiments, particularly the Black Watch and the Camerons, were never more worthy of the growing reputation of the Highland soldiers—a reputation that was to shine still brighter at Fuentes de Onoro, Quatre Bras, and Waterloo.

CHAPTER XI
WITH THE CAMERONS IN THE PENINSULAR
(1810-1814)

I hear the pibroch sounding, sounding,

Deep o'er the mountain and glen,

While light springing footsteps are trampling the heath,

'Tis the march of the Cameron Men.

Regimental March.

The 1st Battalion of the famous Cameron Highlanders was founded in 1793 by Alan Cameron of Erracht, Inverness-shire, and owed its formation to the danger of invasion from France. The 2nd Battalion was not embodied until 1897.

The Camerons have not seen so much service as the other Highland regiments, but have always displayed daring bravery.

As we have seen in our last chapter the regiment won battle honours at Corunna, but at Fuentes de Oñoro it established a reputation.

Between the years 1809 and 1813 Wellington was in command of three armies in the Peninsular—his own English army, an admirable veteran force, the Portuguese troops commanded by Beresford, and the Spaniards. The latter were not very serviceable in the field, but had a perfect genius for guerilla warfare, and as they knew the country intimately and were not compelled to keep together, they proved a constant menace and irritation to the French, threatening their communications, cutting off their supplies, and sniping soldiers on the march or in camp. Wellington was anxious to establish his base in Portugal, and from there to push back the French until Spain was free. This task occupied him for four years, but in that time he was fighting not only for England but for Europe as well. The Peninsular War may appear a very small campaign in comparison with the vast movements of Napoleon, but it was sapping the strength of France. It drained Napoleon's forces of some of their best and most reliable troops, and humiliated them in the eyes of the world. Napoleon might be victorious himself, but his arms and his generals suffered one defeat after another at the hands of Wellington. The legend of invincibility was broken, and all over Europe hope sprang into life once more.

The Highland regiments did not leave for Portugal in a brigade. The Camerons were with Wellington at Busaco on September 25, 1810, whereas the 2nd Battalion of the Black Watch did not embark for Portugal until April 1812.

The Camerons were commanded by Major-General Alan Cameron, and resisted the advance of the French general, Massena, prior to the retirement of the British army behind the lines of Torres Vedras. The long winter broke the strength of the enemy, and in the spring the battle of Fuentes de Oñoro was fought. In this action the following Highland regiments were engaged—the Highland Light Infantry, the Gordons, the 1st Battalion of the Black Watch, and the Camerons. Perhaps more than any other regiment the Camerons excelled upon that day.

Wellington had already invested the fortress of Almeida, and to break the advance of Massena he occupied the district between the two villages of Fuentes de Oñoro in Spain, and Villa Formosa in Portugal. It was on May 3 that Massena hurled his assault upon the former, where the Camerons and the H.L.I. were stationed.

Throughout the whole of one day the French strove to capture the village, and at times it was touch and go whether the British would not be compelled to evacuate the place.

A Cameron Highlander, who fought in the action, has recorded his experiences. "The village," he says, referring to the initial stage of the engagement, "was now vigorously attacked by the enemy at two points, and with such a superior force, that, in spite of the unparalleled bravery of our troops, they were driven back, contesting every inch of the ground. On our retreat through the village we were met by the 71st Regiment (H.L.I.), cheering and led on by Colonel Cadogan, which had been detached from the line to our support. The chase was now turned, and although the French were obstinately intent on keeping their ground, and so eager that many of their cavalry had entered the town and rushed furiously down the streets, all their efforts were in vain; nothing could withstand the charge of the gallant 71st, and in a short time, in spite of all resistance, they cleared the village."

But that was only the initial attack. Upon May 5, Massena came seriously to the assault. The light companies had now been withdrawn, leaving the H.L.I. and Camerons to hold the position.

In the morning the fiercest attack was made by the French. For a time they carried everything before them. The English cavalry was driven back, Ramsay's horse artillery being cut off, and apparently captured. Mad with victory the French squadrons came full at the British infantry. Two companies of the Camerons were taken after a gallant resistance. The flood of the enemy passed on, obliterating the detachments of the defenders as surf covers the shore. Backwards the remainder of the Camerons and H.L.I. were forced, till at the chapel they made their stand. That day was full of brilliant incidents. One of the most dramatic and picturesque was the return of Ramsay, with his artillery cleaving the ranks of the French as a scythe cleaves the grain. Another was the spirit with which the Black Watch met the French cavalry as they galloped in dense squadrons upon the British lines. Down went their bayonets, the Highland ranks stood grim and unshaken as a granite rock. The cavalry flung themselves with desperate bravery upon the steel, recoiling towards their own lines, broken and defeated.

In the meantime the Camerons were carrying on their forlorn struggle, and at the climax of the battle they suffered their greatest loss. Captain Jameson has recorded how "a French soldier was observed to slip aside into a doorway and take deliberate aim at Colonel Cameron, who fell from his horse mortally wounded. A cry of grief, intermingled with shouts for revenge, arose from the rearmost Highlanders, who witnessed the fall of their commanding officer, and was rapidly communicated to those in front."

The rage of the Highlanders knew no bounds. They flung themselves upon the French, who, surprised by the desperate vigour of the charge, were driven back. Supported by the H.L.I., the Camerons turned the scales at this point, and with the arrival of Wellington's reserves the battle of Fuentes de Oñoro was won.

Ciudad Rodrigo was the next place to fall. We are told that the story of the assault can never be adequately described, and the bravery and determination displayed by the British troops was beyond all praise. It was certainly a masterly feat to assemble 40,000 men about the fortress of Castile without arousing the suspicion of the enemy, and following this up by a successful assault, capturing the stores and artillery of Marmont's forces.

In a similar manner Badajoz was surrounded by 30,000 men, and three attacks were planned—on the right by Picton, in the centre by Colville, and on the left by Leith. The soldiers swarmed up the ruins in the broken walls, to be hurled down again and again by the besieged. With dogged courage they still persisted, and carried the place by storm, with a loss of 2000 killed and wounded. Portugal was saved.

It was early in June that Wellington began to move towards Salamanca. Of that engagement Napier has written: "Salamanca was the first decisive victory gained by the Allies in the Peninsula. In former actions the French had been repulsed; here they were driven headlong, as it were into a mighty wind without help or stay ... and the shock reaching even to Moscow heaved and shook the colossal structure of Napoleon's power to its very base."

For their part in this battle the Camerons and H.L.I. were allowed to add the name 'Salamanca' to their battle honours.

Although the wars in the Peninsula were not 'Highlanders' battles' in the way the Crimean and Indian Mutiny campaigns were—yet the regiments principally engaged, namely the Black Watch, Camerons, Gordons, and H.L.I., fought with the greatest distinction and gallantry.

On September 9, 1812, the Black Watch and Camerons stormed the hill of San Michael, carrying ladders and splicing them together under the very walls. A terrific fire was opened on them as they ascended, and for a long time every man who clambered to the top of the ladder was certain of death. This signal slaughter so discouraged the Portuguese that they would on no account support the Highlanders, and for this reason their loss of life was of no avail, as it was impossible to storm the garrison without reinforcements. And so Burgos was doomed to be a failure, and the retreat began. The loss of the 42nd in the storming of San Michael was exceedingly heavy, and with the abandonment of the siege the allied forces gave up the attempt and withdrew to the frontier of Portugal, where winter quarters were established.

In 1813 Wellington set his face towards France. With Graham were the Black Watch, the Camerons, and the Argyllshire Highlanders. Colin Campbell, who had been with Moore, and who was to see service in the Crimea and in the Mutiny, was in one of the battalions under Graham.

On the 20th of June Wellington was nearing Vittoria, while Graham, who had been despatched southward, was to attack the French right and force the passage of the Zadora. Graham approached this valley of the Zadora on the 21st, but before advancing it was essential that the enemy's troops should be driven across the river.

This was accomplished successfully, and by this action Graham cut off the French from their only way of retreat to Bayonne, and the only possible road was rendered altogether impassable by the confusion of the troops and baggage. As an authority has pungently written, "Never was there a defeat more decisive, the French were beaten before the town, and in the town, and through the town, and out of the town, and behind the town"; indeed so thoroughly were they beaten that the whole French force at Vittoria relinquished its baggage, guns, stores, and papers, making it impossible to know what was owing or what was to be done, while even the commanding officers suffered considerably from an absence of clothes. In this action the H.L.I. lost very heavily. Their commanding officer, Colonel Henry Cadogan, gave them the lead, and almost immediately was mortally wounded. Like Wolfe at Quebec, his sole anxiety was whether the French were beaten, and the same answer was given him, "They are giving way everywhere."

On that eventful day the H.L.I. lost 400 officers and men, the toll of gallantry commemorated in the jingle:

Loud was the battle's stormy swell,

Where thousands fought and many fell,

But the 71st they bore the bell,

At the battle of Vittoria.

During the campaign of the Pyrenees the Highland regiments were not members of the brigades that saw most of the fighting. We have dealt with their achievements under Graham, and we must not forget that the 42nd were rewarded with the word 'Pyrenees' to commemorate the success of their arms, but on the whole the brunt of the fighting fell to other troops.

In September San Sebastian was taken, and on October 7 the passage of the Bidassoa was carried, upon which the British troops caught their first glimpse of the country of France, and, rushing up the slopes on the other side of the river, carried the Croix des Bouquets stronghold.

Along the river Nivelle rose the French lines of fortifications, but the British troops, in no way disheartened, forded the river on November 10, and carried the position by storm. It was for this action that the Royal Highlanders display the word 'Nivelle' upon their regimental colours. The humiliation which Soult suffered was in no way lessened by the desertion of his German troops, who, learning that their country had decided to throw off the tyranny of France, marched over to the Allies. Presently the French fell back towards Orthez, but a severe defeat compelled Soult to retire altogether from the coast towards Toulouse, after a loss of some 8000 men. By the first week in March the Allies were in hot pursuit, with Beresford threatening Bordeaux.

The campaign was approaching its final stages, and it was high time. "The clothing of the army at large," records a Highlander, "but the Highland Brigade in particular, was in a very tattered state. The clothing of the 91st Regiment had been two years in wear, the men were thus under the necessity of repairing their old garments in the best manner they could. Some had the elbows of their coats mended with grey cloth, others had one-half of the sleeve of a different colour from the body; their trousers were in equally as bad a condition as their coats. The 42nd, which was the only corps in the Brigade that wore the kilt, was beginning to lose it by degrees. Men falling sick and left in the rear frequently got the kilt made into trousers, and on joining the regiment again no plaid could be furnished to supply the loss....

"It is impossible to describe the painful state that some shoeless men were in, crippling along the way, their feet cut or torn by sharp stones or brambles. To remedy the want of shoes, the raw hides of the newly-slaughtered bullocks were given to cut up on purpose to form a sort of buskins for the bare-footed soldiers."

The writer finishes his reflections upon a cheerful note—just as true to-day as it was a hundred years ago. "We were getting hardier and stronger every day in person; the more we suffer the more confidence we feel in our strength; all in health and no sickness."

On April 10, 1814, came the first movement towards the last decisive battle of Toulouse, and the final and culminating victory of the arduous Peninsular War was about to take place. Wellington was in command of some 40,000 Anglo-Portuguese troops, 12,000 Spanish troops, and 84 pieces of cannon. Under Soult were some 38,000 men, in addition to which there were the National Guard of the city, while 80 guns defended the formidable ramparts constructed by the townsfolk of Toulouse. Wellington advanced the Spanish, who, displaying great courage, were successful in driving the French back on to their own fortifications.

At the same time the lines of redoubt on the right were taken and carried by General Pack's brigade with the Black Watch, Camerons, and Argylls. Unfortunately the Spaniards were not sufficiently experienced or proven to withstand the fire from the French batteries, and for a time were disorganised. On the extreme right Picton had not been any more successful.

This repulse of the Spaniards disarranged to some extent the plan of attack, and Beresford's artillery was hurried up to shell the heights. After a brief rest the assault again began. With heroic courage the Spaniards advanced in the teeth of a heavy fire, but in each case were repulsed. General Pack's brigade was then ordered to attack the works at the two centre redoubts under the full range of the enemy's fire. It is recorded that they did not return a shot, but advanced with perfect steadiness. Before the Highlanders lay the enemy's entrenchment, while "darkening the whole hill, flanked by clouds of cavalry, and covered by the fire of their redoubt, the enemy came down on us like a torrent, their generals and field-officers riding in front, and waving their hats amidst the shouts of the multitude, resembling the roar of an ocean."

The Highlanders, unmoved by the spectacle, fired a volley which was returned by the French, then without pause charged the position, taking the redoubt. It was a brilliant piece of work, carried out mainly by the Black Watch and the Camerons.

Shortly after, General Pack rode up and uttered the following words: "I have just now been with General Clinton, and he has been pleased to grant my request, that in the charge we are now about to make upon the enemy's redoubts, the 42nd shall have the honour of leading the attack. The 42nd will advance."

During the next few minutes the artillery poured their fire upon the Black Watch. Men fell in heaps. There was only one thing to do before the regiment was annihilated, and that was to rush the batteries. Not a hundred of the 500 who had started were left when the redoubt was taken. But it was impossible to hold such a position with only a handful of men. The remnant of the Black Watch retired towards the Argyllshires, who were in position near a farmhouse. The enemy, determined to recover the lost ground, nearly achieved their purpose. With a force of some five or six thousand men advancing under sheltered ground they rushed impetuously upon the Black Watch, who were forced by sheer weight of numbers to fall back upon the 91st. It was but a momentary retirement. Suddenly, irresistibly, the two Highland regiments crashed upon the disordered front of the enemy. Panic overcame the French. Victory was assured.

It was the Highland regiments, and the Black Watch above all, that, in Fitchett's opinion, saved Wellington from a reverse at Toulouse. Anton relates that, having once started towards the French entrenchments over ground difficult to manœuvre on, it would have meant annihilation to retreat. It was only the invincible character of the Highlanders' charge that carried them to victory.

Toulouse was still within the range of the British artillery, and Soult decided to evacuate that evening, in order to avoid a siege without very much chance of holding out long. It was humiliating for a Field-Marshal of France to surrender the capital of the second Province, within whose walls a veteran army, that had already conquered two kingdoms, had rushed for protection following a series of defeats at the hand of Wellington.

The troops of Great Britain had come to the liberation of Spain and Portugal; had fought eight pitched battles against commanders only second to Napoleon, and had "out-manœuvred, out-marched, out-flanked, and overturned their enemy." There only remained the decisive actions of

Quatre Bras and Waterloo to convince Napoleon himself that the British Army and the British leader were not to be despised.

Toulouse was the final battle and the decisive victory of the Peninsular War. In a manner, however, Toulouse was more spectacular than serviceable, for eight days before the action took place Napoleon had resigned his crown; and while Wellington was beating back Soult step by step, first to the Pyrenees, then to Vittoria, to San Sebastian, and then to Toulouse, the enormous forces of the Allies were with the same inevitable progress driving the army of Napoleon towards Paris. Beaten in the field, and distrusted in Paris, he decided that the time had come to throw himself upon the mercy of the Allies, if by abdicating his throne he might at least retrieve some hope of the accession of his little son. The Allies in due course occupied Paris. Napoleon, deserted even by his wife, reached the little Isle of Elba, and Louis XVIII.—brother of that tragic Louis who was executed twenty-one years previously—ascended for a brief time the throne of France.

BATTLE HONOURS OF THE (QUEEN'S OWN) CAMERON HIGHLANDERS

Egmont-op-Zee, Corunna, Busaco, Fuentes de Oñoro, Salamanca, Pyrenees, Nivelle, Nive, Toulouse, Peninsula, Waterloo, Alma, Sevastopol, Lucknow; Egypt, 1882; Tel-el-Kebir; Nile, 1884-1885; Atbara, Khartoum; South Africa, 1900-1902.

Raised in 1793. From 1873 to 1881 the 79th (Queen's Own Cameron Highlanders) Regiment.

The 2nd Battalion raised in 1897.

CHAPTER XII
THE GORDONS AT QUATRE BRAS
(June 16, 1815)

There was a sound of revelry by night,

And Belgium's capital had gather'd then

Her Beauty and her Chivalry, and bright

The lamps shone o'er fair women and brave men;

A thousand hearts beat happily: and when

Music arose with its voluptuous swell,

Soft eyes look'd love to eyes which spake again,

And all went merry as a marriage-bell;

But hush! hark! a deep sound strikes like a rising knell!

BYRON.

Towards the end of 1814 there was an interesting assemblage of emperors, kings, generals, and representatives of the people at Vienna to settle once and for all the future peace of Europe. There was not a great deal of sympathy between the Allies, and now that Napoleon had shot his bolt, and was apparently for ever humiliated, disputes soon took the place of friendly overtures, while the Congress promised to disagree as ardently as any other peaceful gathering before or since. Napoleon, fretting at Elba, learnt how matters stood, and decided with his amazing promptitude that the day had dawned that might carry with it his re-accession to power.

In France Louis XVIII. was little better than a shadow upon a throne. The reaction that had set in against Napoleon at the time of his abdication had been altogether submerged by the impatience with which the French people regarded the deliberations of the Allies. The pride of France was touched, and the pride of France has ever soared very high. Like many another exile Napoleon by his absence attained a greater hold upon the imagination of his countrymen than he had ever possessed before. Those old soldiers who had been victorious under his standards were never tired of foretelling the time when the 'Little Corporal' would again return and sweep all the armies of the Allies before him like forest leaves. We may be perfectly sure that Napoleon was now, as always, in touch with the spirit of

France, and that when he struck it was with everything as much in his favour as could be.

On a dark March evening, when the British war-ships were riding at anchor, and no whisper of danger reached the watching sailors, he left Elba and set foot upon the shores of France. The news of his arrival sped like wildfire through every village of the south, and was flung from lip to lip until it reached Paris itself. The mere presence of Napoleon, without arms, without money, without anything to win back an Empire, sent Louis XVIII. scurrying into exile!

It was a triumph indeed. But Napoleon was not foolish enough to ignore the apprehensions of the French people; whatever feelings were hidden within his own heart he stifled them for the moment under a pretence of peace. It was England who refused to discuss the situation on any terms. Napoleon was declared an outlaw and the enemy of Europe. As our countrymen pledged themselves a hundred years later to crush and overthrow Prussianism, so they pledged themselves then to fight until the danger was averted. The arrival of Napoleon had been so swift that it was quite impossible to assemble the Allies. The Austrian and Russian forces had to travel great distances, and only the Prussian army on the Rhine under Blücher, the English in Belgium under Wellington, with some Hanoverians, Belgians, and Dutch, were ready to withstand the swift onrush of the French.

With his unerring judgment Napoleon grasped the situation. He realised, like those German hosts in the summer of 1914, that he must win, if win at all, by forced marches and forced battles. His army was a small one, but was largely composed of veteran troops. It was perfectly within reason to achieve the separation of the forces of Wellington and Blücher, and defeat them in turn. The enthusiasm with which Napoleon was greeted by the French soldiers is one of the most remarkable episodes in history. To them he was the son of New France, the invincible 'Little Corporal.' When he left Paris to join the army he uttered these memorable words: "I go," he said, "to measure myself with Wellington," and when he arrived at the Imperial Headquarters he sent this message to his troops:

"Soldiers! We have forced marches to make, battles to fight, troubles to encounter; but, with firmness victory will be ours. Rejoice, the honour and the happiness of the country will be recovered! To every Frenchman who has a heart, the moment has now arrived to conquer or die!"

Napoleon aimed at the occupation of Brussels, then in the hands of the British, and there is no doubt that his intention was to surprise Wellington's army by the rapidity of his advance. There is also little question that if he had succeeded in taking Brussels, a great part of Belgium would have risen in his favour. An examination of the map will show how many roads there are converging upon Brussels from the French frontier, and it was unknown to Wellington upon which Napoleon might march. Accordingly the English Commander-in-Chief distributed his forces so that he could concentrate upon any single point.

It would be foolish to praise one Highland regiment above another, for prowess is largely a matter of opportunity. In the action at Quatre Bras both the Gordons and the Black Watch were beyond praise, while at Waterloo the former took romance as it were by the stirrup iron, and added a new glamour to the old tale of Scotland's glory.

At ten o'clock on that eventful night, when the dance in Brussels was at its height, Colonel John Cameron, commanding officer of the Gordons, left the ballroom and went to his quarters. Early on June 16, amidst torrents of rain, the 92nd marched out of the city for the impending conflict. The bagpipes screamed through the streets, bringing many a face to the windows to watch how the Gordons went to face Ney at Quatre Bras. They took up position near a farmhouse, where soon after their arrival the Duke of Wellington himself rode up to Colonel Cameron, and congratulated him upon the appearance of his men, checking for a while their impatience.

At Quatre Bras when the fight was high,

Stout Cameron stood with wakeful eye,

Eager to leap, as a mettlesome hound,

Into the fray with a plunge and a bound.

But Wellington, lord of the cool command,

Held the reins with a steady hand,

Saying, "Cameron, wait, you'll soon have enough—

Give the Frenchmen a taste of your stuff,

When the Cameron men are wanted."

In front of the farmhouse there was a ditch, and this the Gordons were ordered to defend, together with the outhouses and other buildings. They had hardly got into position before the attack commenced, and the Highlanders found themselves confronted by the forces of Marshal Ney. Their ranks were raked for a considerable time by the French artillery. This was only supplementary to a desperate charge by the French cavalry, at that time unrivalled in Europe. The chasseurs managed to work their way behind the Gordons, and Wellington was compelled to leap a fence to avoid capture. But the Frenchmen never broke out again. The 92nd accounted for them.

Meanwhile the 42nd—which with three other regiments formed Pack's brigade—were brought up after a very long march and flung into the heat of the fighting, changing commanders no less than four times. Confused, separated, seeing their officers fall on all sides, they endured sufficient hammering to break the confidence of many a disciplined regiment; but the ranks of the Black Watch had never been broken, and they remained perfectly staunch until, in its turn, the French cavalry was shattered upon their bayonets.

Anton, who served in the Black Watch, relates how they marched out of the ancient gate of Brussels and entered the forest of Soignes. Shortly afterwards the frightened peasantry ran chattering past them, saying that the enemy were advancing. Then General Pack came galloping up, and reproved the Colonel for not having the bayonets fixed. A few minutes later the Belgian skirmishers came dashing helter-skelter through the open ranks of the 42nd, and next instant the Highlanders were confronted with their pursuers.

At the sight of the grim faces of the Black Watch the French fell back for the time being, while the Highlanders advanced, at which Marshal Ney ordered a regiment of Lancers to break upon their flank. They came with such rapidity that they almost took the Highlanders off their guard. "We instantly formed 'rally-square,'" says Anton. "Every man's piece was loaded, and our enemies approached at full charge, the feet of their horses seemed to tear up the ground. Our skirmishers having been impressed with the same opinion that these were Brunswick cavalry, fell beneath their lances, and few escaped death or wounds. Our brave Colonel fell at this time pierced through the chin until the point of the lance reached the brain. Captain Menzies fell covered with wounds, and a momentary conflict took place over him. He was a powerful man, and, hand to hand, more than a match for six ordinary men.... Of all descriptions of cavalry, certainly the Lancers seem the most formidable to infantry, as the lance can be projected with considerable precision and with deadly effect without bringing the horse to the point of the bayonet, and it was only by rapid and well-directed fire of musketry that these formidable assailants were repulsed."

The Gordons having repulsed the cavalry at the point of the bayonet, awaited the advance of the veteran French infantry.

Their vigil was soon rewarded. The Duke of Wellington, perceiving that some French had gained a footing in the farmhouse which was of such strategic importance, shouted to their commander, "Now, Cameron, is the time; take care of the road." Major-General Baines riding up shouted,

"Ninety-second, follow me!" The order to charge was given, and the 92nd, leaping from the ditch, rushed forward impetuously upon the enemy, hurling them back at the point of the bayonet. The victory was won, but at great cost to the Gordons, for Colonel Cameron was shot by a bullet fired from one of the upper windows of the farmhouse, and was soon beyond human aid. He was conveyed to the village of Waterloo before he died, with the words: "I die happy, and I trust my dear country will remember that I have served her faithfully." It is worth while recalling once again that powerful verse written by Sir Walter Scott:

Through shell and shot he leads no more,

Low laid 'mid friends' and foemen's gore;

But 'long his native lake's wild shore

And Sunart rough and high Ardgour

And Morven long shall tell,

And proud Ben Nevis hear with awe

How upon bloody Quatre Bras

Brave Cameron heard the wild hurrah

Of conquest, as he fell!

The losses suffered by the Highland regiments had been very heavy, but they had won deathless prestige. Out of all the forces engaged Wellington selected four regiments for special mention. The Black Watch, the Gordons, and the Camerons were of that proud body. During this time the French and the Prussians had been engaged at the battle of Ligny, and although Blücher had superior forces to Napoleon he had lost the day, though had not actually suffered a defeat. After the action the Prussians retreated towards Maestricht in order to maintain their communications with Wellington's army. Unfortunately for the British, the despatch-rider who was sent to inform Wellington that the Prussian army was in retreat did not reach him, and it was not until the 17th, at Quatre Bras, that the British General heard the result of the battle of Ligny. This news—that Napoleon had defeated Blücher—was something of a shock to Wellington, who had hoped, with Prussian support, to make a definite attack upon the French.

The Gordons At Quatre Bras

After the indecisive action at Quatre Bras, Wellington decided to march his army towards Brussels, and attempt to restore communication with Blücher. He despatched word to him that he intended to halt at Mont St. Jean, but only on condition that Blücher would pledge himself to the extent of 25,000 men. The Duke of Uxbridge covered the retreat of the British forces—for there is no denying that it was in the nature of a retreat—and the army halted for the night close to a little village that has gone down to history under the name of Waterloo.

BATTLE HONOURS OF THE GORDON HIGHLANDERS

Mysore, Seringapatam, Egmont-op-Zee, Mandora, Corunna, Fuentes de Oñoro, Almaraz, Vittoria, Pyrenees, Nive, Orthez, Peninsula, Waterloo; South Africa, 1835; Delhi, Lucknow, Charasiah; Kabul, 1879; Kandahar, 1880; Afghanistan, 1878-1880; Egypt, 1882, 1884; Tel-el-Kebir; Nile, 1884-1885; Chitral, Tirah; South Africa, 1899-1902; Ladysmith, Paardeberg.

1st Battalion, raised 1758, was disbanded. Re-formed 1787 as the 75th (Highland) Regiment of Foot. From 1862 to 1881 the 75th (Stirlingshire) Regiment.

2nd Battalion, raised 1794, as the 100th (Gordon Highlanders) Regiment of Foot. From 1861 to 1881 the 92nd (Gordon Highlanders) Regiment of Foot.

CHAPTER XIII
WITH WELLINGTON AT WATERLOO
(June 18, 1815)

In vain did cuirassiers in clouds surround them,

When, cannon thundering as the ocean raves,

They left our squares unmoved as they had found them,

Firm as a rock amidst the ocean's waves.

NORMAN MACLEOD.

Many have been the explanations of Napoleon's failure at Waterloo. It has been said that his star was on the wane and his health undermined, that he entrusted his fortunes to incompetent generals such as Ney and Grouchy, that his troops were not the soldiers of the early campaigns. But the truth of the matter is that Napoleon was beaten here as his troops had been beaten in the Peninsular simply by the dogged front of the British infantry. We have seen how the Highlanders withstood the cavalry at Quatre Bras, how they stormed the French position at Toulouse, how they were the better men at Fuentes de Oñoro. They were not alone in that quality of endurance and nerve. Throughout the whole British Army there was a confidence in itself that has remained till this day, and which is possessed by no other soldiers in the world. A remarkable testimony to this was made by General von Müffling, a Prussian officer, who in the curious changes of time was attached to Wellington's staff. "For a battle," he says, "there is not perhaps in Europe an army equal to the British; that is to say, none whose discipline and whole military tendency is so purely and exclusively calculated for giving battle. The British soldier is vigorous, well-fed, by nature both brave and intrepid, trained to the most rigorous discipline and admirably armed. The infantry resist the attacks of cavalry with great confidence, and when taken in flank or rear, British troops are less disconcerted than any European army."

"Marshal Bugeaud," says Captain Becke in his Napoleon and Waterloo, "has left it on record that 'the British infantry are the best in the world,'—however, he was careful to add this significant statement—'But fortunately there are not many of them.'"

It is probable that Napoleon was misinformed regarding the strength of Blücher's forces, or else he underrated the efficiency of the Prussian army. At any rate he was satisfied with instructing Marshal Grouchy to occupy himself in the pursuit of Blücher while he dealt with Wellington. It has been stated that Grouchy failed in his duty, and that had he carried out the Emperor's instructions Wellington might have been unable to withstand the furious assault of Napoleon's veterans. But the French offensive was fairly checked before ever Blücher arrived.

In the meantime Wellington prepared for battle, having as implicit a trust in Blücher as had long ago existed between Marlborough and Eugene. Throughout the long day at Waterloo he maintained his ground in perfect composure and confidence, knowing that the Prussians were nearing him at every hour.

The strength of the army under Wellington was 50,000 infantry, 12,000 cavalry, 5000 odd artillery, with 156 guns. But of this number only 24,000 were British, and to quote from Napier: "A French soldier would not be equal to more than one English soldier, but he would not be afraid to meet two Dutch, Prussians, or soldiers of the Confederation."

In the Military and Naval Museum in Whitehall there is a most admirable plan of the field of Waterloo of considerable size and drawn to scale, and more instructive than pages of explanatory notes. But to put the matter quite simply, there was a valley some three miles long, varying in breadth here and there, while in close proximity to this valley ran a chain of hills in parallel direction on each side. The British forces were ranged on the north with the French army on the southern range, where their artillery confronted each other, while the advances of horse and foot were made over the valley underneath. The village of Mont St. Jean was behind the centre of the northern hills, and the other village, La Belle Alliance, behind the southern range. Then there was a broad highway—a very important feature of the battle—leading from Charleroi to Brussels, and passing through both these villages, thus bisecting the English and the French lines. This road was the proposed route by which Napoleon hoped to reach Brussels, but was in reality to be the line of his retreat.

There were also some other important hamlets which were taken and retaken in the course of the day, on the right wing the Flemish farmhouse of Hougoumont, with its outbuildings, affording cover to whichever force was in possession. In the centre lay La Haye Sainte.

Napoleon has criticised Wellington for occupying the position he did. Strategically he believed that it was a treacherous one, as it could not afford him any retreat. On the other hand, it was a protection for Brussels, and in after years Wellington himself remarked: "They never could have beaten us so that we could not have held the wood against them." He referred to the forest of Soignes, which certainly would have afforded cover for artillery against overwhelming forces.

On the morning of the 17th the 42nd marched from Quatre Bras to the undulating height of Mont St. Jean. On arriving there Wellington said, "We shall retire no farther." This was the first occasion on which the English Commander had come into personal contact with Napoleon. Not since Scipio and Hannibal at Zama had two such military giants met face to face—Napoleon, who had swept victorious over Europe; Wellington, who, on a lesser scale, had, upon the fields of Spain, driven the greatest French marshals before him. And now, upon the eve of this great battle, Wellington stood upon high ground perfectly imperturbable, while not so far away Napoleon passed along his line, receiving tumultuous cheers, inspiriting his soldiers to carry the English position by assault, firm in the belief that if his veteran troops by their very prestige could fling back the English lines, the victory was as good as won. Certainly it was a manœuvre that had always, or nearly always proved successful against the armies of other nations, but had always failed in the Peninsular against the British soldier. The French formation on this occasion can best be compared to and was inspired by the same motive as the Prussian formation a hundred years later—it relied upon the discipline of men advancing in mass to carry a position at the point of the bayonet. The British army was in line.

Much has been made in recent years of the part that the Belgians played at Quatre Bras and Waterloo, and it is only fair to a nation so closely associated with us to-day to point out that had not the Dutch-Belgian forces withstood Ney's first furious attack at Quatre Bras, British aid might have come too late to stem a disaster.

Upon the field of Waterloo the Dutch-Belgian brigade went into the action 18,000 strong, and lost 90 officers and 2000 odd men. The Dutch-Belgian troops were placed in front of Picton's division, a hopeless position to withstand the full weight of the French bombardment and d'Erlon's attack. That they failed is no reflection upon their gallantry. After their retirement past Picton's division they returned to take an important share in the action.

The battle commenced at noon on June 18, 1815, after a night of terrible rain, and Napoleon opened the engagement by despatching his brother Jerome to attack the farmhouse of Hougoumont. The French poured down the southern heights, moving forward in unbroken regularity, only to find—as the Prussian Guard were to find long after at Ypres—that the British Guards were invincible. Meanwhile, under Sir Denis Pack were the Black Watch and the Gordons, holding the line to the left of the road to Brussels. Following the attack launched on Hougoumont came the second attack, which was directed against Picton's division. The story of how the comparatively small force under his command managed to withstand this attack, and how the Scots Greys poured like a river upon the confused French soldiery is an immortal incident in the history of the British Army.

After beating back the enemy, the command was given to the Highlanders to open ranks, and a few minutes later the Greys passed through, leaped the hedges, and prepared to charge the enemy. Presently a galloper rode up with the command, "92nd, you must charge, for all the troops on your right and left have given way."

The Gordons, though exhausted with hard fighting, prepared to advance, and the Scots Greys assembled with them. The bagpipes struck up as the Greys passed into the ranks of the 92nd, and with one accord, and shouting "Scotland for ever!" the Gordons gripped the stirrups of their comrades and swept into the mad charge. Horse and man together, nothing could withstand that—for the glory of Scotland they were ready to win through or die in the thick of the fight.

The French column was struck to the ground. Two French eagles and 2000 prisoners were within a few minutes in the hands of the British. Sir Denis Pack rode up with the memorable words, "Highlanders, you have saved the day!"

But the Highlanders had not matters all their own way. For hours they stood under a harassing fire, and to quote General Foy: "We saw those sons of Albion formed up on the plain between the woods of Hougoumont and the village of Mont St. Jean. Death was before them and in their ranks, disgrace in their rear. In this terrible situation neither the cannon-balls of the Imperial Guard, discharged almost at point-blank, nor the victorious cavalry of France, could make the least impression on the immovable British infantry."

At last, upon the far horizon to his right, were seen the dim moving columns of the Prussians coming to the aid of Wellington. Grouchy did not appear, and Napoleon, knowing that he must achieve success now or never, opened a furious artillery fire upon the opposing lines. It was now 3.30 in the afternoon, and no part of the British position had been lost. The French Cuirassiers were advanced against the English guns, and were decimated in their fruitless attacks on the right. Meanwhile the Prussians had attempted to carry by assault the village of Planchenoit, an important strategical position in the line of Napoleon's retreat towards the frontier. A terrific conflict was waged here, for which Napoleon was compelled to devote some of his finest troops. It became all along the line a question of who could stand the hardest pounding. At last Napoleon, mounting his white horse, Marengo, started out from the farmhouse, in which he had remained studying his maps, and rode to the spot where his veteran Guard were to march past on their way into action. It was one of the most, if not the most dramatic moment in military history. Standing upon a hillock, a figure beloved by all the war-worn troops of France, he merely pointed his arm towards the distant lines of the enemy, as though he would point to them the place of honour. It was enough. They passed him with thunderous tread and loud shouts of "Vive l'Empereur!" and so marching down the slope, formed up for their famous assault. Just as the Coldstreams received in silence and flung back again the furious onslaught of the Prussian Guard at Ypres, so Maitland's Brigade and the British Guards awaited the attack. The Frenchmen passed perfectly steadily across the open, shelled unceasingly by the British guns, and fired upon by the British infantry. They were quite unshaken. When Ney's horse crashed to the earth beneath him he pointed the way on foot. It was like the tramp of a deathless army.

The British Guards were lying down to avoid the fire of the French artillery, but when the French came within some fifty yards one of the British officers cried, "Up, Guards, and at them!" at which historic words the British leapt to their feet and poured a round upon the French column. The Old Guard, unbroken, undismayed, advanced at a charge, but Maitland's men never ceased pouring volley after volley into their crowded ranks. In an attempt to form into open column, the enemy became disorganised. The opportunity was not missed by their opponents. With a loud cheer the British charged, driving the exhausted Frenchmen back. Their position was tragic. All this time their left flank was receiving an unremitting fire from the English infantry. It was impossible under such circumstances for even veteran troops, such as Napoleon's Guard, to remain in action, and the sight of the broken ranks of the flower of the French Army created more panic amongst the other troops than almost any feature of the battle. They were beaten but not dishonoured. How great then must their reverse have been!

Napoleon hastily advanced his remaining battalions, and shortly after Wellington knew the moment had dawned for the advance. The whole British line moved forward, having endured a ceaseless artillery fire for nine long hours, having repelled the impact of cavalry, and repulsed the French Guard. Wellington himself headed the advancing troops, and when warned of the danger replied, "Never mind, let them fire away; the battle's won, and my life is of no consequence to me now."

The pipes struck up, the bugles sounded, the drums rolled above the noise of feet. Away went the English Guards, the Black Watch, the Camerons, the Gordons, the Rifles—the triumphant British Army. The whole French line was swept back in confusion. The Old Guard still rallied, protecting Napoleon himself in one of its squares. But the day was lost, and soon the Emperor joined the rabble of fugitives and set his face towards Paris. The hour of his destiny had struck.

It was near La Belle Alliance that Wellington met Blücher. It was decided that, as the Prussians were not so exhausted as the British, they should follow up the flying French. Anton has given a little picture of the end of the day. "Night passes over the groaning field of Waterloo, and morning gives its early light to the survivors of the battle to return to the heights of St. Jean, on purpose to succour the wounded, or bury the dead. Here may be seen the dismounted gun, the wheels of the carriage half sunk in the mire; the hand of the gunner rests on the nave, his body half buried in a pool of blood, and his eyes open to heaven whither his spirit has already fled. Here are spread promiscuously, heaps of mangled bodies—some without head, or arms, or legs: others lie stretched naked, their features betraying no mark of violent suffering. The population of Brussels, prompted by a justifiable curiosity, approach the field to see the remains of the strangers who fell to save their spoil-devoted city, and to pick up some fragment as a memorial of the battle, or as a relic for other days."

Well might little Peterkin ask then as now, "But what good came of it at last?" Another passage I cannot resist quoting. It is from the narrative of a soldier in Dr. Fitchett's Wellington's Men, and relates to the march on Paris following Waterloo. "At noon arrived in the neighbourhood of Mons, where we overtook the Greys, Inniskillings, Ross's troop of horse artillery, and several other corps, both of cavalry and infantry.... The Greys and the Inniskillings were mere wrecks—the former, I think, did not muster 200 men.... We crossed after the Greys, and came with them on the main road to Maubeuge at the moment a Highland regiment, which had come through Mons, was passing. The moment the Highlanders saw the Greys an electrifying cheer burst spontaneously from the column, which was answered as heartily; and on reaching the road the two columns became blended for a few minutes—the Highlanders running to shake hands with their brave associates in the late battle...." The battle of Waterloo was the culmination of many years' conflict between the English and the French, and the final struggle between Napoleon and Wellington. We have seen how the rivalry with France was fought to a finish in Canada and the West Indies, in India, in the Peninsular, and on the Continent. After Waterloo there was peace for many years. Napoleon, banished to St. Helena, was soon to die, and remain as a deathless memory amongst the old veterans of the armies he had led to victory. Wellington was to win new triumphs, though infinitely less enduring, in political life, and to lose the fickle popularity of an English mob, dying long after in 1852. The Highlanders, who had fought almost unceasingly for many years and in many parts of the world, and whose gallantry at Waterloo brought them new laurels, were mainly engaged upon home service until a new generation heard in the far Crimea the melancholy beating of the drums of war.

CHAPTER XIV
THE HIGHLAND BRIGADE AT THE BATTLE OF ALMA
(September 20, 1854)

"Leave me, comrades—here I drop;

No, Sir, take them on;

All are wanted—none shall stop;

Duty must be done:

Those whose guard you take will find me,

As they pass below."

So the soldier spake, and staggering

Fell amid the snow,

And ever, on the dreary heights,

Down came the snow.

HENRY LUSHINGTON.

The years following Waterloo were free from war, but full of domestic unrest. The National Debt had risen from under 240 millions to over 860 millions, while the end of hostilities brought with it a fall in corn, a renewal of foreign competition in trade, and a tremendous increase in unemployment. Riots and plots abounded; the introduction and development of machinery was blamed for throwing people out of work. There was even, in the Cato Street Conspiracy in 1820, a futile idea of murdering the Cabinet.

In 1832 the famous Reform Bill was passed, resisted to the last by Wellington and the Tories, while the Abolition of Slavery followed soon after. In 1837 Queen Victoria came to the throne.

In 1854 the Crimean War broke out, after a peace in Europe lasting practically forty years.

The trouble in the Crimea was entirely political. England feared that Russia would crush Turkey and plant herself upon the shores of the Eastern Mediterranean. France was also alarmed and, to prevent the Czar overwhelming the Sultan, united her forces with the British. For two years they fought together as allies. In former chapters we have followed in the footsteps of Wolfe, of Moore, of Abercromby, and of Wellington, and now we meet, though not for the first time, a great Scots soldier in Sir Colin Campbell. He linked the Peninsular Campaign of 1809 with the Indian Mutiny of 1857, handing on the sword to Roberts, who in his turn was to be succeeded by Sir John French. Of Roberts and Wolseley and Lord Kitchener we will hear a great deal soon enough. It is of Colin Campbell, of Balaclava and Lucknow, that the next few years are full.

Colin Campbell was born in Glasgow on the 20th of October 1792. He was not sixteen when he joined the army as an ensign, and sailed at once for Portugal, receiving his baptism of fire at Vimiera. He served under Sir John Moore, taking part in the historic retreat to Corunna. Later on he was in the miserable Walcheren Expedition, and contracted a fever which visited him every season for thirty years afterwards. He was at the battles of Barossa and Vittoria, and in July 1813 served at the siege of San Sebastian. There he was severely wounded and was compelled to return to England, but on his recovery he sailed for Nova Scotia to join his regiment. He won experience in America, Gibraltar, and the West Indies; took part in the battles of Brandenburg and New Orleans, and fought in the Chinese War. Just as Lord Roberts was enjoying well-earned repose in 1899, Campbell contemplated retirement when his most important and historic work lay ahead. "I am growing old and only fit for retirement," he wrote when the Crimean War and the Indian Mutiny still lay buried in the future. He was sixty-two years of age when, in 1854, he was appointed Commander-in-Chief of the Highland Brigade, and found himself in the proud position of leading the Black Watch, the Camerons, and the Sutherland Highlanders.

After a trying voyage, in which the troops suffered severely from sickness, the Black Sea was reached on the 19th of September 1854. The landing was accomplished in safety, and it was learned that the Russians were holding a very strong position on the left bank of the Alma, a shallow river confronting them a few miles distant. The Russian forces were well posted, strong in artillery, and numbering some 40,000 men and 106 guns. The attack was launched without delay. The French advanced on the right, and the British on the left. In this manner the West drew near to the East, and everything hung upon the success of the assault. Had the attacking columns suffered a reverse it would have been exceedingly difficult to save a retreat from degenerating into a rout. The Russians fully expected to drive their enemies into the sea.

Before the action Sir Colin Campbell rode up and joined the ranks of his Brigade, giving his men some words of advice before the advance commenced, begging them to keep their heads, and remember the land of their forebears.

Facing the British troops was a high entrenched slope upon which the Russians awaited their attack. "Now, men," said Sir Colin, "the army will watch us; make me proud of the Highland Brigade."

The soldiers were confident of success. "When," records Kinglake, "the command travelled on along the ranks of the Highlanders it lit up the faces of the men one after another, assuring them that now at length, and after long expectance, they would indeed go into action. They began obeying the order, and with beaming joy, for they came of a warlike race; yet not without emotions of a graver kind; they were young soldiers, new to battle."

Upon the right of the Highland Brigade were the Guards, while between the Coldstreams and the Black Watch rode Sir Colin Campbell. While they stood there the muffled thunder of guns on their right told every man that the engagement had already started, and that far away their French allies were already in action upon the Russian front. To the left of Sir Colin Campbell was a gorge where the enemy had constructed a large redoubt, flanked on each side by artillery upon the heights, while in support of the artillery were large numbers of troops. This redoubt was defended by fourteen heavy guns. The advance began under a merciless fire, but so fierce was the attack that the enemy were compelled to retreat until their reserves were called up, when they outnumbered the British by twenty to one. It was at this critical moment, when a reverse seemed inevitable, and the light troops engaged were recoiling, that Sir Colin Campbell shouted, "Forward, the 42nd!"—the bagpipes struck up, and the advance of the Highland Brigade commenced. Against his three battalions in echelon were twelve regiments of Russians in mass. But without a halt, without a pause, the 42nd forded the River Alma and faced the heights, advancing steadily and without faltering, the Sutherlands in the centre and the Camerons upon the left flank. For a few moments Sir Colin Campbell halted the Brigade to let them recover their breath, and then giving the order, "Advance firing"—a manœuvre in which the Black Watch were greatly expert—they drew nearer to the closely packed forces of the enemy. It was inevitable that they should lose very heavily, and that the fire that was opened upon them should be exceedingly hot, but always into the dense clouds of smoke that floated between the intervening distance the 42nd advanced. The time was nearly ripe.

"Charge!" cried Sir Colin, and down went the steel line of bayonets. But instead of a clear front a new situation arose which called upon all the strategic skill of the Scottish leader to avert disaster. The solitary regiment of the 42nd was not only faced by the hosts of Russians on their front; other battalions of the enemy were on the move preparing to attack upon the flank. Instantly he turned to the Sutherlands, ordering them to protect the flank of the Black Watch. In perfect order, amid the thunder of the conflict, the two Highland regiments charged straight at the enemy. It is difficult to believe that the Russians should have retired before two battalions with only one other in support, but they did. Whether it was the appearance of the Highlanders, or the invincible character of their advance, one cannot say, but after a momentary wavering the enemy gave way to panic. And then upon the other flank of the Brigade the Russians threatened a similar movement.

Again Campbell saved the situation and this time by calling up the Camerons. Kinglake has given a vivid impression of the effect of this new force of kilted troops appearing out of the smoke. "Some witchcraft," he says, "the doomed men might fancy, was causing the earth to bear giants. Above the crest or swell of the ground on the left rear of the 93rd yet another array of the tall bending plumes began to rise in a long ceaseless line, stretching far into the east; and presently, in all the grace and beauty that marks a Highland regiment when it springs up the side of a hill, the 79th came bounding forward without a halt, or with only the halt that was needed for dressing the ranks, it advanced upon the flank of the right Sousdal column and caught the mass in its sin—caught it daring to march across the face of a Highland battalion—a battalion already near and swiftly advancing in line. Wrapped in the fire thus poured upon its flank the hapless column could not march—could not live."

The Russian force was indeed in a position that was not tolerable, and its rout was complete and immediate. And now the three Highland regiments, with Sir Colin in the centre, extending in open order for nearly a mile, swept forward in perfect formation against the confused masses of the Russian army, to whom they presented a never-ceasing wave of soldiers, with (to their imagination) unending supports that would spring up just as readily as on the two occasions that they had attempted an outflanking movement. To the horror of their troops in reserve, who could well see how great was the difference numerically between their comrades and the British, the Russians took to their heels, overwhelming their own supports and carrying everything before them in their blind panic. The Highland Brigade had turned the scales, and the time was ripe to convert defeat into disaster. The cavalry were advanced to harass the broken Russian columns; the artillery commenced to shell their shattered ranks.

But, as Sir Colin wrote to a friend, "it was a fight of the Highland Brigade. Lord Raglan came up afterwards, and sent for me. When I approached him I observed his eyes to fill and his lips and countenance to quiver. He gave me a cordial shake of the hand. The men cheered very much. I told them I was going to ask the Commander-in-Chief a great favour—that he would permit me to have the honour of wearing the Highland bonnet during the rest of the campaign, which pleased them very much. My men behaved nobly. I never saw troops march to battle with greater sang-froid and order than those three Highland regiments."

Not long after, when Sir Colin Campbell was returning, he addressed the regiments of the Highland Brigade, never thinking how soon he would be called upon to lead them again. "Our native land," he said, "will never forget the name of the Highland Brigade, and in some future war that nation will call for another one to equal this, which it will never surpass."

It was indeed a victory to be proud of. Three regiments had put to rout no fewer than twelve battalions, including the famous division of picked Czar's Infantry.

The Russians retreated before the Highland advance across the Belbec River, falling back towards Sevastopol, a strongly fortified place upon the shore of the Black Sea. It is probable that had the pursuit been carried out energetically, as Lord Raglan advised, the Russians would have been utterly dispersed, and the war concluded, but the delay enabled them to enter Sevastopol at their leisure, and in consequence of this movement the Allies decided to march across the Peninsula to Balaclava, and by forcing the action from that point to invest the Russian forces in Sevastopol by land and sea.

CHAPTER XV
THE 'THIN RED LINE' AT BALACLAVA
(October 25, 1854)

Gae bring my guid auld harp ance mair, gae bring it free and fast,

For I maun sing anither sang, ere a' my glee be past.

And trow ye, as I sing, my lads, the burden o't shall be,

Auld Scotland's howes, and Scotland's knowes, and Scotland's hills for me;

I'll drink a cup to Scotland yet, wi' a' the honours three.

Scotland Yet.

In the Crimean campaign the regiments in the Highland Brigade chiefly concerned were the Black Watch, the Camerons, and the Sutherland Highlanders. At the battle of the Alma we have seen how the glory of the first advance rested with the 42nd, and the brunt of the flanking movements upon the Sutherlands and Camerons. In the siege of Sevastopol the 42nd and 79th were engaged in fatigue duty and in the trenches, the 93rd lying before Balaclava with Sir Colin Campbell. It was their good fortune to meet the Russians once again in the open. It was an amazing achievement that two ranks of Highlanders could attack and defeat twelve battalions of Russian infantry. An even greater achievement was it when the 93rd resisted successfully without supports the furious onslaught of the Russian cavalry.

The battle of the Alma was thus the first and last engagement in which the Highland Brigade fought together during the Crimean War. For two miserable winters they, with the other regiments of the British and French forces, were to endure privation and hardship such as had probably never before been experienced in a British campaign. The bitter cold, the lack of food, the absence of all hospital arrangements made the siege of Sevastopol one of the most ghastly tragedies in English history. Cholera, dysentery, with every other form of illness consequent on exposure and lack of sanitation, proved a more deadly antagonist than the Russian guns. Whatever the sufferings our soldiers had to endure in the trenches during the winter campaign of 1914-15, they were provided with good food, expert medical attendance, and, so far as was possible, with the relief and exchange of fatigue duty. In the Crimea no army was ever in a worse plight for the merest necessaries of life, and until Florence Nightingale was inspired to leave England for the hospital field there was very little hope of recovery from sickness. But then as now the various British regiments took their part in the trench work without complaint and in good heart—and when possible with the greatest distinction.

The 93rd Sutherland Highlanders were raised in 1799, and sailed for the Cape of Good Hope in 1806. After that they saw little active service of any distinction until the Crimea, though their sister regiment the Argyllshire Highlanders, raised in 1794, took part in the Peninsular War, but not in Waterloo. The two regiments became the 91st and 93rd Argyll and Sutherland Highlanders in 1881.

The Sutherland Highlanders took up their position before Balaclava with the knowledge that it was of first-rate importance to the safety of the whole army. The outer line of defences was held by some 5000 Turks; between the outer line and the inner line were 1500 cavalry, while the 93rd lay in front of the village of Kadikoi. The importance of Balaclava lay in its position. Lying upon the sea coast, it was not merely in communication with the outer world, but the only channel by which the Allies could receive their ammunition and stores. Were the Russians to take possession of Balaclava they would cut the British lines of communication at one swoop. It was therefore practically certain that sooner or later an attack would be made, and on the night of the 24th Sir Colin was informed by the Turks that the Russian advance was imminent. It came with the breaking of dawn, when the grey hordes of the enemy were seen flocking like ghosts down the hill-side, moving forward toward the Turkish redoubts. Compared with the little force defending Balaclava, the number of the enemy was infinitely superior, comprising 25 battalions of infantry, 34 squadrons of cavalry, and 78 guns. Presently their artillery found the range of the troops in the first redoubt, and in a very short time the Turks were in flight. Once this line of fortifications was taken it was hopeless to hold the corresponding flanks. The whole first line was beaten within a few minutes. The Sutherlands, drawn up under Sir Colin Campbell, stood at attention watching the fleeing columns of the Turks heading directly towards them. Perceiving that the Highlanders were perfectly at their ease, the Turks made a feeble rally and formed on either flank. The Russian advance was continued without halt, and their guns soon opened on the 93rd. To prevent unnecessary loss, Sir Colin drew back the regiment behind the slope of the hill, and from there awaited the next move. Presently the enemy's cavalry, leaving the main body, galloped straight for his position. The moment of trial had come. Instantly he drew up the Highlanders in a line only two deep, shouting to them, "Now, men, remember there is no retreat from here. You must die where you stand!" at which there was a low murmur, "Ay, ay, Sir Colin; an need be, we'll do that!" The whole line was advanced to the top of the hill, a movement that so excited the men that they nearly charged the Russians.

But that was not Sir Colin's intention, and halting them he calmly awaited the onslaught of the Russian cavalry, merely giving the order for the Sutherlands to stand in line. The noise of the thundering hoofs grew ever louder. It echoed in the ears of the Turks, and as dense masses of horses bounded in all their picturesque strength towards them, they broke on the instant and ran in a frenzy of terror to the rear, extending their hands to the vessels riding at anchor, and shouting in their panic, "Ship! ship!" To the Eastern mind it seemed the merest folly to await such a crash of cavalry.

But not a man of the 93rd moved. Just as the French Cuirassiers at Quatre Bras had come flaunting their swords and breastplates in the sunlight, so the Russian cavalry, on that winter's morn, came rushing in their hundreds upon the 'thin red line.' Lord Wolseley has written that the pace of their advance must have been three hundred and fifty yards a minute, while behind them squadron upon squadron—like the successive waves of a sea—raced their supports. "In other parts of the field," an eye-witness has recorded, "with breathless suspense every one waited the bursting of the wave upon the line of Gaelic rock." Suddenly, when it was feared the Highlanders in their forlorn bravery were already overwhelmed, the splutter of fire passed down the line. It was done without flurry or haste, but the effect was incalculable. The whole front rank of the cavalry stumbled and recoiled; horses and men fell, the second rank was baffled and helpless, the speed was in an instant checked, and the Sutherlands, calmly reloading, discharged a second volley into the enemy. But the Russians were not beaten so easily. Breaking away, a detachment of cavalry cantered off to attack the 93rd on the flank. Quite calmly Sir Colin wheeled a company of his men to face them. This was done without any confusion, and another volley decided the action. It was stated afterwards that although few of the Russians were killed, nearly every man and horse was wounded. It had been a desperate moment, for, as Kinglake remarks, "the advance of the Russian squadrons marked what might well seem at the moment to be an ugly if not desperate crisis in the defence of the English seaport. Few or none at the time could have had safe grounds for believing that, before the arrival of succours, Liprandi (the Russian Commander) would be at all once stayed in his career of victory, and in the judgment of those, if any there were, who suffered themselves to grow thoughtful, the whole power of our people in the plain and in the port of Balaclava must have seemed to be in jeopardy; for not only had the enemy overmastered the outer line of defence and triumphantly broken in through it, but also, having a weight of numbers, which for the moment stood as that of an army to a regiment, he already had made bold to be driving his cavalry at the very heart of the English resources. If, in such a condition of things, some few hundreds of infantrymen stood shoulder to shoulder in line confronting the victor upon open ground, and maintaining from first to last their composure, their cheerfulness, nay, even their soldierly mirth, they proved themselves brave men by a test that was other than that of sharp combat, but hardly less trying."

After Balaclava the Highland Brigade were employed in besieging Sevastopol, and on September 8, 1855, a scheme was nearly carried into effect that might have resulted in the fall of the Russian position by assault. Sir Colin Campbell drew out a plan in which the Black Watch were to advance to the attack, while the remainder of the division supported them. About midnight on the 8th, therefore, when the fire of the Russian troops had become almost silent, a little party went forward to the Redan to reconnoitre. To their astonishment there was no one to be seen, save the wounded and the dying. In the silence of the night the Russian forces had evacuated, leaving Sevastopol to fall into the hands of the Allies.

There is little more to tell of the part that the Highland Brigade took in the Crimean campaign. After the fall of Sevastopol the Black Watch was stationed at Kamara until peace was declared, and in due course arrived in England, accompanied by the Camerons and the Sutherlands. They little knew what trials lay before them. Already in the far-distant land of India the clouds were beginning to gather upon the horizon. Already in many a silent street the whisper was passing from lip to lip that was destined, within a few short months, to reverberate down the passages of Time.

CHAPTER XVI
WITH HAVELOCK TO LUCKNOW

I have been forty years in the Service, I have been engaged in actions seven-and-twenty times, but in the whole of my career I have never seen any regiment behave so well as the 78th (Seaforth) Highlanders. I am proud of you. I am not a Highlander, but I wish I was one.

HAVELOCK.

It was in the early months of 1857 that there were the first ominous signs of unrest in India.

We have already seen how our power in India was founded upon the position held by the traders of the East India Company; we have also read of Dupleix, the French Governor; of Robert Clive, who held Arcot for fifty days against thousands of the enemy; of the battle of Plassey, and the 'Black Hole' at Calcutta; we have dealt very briefly with the victories of Wellesley, but between the early part of the nineteenth century and 1857 there had been little actual conflict, while the progress of the British Government had been well sustained.

During these years the native army had been very largely increased in numbers, while the British forces had hardly altered. In Bengal there were twenty Sepoys for every English soldier, and naturally enough the Crimean War had not been a favourable time to increase our garrison. It is difficult to say whether the Russian campaign had any political effect upon the Indians, but it is probable that it gave an impetus to the general unrest. Railways, telegraph wires, with all the other new appliances that were being first introduced at this time, were regarded with the deepest hatred and suspicion.

Finally in the early part of 1857 it was rumoured amongst the Sepoys that a plot had been laid by the Government to crush their religious scruples by stealth. Certain Indians hold the belief that they lose their caste if the fat of a cow or a pig passes their lips. It was necessary, so it was stated, in using the new Government cartridge to bite it with the teeth before ramming it home down the barrel. The grease upon this cartridge was discovered to contain forbidden ingredients.

But it must not be taken for granted that these cartridges were the sole cause of the Indian Mutiny. They were not a cause so much as a fuse to set India ablaze. There was sufficient aggravation to play upon the feelings of thousands of fanatical people. "The real motive of mutiny," says G. O.

Trevelyan, "was the ambition of the soldiery. Spoilt, flattered, and idle, in the indolence of its presumed strength, that pampered army thought nothing too good for itself, and nothing too formidable."

In utter secrecy, an emblem of unity like a kind of fiery cross passed from one Sepoy regiment to another. Something was happening, and it is foolish to believe that those in authority were altogether in the dark. But the Crimean War was raging, and it was hardly the time to act. Men like Sidney Cotton, Edwardes, Chamberlain, and, soaring above them all, John Nicholson, were not the kind of men to be blind to the state of affairs, or to be taken wholly by surprise. Nicholson, by an investigation of the native letters passing through the post-office, was well aware of the magnitude of the conspiracy. Young Frederick Roberts, who at this time was acting Deputy-Assistant-Quartermaster-General, wrote: "He impressed me more profoundly than any man I had ever seen before, or have ever met since. I have never seen any one like him; he was the beau-ideal of a soldier and a gentleman. Above all others, I had for him the greatest admiration and the most profound respect."

Nicholson had gone out to India as a boy of sixteen. He was a man of very imposing presence, very reserved, and inspiring amongst the natives the greatest possible admiration and hero-worship. He made few friends, faced conspiracy and disturbances night and day; a man whose self-reliance was only equalled by his courage, and whose name has gone down in India as a kind of super-man, removed above the level of his contemporaries.

It was Meerut, well called 'the cradle of the Indian Mutiny,' that set flame to the fire that was to rage across India. The cavalry there refused point-blank to use the cartridges, for which insubordination the colonel placed several under arrest. For a time everything seemed to be quiet enough, and then on the next day (a Sunday) the native regiments decided to rise and put the English to the sword.

The bells were ringing for evening service and the English officers and their wives were making their way to church, when out of the silent night there thundered the alarming rattle of rifle shots and the doleful roll of drums. Dense masses of smoke circled heavenwards from the native quarters.

The Mutiny had taken birth.

Sepoys, turned suddenly into a maddened crowd of fanatics, shot their rifles in all directions. With that confidence in their men which was such a pathetic feature of the Mutiny, the English officers hurried towards their regiments, and fell riddled with bullets. The cry, 'To Delhi! To Delhi!' arose, and to the ancient city of kings the rebels set out. Delhi was the Mecca of revolt, from whence the trouble was to spread like the wings of the morning. It was already a rendezvous for the rebels from all parts of the country.

Meerut was not only the cradle of the Mutiny; it was also in a manner the death-warrant of the deserted English people in Delhi. There was a comparatively strong force of British troops in Meerut, but for one reason or another—principally, one gathers, because their commanding officer was so very aged—they did not attempt the succour of the English in Delhi. Had they done so they would have taken the Sepoys in their hour of mutiny and probably scattered them. It would have been no formidable task. All along the roads to Delhi were streaming rebel cavalry and infantry, riding at their ease, and the English troops could have had everything their own way. As it was, they made no move, and soon news came to Meerut of the terrible massacre at Delhi. Every European—man, woman, and child—on whom the rebels could lay their hands had been murdered. Well said was it, 'The sorrow was in Delhi, the shame in Meerut.'

When the outbreak of the rebellion and the news of the Delhi massacre were reported to General Anson, Commander-in-Chief in India, he said that at any cost Delhi must be regained. It was the only way of preserving the prestige of the English race. Without delay, General Barnard was placed in command of the force, and on June 7th united his troops with those at Meerut. In due course he advanced against Delhi, taking up a position upon a commanding plateau, which stood like a revolver pointing at the heart of the city.

It was Delhi that was the heart of the Mutiny, and coupled with the name of Delhi is that of John Lawrence, the brother of the defender of Lucknow. Truly has Dr. Fitchett said, "At Cawnpore and Lucknow the British fought for existence. At Delhi they fought for empire."

To besiege Delhi, no matter with how small a force, was to maintain British supremacy from the very start. The man who had made that possible was John Lawrence. He it was who founded the Punjaub Frontier Force, who inspired Nicholson, Edwardes, and Chamberlain, who, in a word, prepared for the trouble while it was barely a cloud upon the horizon. He it was who brought 50,000 Sikhs into the war, and "through him," wrote Canning, "Delhi fell."

It is not within our subject to deal with the siege and storming of the city. The few details that follow must only be regarded as rough indications of the conflict. As the heart of the Mutiny it would require a greater canvas than it is possible to give here.

The Ridge commanding Delhi formed not only a point of vantage but also a rampart of defence, standing some 60 feet over the city. Even then the situation was critical. The British forces were plagued with cholera, and possessed guns which could not be relied upon to fire with accuracy. It was a struggle between a mere handful of men on an open plateau and a fierce and relentless army secured behind fortifications.

For nearly six weeks the Delhi Field Force held its own on the Ridge, suffering attacks almost daily, and carrying out sorties that were sometimes successful, but were always accompanied by great loss of life, and holding on like grim death till the city should fall into their hands.

On August 7 John Nicholson arrived, bringing with him some artillery and cavalry, and also the wonderful corps of Guides. News from the rest of India was in no way cheering. During the siege of Delhi, Sir Henry Lawrence had fallen, Lucknow was not relieved, and Havelock was as yet far away. Perceiving the gravity of the position, Nicholson decided that the Sepoys must receive a blow from which they could not recover. "Delhi," he said, "must be taken, and at once."

The news of the massacre at Cawnpore, with all its tale of horror, had already reached the troops, and they set out with renewed determination, led by John Nicholson, "a tower of strength, a guiding star," who, at the head of the troops, was the first to set foot upon the broken rampart. The advance of the British was irresistible, but it brought with it an irreparable loss. "It was almost more than I could bear," says Roberts; "other men had daily died around me, other comrades had been killed beside me, but I never felt as I felt then. To lose Nicholson seemed to me at that moment to lose everything."

It was at sunrise on the morning of the 21st of September, after days of hand-to-hand fighting in the streets of Delhi, that the British at last gained the ascendancy, but with the accomplishment of their long endeavour had come the death of Nicholson.

The news of this victory—and it was a great victory at such a time—passed through the whole of India and thence to England. After weeks of fighting not only Sepoys, but also the ravages of cholera, 10,000 troops had attacked and carried a city defended at every point, losing 3000, and with them one of the greatest men that have ever defended the British flag.

The conquest of Delhi was the conquest of revolt, and a handful of British soldiers had made possible the re-establishment of the British flag.

They carried Delhi city—

Men whose triumphant arms

Filled all the land with wonder,

And stirred with strange alarms

The Pathan in his fastness,

Or where by Jumna's tide

The bold front of rebellion

Had flourished in its pride.[8]

Whilst this long siege was in operation much had happened elsewhere. At Lucknow Sir Henry Lawrence had delayed an outbreak for a considerable time. His influence over the Sepoys was very great, and it was only because of the success of the rebels elsewhere that they eventually decided to fling in their lot with the rising.

Lawrence had been left very much to himself during the earlier stages of the Mutiny. Hearing of the outbreak at Meerut and the fall of Delhi, he knew that in his isolated position he must act on his own initiative, and accordingly decided that he would concentrate the little force of British troops—together with their wives and families—in the Residency, the most hopeful place, in his opinion, for a small force to defend. Here he stored grain and built ramparts and trenches, and when by the end of May the Sepoys were in revolt, he was prepared to fight to the last.

At Cawnpore, where Nana Sahib, an Indian inspired by the deepest hatred of the English, was in command of the rebels, things were no more promising. Early in June the first signs of insurrection were visible, and the British, under Major-General Sir Hugh Wheeler, fortified themselves as best they could in a hospital barracks, where they were speedily besieged. It was a most ill-chosen place to make a stand. Their sufferings were terrible, but for all that they held out for eighteen days, after which, influenced by the frail hope that the women and children would be spared, General Wheeler came to terms with Nana Sahib. No word had reached them that they would be relieved or that Havelock was already on the road to Cawnpore. Trusting to the word of Nana Sahib, the garrison marched out—300 women and children, 150 soldiers, and the same number of civilians. For the terrible details of what followed one can best refer to Trevelyan's Cawnpore.

"All the world knows of the cruelty that awaited them," he writes. "They were permitted to embark in boats, and no sooner had they done so than the Sepoys opened fire. Those who were not slaughtered were conveyed ashore again and imprisoned. The white-haired General, the English officers and the civilians were speedily shot. But there still remained 122 women and children, who were placed in the Assembly Rooms, and here, and into this room—while Havelock was almost at hand—there were sent seven men to massacre the women and children and fling their bodies into a well. This hideous duty was not performed by the Sepoy soldiers, but by certain hirelings who were heavily paid by Nana Sahib."

It was at this stage, when Lucknow was the next point of attack and Cawnpore had already fallen, that Havelock set out from Calcutta, where he had been preceded by the 78th Seaforth Highlanders.

The Persian campaign of 1856-57 was of little importance, but it is interesting as the scene of some activities—one cannot rate the foe more generously—on the part of the 78th Highlanders under Havelock and Outram, both fated to bear a great share in repressing the Mutiny. At Kooshab the "Ross-shire Buffs," as the regiment was called, distinguished themselves by routing the Persian force most ignominiously. In consequence of this action Havelock was greatly impressed with their courage and stamina. "There is a fine spirit in the ranks of this regiment," he wrote. "... I am convinced the regiment would be second to none in the service if its high military qualities were drawn forth. It is proud of its colours, its tartan, and its former achievements."

It was with this veteran battalion that Havelock set out for Cawnpore.

Havelock was instructed that he should first quieten all disturbances at Allahabad, and then not lose a moment in relieving Sir Henry Lawrence and General Wheeler. His force was a comparatively insignificant one, lacking cavalry altogether, its guns drawn by cattle, and numbering only 1400 British soldiers. He was marching through a hostile country, and certain to encounter hundreds of thousands of well-armed Sepoys. Soon enough news came of the massacre of Cawnpore, but trusting that some at least of the garrison were still holding out, he struggled onward.

To return to Lucknow. The whole ambition of the rebels was now bent upon its destruction. Sir Henry Lawrence, driven to despair by the thought of what might happen to his helpless women, had made one sortie, which, unfortunately, had been heavily repulsed. He had been overpowered by numbers, and compelled to fight his way back into the Residency. So far everything was favouring the Sepoys.

The long and arduous siege began, and had it not been for his presence, it is doubtful whether the little force could have cherished the courage to hold out. To the last he urged them most earnestly never to surrender.

Early in July Lawrence was fatally wounded, and three days later died, leaving the heartbroken garrison to carry on the defence. Upon his tomb were written these simple and moving words: "Here lies Henry Lawrence, who tried to do his duty."

On the 12th of July Havelock encountered the rebels. It was the first time that the Sepoys had come in contact with an efficient British force, but when they saw the Highlanders they cried to each other that here were the wives of the men slain in Cawnpore and Delhi. It is recorded that after a brief acquaintance with the Seaforths the Sepoys would willingly have fled from the English "women," but there was no escape. Havelock ordered his men to charge, and to go on charging, and although the enemy were in a strong position and admirably armed, they were quite unable to resist the artillery and infantry that faced them. For twenty-four hours the British had been marching, and for as long a time they had tasted no food, but on the morning of the 15th they set out again upon their advance on Cawnpore. Again and again they confronted the enemy in ever-increasing numbers as they began to near the city. At last on the night when they came within twenty-three miles of Cawnpore, and fell upon the ground to snatch a little rest, Nana Sahib, hearing of their swift approach, signed the death-warrant of the hapless women and children. The next day—the 18th of July—saw the advance upon the city. "The rays of the sun," says one writer, "darted down as if they had been concentrated through a lens." After all their privations and their unconquerable march how tragic was their victory to prove.

In the meantime, the Indian army, composed of 5000 men with 8 guns, had come out to meet Havelock, and it was well for the British that Nana Sahib was anything but a competent general. The Indian leader had settled very definitely in his mind where Havelock was certain to attack him, and he made his plans accordingly. Fortunately Havelock was perfectly aware of this, and the Sepoys learnt his real intentions too late. One thing, however, was necessary, and that was the muzzling of the native guns. For this task the 78th Highlanders were chosen. Under Colonel Hamilton they advanced, and when they reached to some eighty yards of the Indian artillery, they brought their bayonets to the charge and flung themselves straight at the gunners. In a few minutes the artillery was in the hands of the British. The Sepoys retreated behind a howitzer. Again the Highlanders were rallied by Havelock, whose words, "Well done, Highlanders! Another charge like that wins the day," rang out like a bugle call. Again the Sepoys broke and set out towards Cawnpore, rallying in a village some little way from the city. Instantly Havelock galloped up to the leading regiments and cried, "Who'll take that village? The Highlanders or the 64th?" The rivalry thus inspired resulted very quickly in the evacuation of the position by the Sepoys, and the whole rebel army fell back towards Cawnpore.

The British were so exhausted by their unceasing march, lack of food, and the terrible sun, that they halted for a breathing-space, and Nana Sahib chose that moment for a final effort, opening fire upon their ranks with a large gun stationed upon the Cawnpore road. The crisis of the battle had come at last. Trevelyan has well pictured what followed. "Then," he says, "the mutineers realised the change that a few weeks had wrought out in the nature of the task which they had selected and cut out for themselves. Embattled in their national order, and burning with more than their national lust of combat, on they came, the unconquerable British infantry. The grape was flying thick and true. Files rolled over. Men stumbled and recovered themselves, and went on for a while, and then turned and hobbled to the rear. Closer and closer drew the measured tramp of feet; and the heart of the foe died within him, and his fire grew hasty and ill-directed. As the last volley cut the air overhead, our soldiers raised a mighty shout, and rushed forward, each at his own pace, and then every rebel thought only of himself. Those nearest the place were the first to make away, but throughout the host there were none who still aspired to stay within push of the British bayonets. Squadron after squadron, battalion upon battalion, these humbled Brahmins dropped their weapons, stripped off their packs and spurred and ran, limped and scrambled back to the city that was to have been the chief and central abode of Sepoy domination.... At nightfall Dhondoo Punth (Nana Sahib) entered Cawnpore upon a chestnut horse drenched in perspiration, and with bleeding flanks. A fresh access of terror soon dismissed him again on his way to Bithoor, sore and weary, his head swimming and his chest heaving."

The battle of Cawnpore was won, but the loss had been considerable, and the massacre of the hapless garrison was to take from the victory all its joy. There are few episodes in our history that have been conducted under more trying circumstances. There have been terrible marches undertaken, but few can be compared to the advance on Cawnpore. As Havelock said in issuing a report to the soldiers: "Between the 7th and 16th you have, under the Indian sun of July, marched one hundred and twenty-six miles, and fought four actions, but your comrades at Lucknow are in peril. Agra is besieged, Delhi is still the focus of mutiny and rebellion."

During the night following the action a thunderous report reached the ears of the British force, to be followed by a dense cloud of smoke. It split the silence of the Indian night and died away. The rebels, before their retreat from the city, had blown up the magazine.

The next day the Highlanders marched into Cawnpore, a deserted city, with all the traces of the horrible thing that had taken place there. "Was it any wonder," says one of the soldiers, "that when men carried back with them to camp a long heavy tress of golden hair, clean cut through as if by the slash of a sharp sword, and showed this token to comrades, who had been fighting and marching, and striving and straining that this thing might not be, was it any wonder that our soldiers swore to exact a merciless retribution as they stood around the dead, but eloquent witness of this oath."

The task that lay before Havelock was one that might have made any man give way to despair. Well might he have said, in the heroic words of Scott: "I see before me a long tedious and dark path but it leads to stainless reputation. If I die in harness as is very likely, I shall die with honour. If I achieve my task I shall have the thanks of all concerned and the approval of my conscience." Death and disease had reduced the numbers of his force to a bare 1500. They were still faced by some fifty miles swarming with the enemy, at the end of which they hoped to rescue the garrison of Lucknow. "The chances of relieving Lucknow," said Havelock, "are daily multiplying against us; the difficulties of an advance are excessive."

CHAPTER XVII
WITH SIR COLIN CAMPBELL AND THE SUTHERLANDS TO LUCKNOW

Pipes of the misty moorlands,

Voice of the glens and hills;

The droning of the torrents,

The treble of the rills!

Not the braes of broom and heather,

Nor the mountains black with rain,

Nor maiden bower, nor border tower,

Have heard your sweetest strain!

The Pipes of Lucknow.

Lucknow was fated to hear of three advances to its relief. The initial attempt by Havelock failed owing to lack of ammunition. He was compelled to return to Cawnpore and wait patiently until the arrival of Sir James Outram.

On the 4th of August Havelock began his second advance towards Lucknow, his force consisting of Highlanders, Fusiliers, and Sikhs. Facing him stretched thirty miles of the enemy's country, the city of Lucknow itself defended by a large army, while a force of the enemy was detached to cut his communications with Cawnpore. Cholera again broke out in the ranks, and the whole situation speedily became impossible. Havelock consulted with his officers and they decided that it would be useless to advance. He therefore fell back upon Mungulwar and appealed to Sir Patrick Grant for reinforcements.

Shortly afterwards the Seaforth Highlanders distinguished themselves in an engagement with the enemy, capturing two of their guns. The Sepoys who threatened Cawnpore next received Havelock's attention, and were defeated, the British falling back again upon the latter.

It was after this second advance of Havelock's that he was superseded by Sir James Outram. No man could have taken over the command with less satisfaction than Outram, but at the same time no man could have made it as bearable to Havelock. In the meantime news was received from

Lucknow that Inglis was determined to cut his way out if the relieving force could not cut their way in. "You must bear in mind," he wrote, "how I am hampered, that I have between 120 sick and wounded and at least 220 women and about 230 children, and no carriage of any description. In consequence of news received I shall soon put this force on half rations; our provisions will thus last us till the end of September. If you hope to save this force no time must be lost in pushing forward."

Havelock instantly called for reinforcements. Sir Colin Campbell, who had landed in Calcutta as Commander-in-Chief, made every exertion to forward the despatch of troops. Before the advance Outram wrote to Havelock, "To you shall be left the glory of relieving Lucknow, for which you have already struggled so much. I shall accompany you only in my civil capacity as Commissioner, placing my military services at your disposal if you please, serving under you as a volunteer."

With this cordiality between the leaders of the Expedition the force set out upon its third, this time the historic, march to save the women and children in Lucknow.

Lucknow is roughly forty-five miles from Cawnpore. The relieving army crossed the Ganges, marched again on Mungulwar, and drove the rebels back to Busseerutgunge. Their advance until September 22—when they were within some sixteen miles of Lucknow—was almost uncontested. The swiftness of their approach took the enemy by surprise. The Sepoys put up a desperate resistance before Lucknow, but by the charge of the Seaforths the bridge was crossed and the city entered. Inside the Residency anxiety grew almost unbearable. They had heard so often rumours and more rumours of relief. Already the garrison knew in their heart that help was coming—eagerly they watched for the first glimpse of a kent face in the dim street below.

Oh, they listened, dumb and breathless,

And they caught the sound at last;

Faint and far beyond the Goomtee

Rose and fell the pipers' blast!

Then a burst of wild thanksgiving

Mingled woman's voice and man's;

God be praised! The March of Havelock!

The piping of the clans!

The rebels had not yet realised how small a force was opposing them, and when they did they rallied again to the attack undismayed. The British pushed on with desperate courage, driving the Sepoys before them, fighting every inch of the way towards the Residency. Night was falling when the last terrible struggle commenced. It was now or never. Already the Residency was almost within hail. The Highlanders, supported by the Sikhs, were in the forefront, and Havelock, placing himself at their head, gave the order to charge. Above the turmoil of the swaying street the thin scream of the pipes pierced the hubbub like the bell of a light-ship over a winter sea. Suddenly the English watchers at the Residency gates beheld the long-looked-for figures of the British soldiery.

Louder, nearer, fierce as vengeance,

Sharp, and shrill as swords at strife,

Came the wild MacGregor's clan-call

Stinging all the air to life.

But when the far-off dust-cloud

To plaided legions grew,

Full tenderly and blithesomely

The pipes of rescue blew!

It was a supreme, a dramatic moment. The gates were flung open, and "from every pit, trench, and battery—from behind the sand-bags piled on shattered houses—from every post still held by a few gallant spirits, rose cheer on cheer—even from the hospital many of the wounded crawled forth to join in that glad shout of welcome to those who had so bravely come to our assistance. It was a moment never to be forgotten. The delight of the ever-gallant Highlanders, who had fought twelve battles to enjoy that moment of ecstasy, and in the last four days had lost a third of their numbers, seemed to know no bounds."

It was mainly by the magnificent efforts of the Seaforth Highlanders that a passage was forced through the condensed masses of Sepoys into the heart of Lucknow and into the Residency itself. "Never did the valour of this gallant regiment shine brighter than in this bloody conflict."

It had been the hope of Sir James Outram that after the relief of Lucknow the garrison would be able to withdraw under safe protection to Cawnpore. Most unhappily, however, it became evident that not only would it be impossible for the troops to force their way out through 50,000 Sepoys, but that, as the provisions and ammunition had been left temporarily in the rear, they were in actual danger of becoming a further drain upon the resources of the Residency. Whatever hope there was that the soldiers could fight their way out, there was little chance that 700 women and children would be able to reach Cawnpore. But what they had brought, however, was perhaps as good as food and arms—the presence of strong hearts and news of Colin Campbell. For six weeks, therefore, Havelock and Outram and the Seaforths were in their turn besieged in Lucknow.

In the meantime, namely the beginning of November, troops had reached India from England, and the officer in command was Sir Colin Campbell, a name associated for all time with the stand of the 'thin red line' at Balaclava. He was sixty-five years of age, considerably younger than Field-Marshal Roberts when he was asked by the Government to go to South Africa. But he was only too ready to start to the support of the hapless garrison. Landing at Calcutta on August 13, he reached Cawnpore on November 3, and on the 9th was already on the road to Lucknow.

Under Sir Colin Campbell were some 4700 men, a small force of cavalry, the Naval Brigade, artillery, and amongst the infantry the veteran Sutherland Highlanders. It is related that when Sir Colin passed before the ranks of the 'thin red line,' preliminary to the advance on Lucknow, he cried, "93rd! You are my own lads. I rely on you to do the work." At which a reply came, "Ay, ay, Sir Colin, ye ken us, and we ken you. We'll bring the women and children out of Lucknow, or die with you in the attempt."

On November 12 the British had reached the Alumbagh. At this point Colin Campbell decided that he would not force his way through the narrow lanes of the city, but would take what was called the Dilkusha Park—a property some two miles to the east of the Residency. Making that his base, he planned to attack the north of the city, forcing his way by the Secundrabagh.

In the meantime Outram had despatched particulars to Campbell regarding the plans of the city. He also sent a guide named Kavanagh. Kavanagh disguised himself as a Sepoy, and dropping out of the Residency at night, passed safely through the hordes of Sepoys, and crossing the river managed to reach the British. Never did his nerve fail him. By mistake he ran into a battery of the enemy's guns. The slightest hesitation would have betrayed the fact that, despite his disguise, he was not an Indian. With the utmost coolness he made a great business of inspecting the guns, and thus disarming the suspicion of the Sepoy soldiers, walked on in a leisurely manner, and in due course reached the British lines. In all the history of heroism in the Mutiny it would be difficult to find a more hazardous undertaking than that of Kavanagh. He was afterwards awarded the Victoria Cross.

On the 15th Sir Colin Campbell made a feint of assaulting the extreme left, but during the night he advanced in another quarter, and by the morning was in full march upon the fortified position to his right. The Secundrabagh was a garden of considerable size, with walls 20 feet high, and reached by a narrow lane. By a dexterous movement the British guns were moved up to the top of this lane, and from thence opened fire upon the walls, and for nearly an hour the bombardment went on. At last a breach was made, and the three regiments of the 53rd, the Sutherlands, and the Sikhs darted forward, each determined to be the first among the enemy. Indeed it is doubtful whether any command was given; the soldiers—straining like dogs upon the leash—were only too anxious to take the first excuse for a charge. It is recorded that a drummer-boy of the 93rd was one of the first to leap over the breach, and as Roberts himself has written, "When I got in I found him just inside the breach, lying on his back quite dead. A pretty, innocent-looking, fair-headed lad, not more than fourteen years old."

Their officers all shot, the Sikhs hesitated. Sir Colin Campbell saved the situation. "Colonel Ewart," he cried, "bring on the tartan!" and at that, says an eye-witness, "the whole seven companies like one man leaped for the wall with such a yell of pent-up rage as I never heard before or since." In the face of this Gaelic charge the Sepoys were driven back into the building. The rebels were hounded back from floor to floor, and from building to building. In the records of war there have been few scenes of slaughter so fierce as that which took place at the Secundrabagh. Hardly a Sepoy escaped, and without pausing, the Highlanders rushed on to the attack of the Shah Nujeef. It took many hours for these positions to be stormed, during which Major Branston was killed, and the late Lord Wolseley—then a promising young officer—took the command. But the tide was on the turn. Gradually the artillery asserted its superiority, and at last Sir Colin Campbell, galloping up to the 93rd, announced that the place must be carried, and that he himself would give them the lead, at which they answered proudly and with a fear for his safety, "We can lead ourselves." But it is doubtful whether it would have been possible to take this position had not the gallantry of Sergeant John Paton, V.C., come to the aid of the Sutherlands. He had discovered a breach in the rampart, and owing to this invaluable news the place was speedily carried. From the point known as the 'Mess-house,' Campbell signalled to the Residency that they were on the eve of their last attack. Full of joy Outram began to advance to meet the relieving force, carrying one building after another until, at last, that memorable scene took place when Havelock, Campbell, and Outram shook hands before the Mess-house.

Havelock, who was profoundly touched, could be heard saying, "Soldiers! I am happy to see you. Soldiers! I am happy to think you got into this place with a smaller loss than I did." But it was no time for speeches of congratulation. There were still the women and children to be saved. Outside the Residency there lurked an enemy five times more numerous than the British troops. Again the besieged saw the Highlanders fight their way in, and again they were to learn that danger still threatened their lives.

The Sutherland Highlanders at Lucknow

After the dramatic entry it was decided that the garrison must be conveyed out of range of the enemy, and so adroitly was this conducted that the Sepoys did not realise until many hours after the Residency was evacuated that the British had evaded them and were in retreat upon Cawnpore.

Havelock, the brave defender of Lucknow, died almost as soon as the withdrawal had begun. He contracted illness through running three-quarters of a mile under a heavy fire to greet the relieving force. As he was dying he turned to Outram with the memorable words: "I have for forty years so ruled my life that when death came I might face it without fear." No loss could have cast a darker shadow over the withdrawal.

With all speed Sir Colin Campbell made his way towards the Alumbagh, where he left Outram with 4000 men as garrison until the final assault upon Lucknow should take place. Until that time came the Alumbagh was to be held as a revolver at the head of Lucknow.

Unfortunately bad news came from Cawnpore, which had been left with a garrison of 500 troops under Windham, a Crimean soldier. It was threatened by Nana Sahib, whose mind was concentrated upon a second massacre, and the defeat of the British troops. Sir Colin Campbell had many perils to face. In his rear lay a hostile country, between Lucknow and Cawnpore a Sepoy force of some 14,000 men might threaten him at any moment, while over Cawnpore there hung a cloud of dangers, known and dreaded. Should Windham be defeated the bridge of boats across the Ganges would fall into the hands of the enemy, leaving Sir Colin with his little force of soldiers and the large number of sick and wounded hopelessly cut off.

It was with these anxious thoughts in his mind that he received a despatch from Windham marked, 'Most urgent,' and indicating that the garrison at Cawnpore were in a perilous state. Campbell knew that if the worst came to the worst, Windham would have fallen back within the entrenchments of the city, which meant that Cawnpore proper would be in the hands of the rebels. It was a hazardous position for any general. Every moment was precious, and Sir Colin appealed to his gallant Highlanders to make all speed. Let us see how they answered the call. With the utmost haste the force laboured on, and in the words of one of them, "The whole army eagerly pressed on towards the scene of danger.... The anxiety and impatience of all became extreme. Louder and louder grew the roar—faster and faster became the march—long and weary was the way—tired and footsore grew the infantry—death fell on the exhausted wounded with terrible rapidity—the travel-worn bearers could hardly stagger along under their loads—the sick men groaned and died. But still, on, on, on, was the cry. Salvos of artillery were fired by the field battery of the advanced guard in hopes that its sound might convey to the beleaguered garrison a promise of the coming aid. At last some horsemen were seen spurring along the road; then the veil that had for so long shrouded us from Windham was rent asunder, and the disaster stood before us in all its deformity."

Roberts was despatched to ascertain if the bridges were still in the hands of the British. He found an officer on guard, and learned from him that Windham was surrounded on three sides. Spurring on he made his way into the entrenchments and delivered his message. There followed a dramatic incident. From far off came the clatter of hoofs. A little party of cavalry, headed by a familiar figure, galloped towards the fort. SIR COLIN CAMPBELL had come himself! His appearance at that critical moment had the same electric effect as the first glimpse of his worn face in the shell-raked streets of Lucknow. Always impetuous, he had no sooner despatched Roberts than he must hasten upon the same errand. Meeting the officer at the bridges he had inquired how matters stood, and received the reply,

"Windham's men are at their last gasp." It was not the sort of remark to make to the commander of the 93rd Highlanders. "How dare you say of Her Majesty's troops that they are at their last gasp?" he roared, and hurrying across the bridges he carried to the disheartened garrison the inspiration of his indomitable personality.

With the breaking of the dawn the plain across the river was white with the tents of the British Army, and in a short time the smoke of battle began to trail across the Ganges. The conflict for the bridges began, and Sir Colin, who fully realised that sooner or later the Sepoys would rightly appreciate the importance of preventing the British crossing the river, stationed Peel and his artillery upon the other bank. The Sutherlands, under a very heavy shell fire, reached the position where the hapless Wheeler had withstood for so long Nana Sahib's soldiery. They were the first to cross, but by the evening the army were on the Cawnpore side of the river.

For a few days they maintained their position there without assuming the offensive, and on December 3 Sir Colin despatched a convoy conveying the sick and wounded to a place of safety.

This settled, the British set about the defeat of the rebels. But before the attack commenced a new regiment reached the troops before Cawnpore. The Black Watch—having marched seventy-eight miles in three days—came into line with the 93rd, and Sir Colin Campbell greeted his old comrades of the Crimea, shaking hands with the officers and speaking to the men. On December 6 the action commenced. Under Sir Colin were some 5000 troops, a small body of cavalry, 35 guns, and opposed to him 25,000 Sepoys.

The engagement opened with Windham's artillery. Presently the Highlanders of the 42nd advanced, their bayonets gleaming white in the sunlight. Driving the enemy before them they made way for Peel and his sailors, together with their 24-pounder. The swift approach of the Highlanders was irresistible, "and so complete," says one writer, "was the surprise, so unexpected was the onslaught, that the chupatties were found heating upon the fires, bullocks stood tied behind the hackeries, the sick and wounded were lying in the hospitals, the smith left his forge, and the surgeon his ward, to fly from the avenging bayonets."

In the meantime the rebel right, struck by an iron hand, was flung into an irretrievable confusion, and took to its heels. "Gun after gun was spiked; cartloads of ammunition lay strewed along the road. For two miles without a check the pursuit was carried on by the 17th battery alone, accompanied by Hope Grant and his staff. Four times in that distance did we go into action to clear our front and our flanks, until General Grant, thinking wisely that we were too far from our supports, determined to wait for more artillery. Then a small cloud coming nearer and nearer was seen on the left, and the head of the cavalry column debouched from a grove. The order for a further pursuit was given; the cavalry spread like lightning over the plain in skirmishing order. Sir Colin took the lead, and the pursuit was continued, taking all the character of a fox-hunt."

After the rout of the enemy came the return of the victorious British troops, who cheered Sir Colin Campbell, as the Kabul-Kandahar Field Force cheered Roberts on the road to Sibi.

"In front," says one writer, "came the 9th Lancers with three captured standards at their head, the wild-looking Sikh horsemen rode in the rear. As they passed the Commander-in-Chief he took off his hat to them with some words of thanks and praise. The Lancers shook their lances in the air and cheered; the Sikhs took up the cry, waving their sabres above their heads. The men carrying the standards gave them to the wind; the Highland Brigade who were encamped close by ran down and cheered both the victorious cavalry and the veteran chief, waving their bonnets in the air. It was a fair sight, a reminder of the old days of chivalry."

With the relief of Cawnpore, there followed a few days in which the army awaited anxiously the order to advance again on Lucknow. The delay was caused by a difference of opinion between Sir Colin Campbell and Lord Canning. The latter was most anxious that Lucknow should be retaken once and for good; Sir Colin, who was ever a methodical soldier, was strongly of belief that it would be better to concentrate the British forces before the advance commenced. Lord Canning won the day, and in the beginning of March 1858 the final assault upon Lucknow took place. By this time the forces of the rebels had been badly broken up and dispirited. The tide had turned, fresh troops were pouring into India, everything was in favour of the British. Instead of the little force which had accompanied Havelock to Lucknow, the British commander had a siege train with guns and ammunition and stores, 30,000 men, and more than 150 guns.

On January 19 the Queen had written to Sir Colin Campbell congratulating him on his Indian campaign, and mentioning in particular the gallantry of the 93rd Sutherland Highlanders. With this letter had come a despatch from the Duke of Cambridge, begging Sir Colin to place himself at the head of the 93rd as their Colonel, which he was only too proud to do. In the attack upon Lucknow and under Sir Colin Campbell were the Black Watch, the Sutherlands, and the Camerons—the Brigade that he had led to victory in the Crimea. The Camerons had arrived shortly before, and were given a cordial welcome by their comrades. The task before the British was a very severe one, despite the large numbers in the field; it was also a very critical one. Should the rebels be completely crushed then the Indian

Mutiny would be virtually at an end, but since the retreat of Sir Colin to Cawnpore their numbers had been greatly strengthened, their fortifications largely rebuilt, and an outer line erected, heavily protected by cannon.

Lucknow was a wonderful city. Dr. Russell, in his Diary in India, has described it as "a vision of palaces, minarets, domes azure and golden, cupolas, colonnades, long façades of fair perspective in pillars and columns, terraced roofs, all rising up amid a calm, still ocean of the brightest verdure. Look for miles and miles away, and still the ocean spreads and the towers of the fairy city gleam in its midst. Spires of gold glitter in the sun, turrets and gilded spheres shine like constellations."

On the 9th of March Sir Colin Campbell opened the engagement that was to prove the most final and the most terrible of the Indian Mutiny. It was given to the Black Watch to lead the attack, while in support were the Sutherlands.

The 42nd advanced in perfect order, their pipes playing 'The Campbells are comin'.' They were received by a hot fire from the rebels, but with the eyes of the army upon them the veterans of the Alma never paused in their stride. The Sepoys did not wait to dispute the matter with them, but fell back towards the city, where the Begum's Palace was to prove the citadel of their defence. The suburbs of Lucknow were quickly in the hands of the British, and the 93rd led the attack upon the Begum's Palace. It was a place of tremendous strength, the walls loopholed and the gateways strongly protected, with an exceedingly deep ditch before the whole front of the position. For a long time the artillery kept up a bombardment of the walls in the frail hope that a breach would be made, and that, as in the attack upon the Secundrabagh, the Highlanders would obtain a foothold. On the following day the artillery suddenly ceased fire, the Sutherlands leapt to their feet, for a few minutes took cover in the building facing the position, and then charged for the ditch. "Every obstacle," says Captain Burgoyne, "that could be opposed to the stormers had been prepared by the enemy; every room, door, gallery, or gateway was so obstructed and barricaded that only a single man could pass at a time. Almost every window or opening that could afford the slightest shelter was occupied by the enemy, and in threading their way through the narrow passages and doorways our men were exposed to unseen foes."

It would appear to have been an almost impossible position to take, but the Sutherlands never flinched, and the more foes and the greater numbers of the enemy that faced them the more did they press on with the bayonet. A hand-to-hand struggle lasting for two hours took place, while above the din of the conflict rang the shrill notes of the pipes of John Macleod—the Pipe-Major of the 93rd. The engagement was very similar to that of the

Secundrabagh, the Highlanders pursuing the enemy from courtyard to courtyard, from room to room, giving no quarter, and expecting none.

Well might the Brigadier write in his despatch, "The Brigadier-General has shared in many a hard-fought action during his service, but on no occasion has he witnessed a more noble and determined advance than was made by the 93rd this day."

By March 20 the rebels were finally driven back, and Lucknow was captured. We must not forget that in the siege the Camerons were also engaged, but in another part of the operations, being included in the division under Outram. There is very little information regarding their share in the engagement, while the 93rd and the 42nd were achieving such memorable work elsewhere. But it is certain, from the Life of Outram, that the Cameron Highlanders engaged in the suburbs of Lucknow managed to repulse the enemy with considerable loss.

Following the storming of Lucknow, Sir Colin Campbell prepared the dispersion of the enemy at Bareilly. This town was to be reached by two columns, converging upon it from different directions, one under the command of General Walpole, with whom were the 42nd and the 93rd, and the other under the command of Brigadier-General John Jones. The first attack by Walpole resulted in a reverse, and the loss of Brigadier Adrian Hope, a most distinguished officer, whose death caused amongst the members of the Highland regiments the deepest resentment and distress. The incident was like that later one of Magersfontein, one that rankled—whether justly or not we cannot say—for many years. The loss of the 42nd was very heavy, and later on Sir Colin Campbell himself took command, advancing upon Bareilly.

On May 5 there was a fierce attack upon the British by the Ghazees, a fanatical tribe, and, as Sir Colin himself said, "the most determined effort he had seen during the war." Uttering their fierce shouts, they flung themselves upon the Black Watch. Colonel Cameron was dragged from his horse; General Walpole was wounded, and had it not been for the presence of Sir Colin Campbell himself, the Highlanders might have been overcome by the fierceness of this attack, being outflanked as well as outfaced by the enemy.

On the following day the British delivered their attack upon Bareilly, practically clearing the position of the enemy. The remnants were dispersed by the 93rd. This action concludes the main features of the Highland regiments' part in the Indian Mutiny campaign.

The 42nd remained in India until January 1868, nearly ten years after the 78th had marched into Edinburgh with the band playing 'Scotland Yet.'

It would not be fitting to conclude a chapter on the Indian Mutiny without recalling the name of Sir Colin Campbell. Broken in health through the toils and anxieties of the campaign, he was compelled to return to England, where he was raised to the Peerage as Baron Clyde. The remaining years of his life were spent in the quiet enjoyment of the honours that were showered upon him by a grateful country, and on August 14, 1863, the great Scottish soldier passed away, and was buried in Westminster Abbey.

THE BATTLE HONOURS OF THE ARGYLL AND SUTHERLAND HIGHLANDERS

Cape of Good Hope, 1806; Rolica, Vimiera, Corunna, Pyrenees, Nivelle, Nive, Orthez, Toulouse, Peninsula, Alma, Balaclava, Sevastopol, Lucknow; South Africa, 1846-1847, 1851-1852-1853, 1879; South Africa, 1899-1902; Modder River, Paardeberg.

The 1st Battalion was raised in 1794 and called the 91st Argyllshire Highlanders.

The 2nd Battalion was raised in 1799 and known as the 93rd Sutherland Highlanders.

The two regiments became the 1st and 2nd Battalions of the Argyll and Sutherland Highlanders in 1881.

CHAPTER XVIII
WOLSELEY AND THE BLACK WATCH IN ASHANTI
(1873-1874)

The Campbells are comin', O ho, O ho!

The Campbells are comin', O ho!

The Campbells are comin' to bonnie Lochleven,

The Campbells are comin', O ho, O ho!

Regimental March.

After the Mutiny we say farewell, as it were, to the Old Guard of the Crimea and India, and hear a great deal about the younger men, Wolseley, Roberts, and White, all of whom had been through the Mutiny, two of them being destined to attain to the highest distinction that the British Army can bestow.

Garnet Wolseley was born in Dublin on June 4, 1833. He lost the use of one eye in the Crimea, served in India during the Mutiny, and in the Chinese War of 1860. In 1861 he crossed to Canada, and in 1870 conquered Louis Riel, the half-breed. In 1873 he led an expedition to Ashanti. There have been many places of horror and oppression in the histories of savage peoples, but it is doubtful whether there was ever a town so foul and brutal as Coomassie, the capital of Ashanti. The shedding of blood was the daily delight and pastime of the king, while murder upon a prodigal scale was to him and to his people a kind of rite. His subjects, instead of rebelling against these practices, delighted in such spectacles, and encouraged Koffi Calcalli, the king, to further outrages and orgies. It was, as some one has called it, 'a metropolis of murder.' So far, however, Britain had not seen her way to interfere, and had she done so, simply on the ground of common humanity, it is probable that other nations would have suspected her of conspiring to take over the country. At last King Koffi, craving for something new, decided that he would attack the English at Cape Coast Castle. Fortunately he was not able to achieve very much, but on the other hand the English were not strong enough to retaliate. This position was rendered all the more dangerous by the policy of toleration, which from the year 1824, when the Ashantis defeated Sir Charles M'Carthy, to the year 1863, when a West Indian regiment failed most signally, had given the natives a poor opinion of the English arms. It was therefore necessary for the safety of the English settlers that an Expeditionary Force should leave for Ashanti. It sailed under the command of Sir Garnet Wolseley, with whom were the Black Watch under Sir John Macleod.

It was no 'picnic,' to quote from a popular expression of to-day; and to give some idea of the country through which the Black Watch marched, I shall quote a paragraph from Sir Henry Stanley's Coomassie and Magdala.

"Coomassie," he says, "was a town insulated by a deadly swamp. A thick jungly forest—so dense that the sun seldom pierced the foliage, so sickly that the strongest fell victims to the malarias it cherished—surrounded it to a depth of one hundred and forty miles seaward, many hundred miles east, as many more west, and a hundred miles north. Through this forest and swamp, unrelieved by any novelty or a single pretty landscape, the British Army had to march one hundred and forty miles, leaving numbers behind sick of fever and dysentery."

To force their way through this fastness of almost impenetrable jungle called for both patience and courage. Wolseley received some assistance from the Fantees, who were enemies of the Ashantis. These natives cut a passage through the forests for the British troops. By the time the Black Watch landed at Cape Coast Castle in January 1874 this preparatory work had been completed.

The Highlanders presented an unfamiliar appearance, being clothed in Norfolk grey, which for several excellent reasons was considered a safer form of dress for the troops than the kilt. Associated with the expedition were officers whose names were soon to become familiar to the whole of the English-speaking race. There were Evelyn Wood, Archibald Alison—future commander of the Highland Brigade—Redvers Buller, all men of sterling quality, while Wolseley, whose long life closed in 1913, was a leader possessed of infinite perseverance and with a genius for organisation.

For a time the Fantees gave their assistance as carriers, and without delay the expedition started into the interior, and, having crossed the Prah River, came in contact with the enemy, who were now only too anxious, were it possible, to come to conciliatory terms with the British. These negotiations failed, and a large number of presumably friendly natives having disappeared, the British expedition were faced by a jungle of ninety miles to their front, at the end of which was the stronghold of King Koffi.

Stanley, who was with the expedition, has related that when they came in touch with the enemy for the first time he turned out to see the Black Watch march past to the attack. "We had but barely finished our breakfasts," he relates, "and buckled our belts on, when our servants informed us that the white troops were close by. Hastening to the square or plaza of the village, we were in time to witness the famous 'Black Watch' come up, all primed and ready for action. This was our first view of the fighting 42nd Highlanders, and I must say I improved the occasion to get a good look at them, as if I had never seen a British regiment in my life. Their march past was done with an earnest determined stride that promised well for their behaviour, whatever might lie at the front."

The Black Watch was under the command of Major Macpherson of Cluny, to whom reference has already been made in a former chapter. He was a descendant of that Cluny Macpherson who, little more than a hundred years before, had been in arms for Prince Charlie.

The forest confronting the Highlanders was intersected by narrow paths, and, in order to advance, and keep in touch with one another, the 42nd availed themselves of these lanes, thus throwing themselves open to a flank attack by the enemy from the dense bush upon either side. They advanced in skirmishing order, firing as they went, unable to see their foe, but knowing very well of his near presence by the hail of slugs that whistled about their heads. For a brief space of time the whole proximity of forest would appear perfectly lifeless, and then, with spurts of fire from every side, a deafening cannonade would be opened. Undaunted, the Highlanders pressed on, firing as they could and when they could, while over their heads the shells of the naval brigade whined and crashed into the trees.

The Ashantis, who so far had reposed the utmost trust in their fetishes, grew at last discouraged with the steady advance of the British. The roadway, over which they had rushed in their headlong retreat, was now bespattered with human blood, while here and there lay the unhappy victims of their sacrifices. Perceiving these significant signs of weakening, the advance of the Black Watch was quickened. Sir Archibald Alison, realising that the turning-point had come, ordered the pipes to strike up, and with the 'Campbells are comin'' the Highlanders charged swiftly after the enemy, who, confronted with lines of cold steel, and deafened by the booming thunder of the great naval guns, made headlong for Coomassie. One who took part in the conflict has well written: "Never was battle fought admitting of less distinction. It is impossible, indeed, to give a picturesque account of an affair in which there was nothing picturesque; in which scarcely a man saw an enemy from the commencement to the end of the fight; in which there was no manœuvring, no brilliant charges, no general concentration of troops; but which consisted simply of lying down, of creeping through the bush, of gaining ground foot by foot, and pouring a ceaseless fire into every bush in front which might contain an invisible foe. Nothing could have been better than Sir Garnet Wolseley's plan of battle or more admirably adapted for the foe with whom he had to deal.

Where he attacked us he found himself opposed by a continuous front of men, who kept his flank attacks at bay, while the 42nd pushed steadily and irresistibly forward. To that regiment belong, of course, the chief honours of the day, but all did exceedingly well."

After this opening engagement Wolseley halted for the night, and on the following day his advance was continued, the River Ordah being reached. Here King Koffi determined to resist the encroachment upon his country and the menace to his capital. It was necessary to throw a bridge across the river, and when this was completed the Rifle Brigade crossed and came into touch with the enemy. For a long time their resistance was so warmly sustained that the British could make no advance, but after seven hours' fighting Wolseley did what in Stanley's opinion he should have done long before, he ordered up the Black Watch. Colonel Macleod, who was in command, gave the order, "The 42nd will fire volleys by companies according to order. Forward!" Immediately there commenced the final advance on Coomassie, throughout which the Highlanders were met by a resistance more determined than ever before.

The arrival of the 42nd turned the scales at once. Their tactics—the front rank firing to the right and the rear rank firing to the left—enabled them to advance without exposing their flanks to the volleys of an invisible foe. Wherever the Ashantis were observed to be huddled together, either in the lanes or in confusion in the bush, the Highlanders charged them with the bayonet, driving them away helter-skelter. Nothing stopped the onward march, and the whole heart went out of the enemy when they realised that it was impossible to distract or confuse the Highlanders by ambuscades on their flanks. To make a stand for their capital—that was the only thing left. All around the British sounded the cow-horns of the enemy giving the signal for retreat.

The result of this swift approach of the 42nd was that all the villages before Coomassie were speedily captured, and Sir Archibald Alison despatched the news to Wolseley, saying that if he were reinforced he could enter Coomassie that night. As Stanley has remarked: "Mere laudation is not enough for the gallantry which distinguished this regiment when in action.... They proceeded along the well-ambushed road as if on parade, by twos. Vomiting out two score of bullets to the right and two score to the left the companies volleyed and thundered as they marched past the ambuscades, cheers rising from the throats of the lusty Scots, until the forest rang again with the discordant medley of musketry, bagpipe, and vocal sounds.... Very many were borne back frightfully disfigured and seriously wounded, but the regiment never halted nor wavered; on it went until the Ashantis, perceiving it useless to fight against men who would advance heedless of ambuscades, rose from their coverts and fled panic-stricken towards

Coomassie, being perforated by balls whenever they showed themselves to the hawk-eyed Scots."

So swift had been their oncoming and so profound the impression they had made upon the Ashantis, that when Coomassie was reached the Highlanders marched into it without opposition, and later in the evening Wolseley himself passed between the lines of the victorious 42nd, who greeted him with cheer upon cheer.

The destruction of the horrible town took place, and without further delay Wolseley led his troops back to Cape Coast Castle.

On March 23 the regiment landed at Portsmouth, where they were the centre of a tremendous enthusiasm. Thus was concluded one of our smaller campaigns, in which the historic Black Watch conducted itself with that resourceful determination and dogged bravery that has ever distinguished it.

CHAPTER XIX
WITH ROBERTS AND THE SEAFORTHS TO AFGHANISTAN
(1878-1880)

Kabul town's by Kabul river—

Blow the bugle, draw the sword—

There I lef' my mate for ever,

Wet an' drippin' by the ford.

Ford, ford, ford o' Kabul river,

Ford o' Kabul river in the dark!

There's the river up and brimmin', an' there's 'arf a squadron swimmin'

'Cross the ford o' Kabul river in the dark.

KIPLING.

It would be quite beyond the scope of this book to deal with the causes that led up to the conflict in Afghanistan, but it would be expedient to glance at the most prominent features of the Afghan trouble. Afghanistan lies at the north of India, and forms the boundary state between the possessions of Russia and of England. For this reason it was compelled to trust neither Russia nor England, and to play a lone hand for its own independence. In 1878 the ruler of Afghanistan was named Shere Ali, a very cunning and unscrupulous man, inspired by the desire to sustain his own independence while siding with the strongest of his neighbours—a policy as old as the world itself.

It was suggested that a British officer should take up his residence at Kabul, and at that Shere Ali for a moment dropped the mask. He opposed the suggestion very strongly, for excellent reasons, since he was in touch with Russia. It instantly became imperative that the Government should act, so they proposed forthwith to send a Mission to confer with Shere Ali. "The Amir must choose," said Lord Lytton, "which of his powerful neighbours he will rely upon, and he must learn that if he does not promptly prove himself our loyal friend we shall be obliged to regard him as our enemy and treat him accordingly. A tool in the hands of Russia I will never allow him to become. Such a tool it would be my duty to break before it could be used." They were courageous words, but uttered rather late.

With Eastern caution Shere Ali did not refuse point-blank to receive the Mission, but was obviously satisfied—as Lord Lytton wrote to Lord Salisbury—that there was nothing more to be got out of the British. For several months the matter was allowed to drop, as England was fully occupied with the threatening of war with Russia over the old question of Turkey. During these rumours of hostilities the Amir, who followed the European Press very carefully, was more and more inclined to throw in his lot with Russia, and with this end in view pushed on the fortifications and the manufacture of guns and ammunition at Kabul. Presently news was received by the Government that a Russian envoy had been welcomed by Shere Ali with demonstrations of the greatest friendliness. One feature of the situation became self-evident. Should war break out Russia would make her attack on India through Afghanistan.

The signing of the Berlin Treaty staved off the war between Russia and England, but the reception given to the Russian envoy by the Amir could not so easily be ignored. Accordingly Lord Lytton decided that a Mission must be received by Shere Ali to prevent the situation appearing as a slight upon the British arms. When Stolieloff, the Russian envoy, was shown the letter he merely remarked to the agitated Amir, "Two swords cannot go into one scabbard." Those words nerved Shere Ali to oppose the passing of the English Mission through the Khyber Pass. It was a humiliating situation, and as Sir Neville Chamberlain wrote in his letter to the Viceroy, "Nothing could have been more distinct, nothing more humiliating to the British Crown and nation." Through their vacillation the Government had now convinced the Amir—as they were later on to delude the Boers—that they would never take action, and as one native Prince remarked with engaging frankness to Chamberlain, "The people say, and we think, that you will still do nothing."

That, quite briefly, was the situation when the Government decided to send a force to Afghanistan. It was composed of two columns—one advancing towards Kandahar, the other by the Kuram Valley. In command of this latter column was Major-General Sir Frederick Roberts, while under him were included the 72nd (the 1st Battalion Seaforth Highlanders), who had already seen service in Central India, and who, together with the 92nd (Gordon Highlanders), will principally occupy our attention during this campaign.

Frederick Roberts was born in India in 1832, being the son of a distinguished soldier, Sir Abraham Roberts, called the 'patriarch of Indian Generals,' while two of his uncles had been in the Navy. He was at the relief of Lucknow and the fall of Delhi. During his long life he saw much service, never meeting with a serious reverse. His last years were employed in a vain appeal for National Service, and his death in 1914 was where he would best have wished it—within sound of the guns.

The advance towards Kabul was naturally somewhat prolonged, owing to the extremely difficult character of the country. It was necessary to carry a great quantity of baggage and commissariat. Everything went smoothly until the Peiwar Kotal was sighted, where the Afghans were at last seen to be in force. It was six in the morning, and very dark, when the sentinels of the enemy were first discovered. There followed a charge by the Highlanders and the Gurkhas, but the main force of the Afghans awaited the attack upon the strongly defended heights of the Peiwar Kotal, which guarded the only approach to Kabul, and which was a kind of crow's nest. "Across the summit or saddle of the steep ascent the enemy had thrown up a battery of field works, the fire of which could rake the whole pass. On either side of the Kotal, on two steep hills, were guns in battery, which could throw a deadly cross-fire upon an ascending force. The troops of the Amir occupied the entire line of the upper hills for a distance of four miles, and at either extremity were guns in position to meet any flank attack that could be made, and lofty and more inaccessible hills covered their line of retreat."

Roberts, determined that he should lose no time in attacking the Afghan position, planned that the Highlanders, the Gurkhas, and the Punjab infantry, with some artillery, should make a flank attack. The remainder of the force held the attention of the enemy in the front. In silence and secrecy the little party set off and attacked at dawn. The type of country through which they were passing was not unlike the Highlands of Scotland when the snow is on the ground. The sides of the hills were thick with boulders and broken foliage, and during the whole of the advance shots were fired from the Afghans concealed behind trees and rocks upon the hill-side.

As soon as the attack had developed the guns came into action, and when the Afghans saw their beasts stampeding and their tents on fire, panic set in. Realising that an assault was threatening their rear, and dreading that they would be surrounded, they speedily evacuated their position. It was a great success, and a Seaforth triumph. For the first time the Afghans had learned that respect for the British soldier that Mr. Kipling has emphasised in the lines:

An' when the war began, we chased the bold Afghan,

An' we made the bloomin' Ghazi for to flee, boys, O,

An' we marched into Kabul, an' we tuk the Bolan 'Issar,

An' we taught 'em to respec' the British soldier.

In a despatch Roberts wrote: "I cannot praise them too highly, the 72nd is a splendid regiment."

That night, after twenty hours of continual marching upon very little food, the troops bivouacked on the saddle of the hill along which the enemy had retreated shortly before. On the following morning it was realised what a very great advantage had been gained in taking this position, an achievement that could only have been won by a high degree of discipline and endurance. Roberts advanced to within four miles of Kabul, and decided that as his force was insufficient he must turn back to Fort Kurum.

He determined to leave a portion of his force to hold the position of Peiwar Kotal during the winter. On Christmas Eve news came that the Amir had been deserted by his army and had set out for St. Petersburg, proposing to place himself in the hands of the Czar. Fate willed it otherwise. He was shortly overcome by illness, dying at Turkestan, and in the confused condition of the country he had deserted it was impossible to know what was hidden in the future.

Shere Ali had been succeeded by his son, Yakub Khan, who was as cunning as his father. He accepted with engaging celerity all the conditions that the British Government laid down, but Roberts strongly suspected that the time was not yet due when peace could be made. The Afghans had not been beaten, and despite public opinion, which, in its accustomed ignorance of the real situation, implored the Government to end the war, he advised most urgently that the campaign to Kabul should continue in the spring.

Soon after this Major Cavagnari was permitted by the new Amir to proceed to Kabul as the British agent. Roberts accompanied him a part of the way, and when they said farewell he turned back and shook hands with him once more. It was in both their minds that in all probability they would never meet again. And so time went on, and not very long after rumours came drifting southwards that there was trouble in Kabul. It was afterwards related that Cavagnari was warned by a native that he should flee. "Never fear," was his answer, "dogs that bark don't bite." "This dog does bite," said the other. As representative of the British Government it was unthinkable that he should consider his own life. "They can only kill three or four of us here," he replied, "and our death will be avenged."

Already his doom was sealed. On September 2nd the Viceroy received a telegram, 'All well.' On September 5 Roberts heard that the Residency in Kabul had been attacked by three regiments, and that Cavagnari and his brother officers were defending themselves as best they could. Roberts was ordered to advance to Kabul, accompanied by the troops that were stationed at Kurum. Things moved quickly after that. One telegram followed upon another, each bearing worse news, and at last came the tragic tidings that the members of the Embassy had been murdered. With Sir Louis Cavagnari, the Resident, were a handful of Englishmen and a detachment of the famous Indian regiment, the Guides. It was of that memorable scene that Sir Henry Newbolt has written:

Sons of the Island race, wherever ye dwell,

Who speak of your fathers' battles with lips that burn,

The deed of an alien legion hear me tell,

And think not shame from the hearts ye tamed to learn,

When succour shall fail, and the tide for a season turn,

To fight with a joyful courage, a passionate pride,

To die at the last as the Guides at Cabul died.

Within twenty-four hours Roberts had left Simla with 5000 men and orders to reach Kabul, while the Amir was warned that the British troops were on their way to avenge the outrage.

The expedition, which included the Seaforths and Gordons, reached Charasiah before the enemy were in force. This place lies some twelve miles from Kabul, but with ridge after ridge of precipitous hill between. Upon this summit the Afghans had placed their guns, while their riflemen had taken cover behind the innumerable boulders to await the advance of the British force. Before Roberts lay the Afghan army thus heavily entrenched, guarding Kabul. He must storm the heights or retreat, and unless he made his attack at once he must permit the enemy to redouble their numbers.

Frequently in the Indian Mutiny the Sepoys, taking for granted that an attack would be made upon one flank or another, stationed their guns accordingly. On this occasion the Afghans, believing that Roberts would concentrate his assault upon their left, laid themselves liable to a surprise.

At the same time it would be difficult to name an enemy more brave, more athletic, and more resourceful than the Afghan, and the task before the British was no enviable one.

Major White of the Gordon Highlanders—afterwards famous as the defender of Ladysmith—went to the attack, covered by the British guns, while General Baker set out to carry the enemy's right. The Gordons started up the steep hill-side, to be suddenly faced by a great number of the enemy—at least twenty to one. They were already exhausted by the severe toil up the hill, and noting their hesitation, White snatched a rifle from one of the men's hands, shot down the leader of the enemy, and as the Afghans wavered the Gordons charged and took the position. It was for this cool action at a critical moment that Major White received the Victoria Cross. Meanwhile, the Seaforths, together with the Gurkhas, had borne the brunt of the attack in another quarter. They struggled onward from ridge to ridge, till at last the Afghans threw up the fight and bolted. The battle of Charasiah was won, but it had taken twelve hours' hard fighting to win it. Daybreak found Roberts on the march, and the Amir, who had had the effrontery to send a message of congratulation to the British commander in the vain hope that it would make things more agreeable when they met, was ready to receive him when Kabul was reached. But the trouble was not over.

The Afghans had taken up another strong position outside Kabul, but in the darkness of the succeeding night, upon the threat of an attack from General Baker, they decided to disperse, and, like all hillmen, vanished into the mist before the dawn. The triumphal entry of Roberts into Kabul was a splendid if melancholy spectacle. He told the people that the British Government had decided not to take revenge for the murder of Cavagnari and his colleagues, but that certain measures would be enforced to ensure peace.

On the next day the Amir walked into Roberts's tent and stated that he wished to resign. As Kabul could not be left without a Governor, Roberts, on behalf of England, proclaimed that Afghanistan would be taken over by the British, and that the future of the people would be decided after a conference.

As might be expected, the Afghans were by no means satisfied with this ultimatum. A guerilla warfare was directed against our troops, and Kabul was besieged by such numbers that it became daily more evident that the position would be soon untenable. It was during these raids and counter-raids that Lieutenant Dick-Cunyngham of the Gordon Highlanders won his Victoria Cross, and Corporal Sellar of the Seaforths was also awarded the coveted honour.

Roberts now found himself in an exceedingly difficult position, being ignorant of the number of the enemy and unable to obtain much information of their movements. As inactivity is often more dangerous than defeat he resolved to lead an attack from two different points, trusting that he could surround the Afghans and win a decisive victory. Had the two columns managed to work in unison the British would have been rewarded with a success. Unfortunately, there was one false move, and, by a blunder, the British force was outflanked and attacked by some 10,000 of the enemy. Compelled to retire in frantic haste, the guns became jammed in the narrow road, and the cavalry were unable to assist them. In the midst of this dangerous situation Roberts arrived to find that his strategy was like enough to turn into a disaster. It was imperative, were the situation to be retrieved, to obtain infantry without delay. A messenger was despatched to Kabul to call up the Seaforth Highlanders. Would they arrive in time before the British troops were annihilated? For there were now less than 300 men and 4 guns confronting 10,000! To win time the English cavalry employed the desperate resort of charging.

"Into a cloud of dust the Lancers disappeared as they headed for the masses of the enemy, and nothing could be seen for a few moments of the fight. Then riderless horses came galloping back, followed by scattered bodies of troopers. They had been received with a terrific fire which had killed many horses and men, and on trying to force their way through the enemy, had been surrounded and beaten back by sheer force of numbers. Even among Roberts and his staff the bullets fell thickly, killing three or four horses and wounding others."

Just in the nick of time appeared the Seaforth Highlanders, amidst the cheers of the Lancers. "It was," says an eye-witness, "literally touch and go as to who could reach the village first, the Highlanders or the Afghans, but our men swept in and swarmed to the tops of the houses, able to check the rush of the enemy, who streamed down on the village like ants on a hill."

In the meantime the other columns that had hoped to join with that of General Baker heard with alarm the mutter of distant artillery, General Macpherson, who was in command, realising that this probably spelt disaster, pushed on with all speed and managed to come to where the Highlanders were fighting at Dehmazung. The British force was thus snatched from a catastrophe that would have raised every Afghan in the country.

After this unsatisfactory engagement Roberts decided that he would take up position in Sherpur, evacuating Kabul since the people there were not to be depended on, and it would be a difficult place to hold. The numbers of the enemy had increased so largely that although many points of vantage had been taken it was decided that concentration within the limits of Sherpur was inevitable. Though Roberts had ample funds of ammunition he could not reassure the Government that for the present any decisive advance could be made. Trenches were hastily thrown up and wire entanglements implanted, and shortly afterwards the attack upon Sherpur commenced. Before dawn the noise, "as if hosts of devils had been let loose," came rolling out of the night, and through the darkness could be dimly seen dense masses of the Afghans rushing upon the British entrenchments, shouting again and again their frenzied battle-cry of "Allah-il-Allah!"

The Gordon Highlanders were one of the first regiments to open fire upon the immense force that threatened them. For three hours, despite the terrible slaughter amongst their ranks, the Afghans rushed again and again to the attack. At last it was evident that a counter-move would be necessary to break the enemy's determination to take Sherpur at all costs. Moving out the cavalry with four guns, Roberts began to shell the outlying villages. Distracted by this manœuvre, the Afghans' assault exhausted itself, and the moment for a counter-attack arrived. Suddenly the cavalry swept down on their crowded masses, and in a moment the enemy were in confused retreat. The end was come. Once in disorder they scattered far and wide, pursued by every available man and horse. By evening all the neighbouring country was perfectly silent, just as though no battle had ever raged. The Afghans had vanished like smoke.

Kabul had been wrecked and plundered by the enemy, but the next day Roberts re-entered the city, made General Hills Governor, and, as he himself said, "the present outlook was fairly satisfactory." But although the natives in the immediate vicinity of the capital were crushed, the tribes at Kandahar were in revolt. General Burrows was forced to retreat to Kushk-i-Nakud, while against him were marching 12,000 men. The result of this engagement was the loss of the guns at Maiwand. It was essential that this disaster should be wiped out, and shortly afterwards Roberts, accompanied by the Seaforths and the Gordon Highlanders, set out on the famous march to Kandahar. The news from Kandahar could not have been worse. The Afghans had completely defeated General Burrows's brigade, and were now besieging the English force under General Primrose in Kandahar. It was imperative that Roberts should relieve Primrose at once, and on the 8th the memorable march commenced. The English force numbered some 10,000 men, selected from regiments of stamina and proved courage.

Only a military genius could have undertaken a march without communication lines, without heavy baggage, and with a hostile army at the end of it. The prospect was not favourable. They were faced by three hundred miles of the enemy's country, the inhabitants of which would be only too ready to fall upon them should an opportunity present itself, and disaster would almost surely turn to annihilation. It would take too long to deal with that eventful march, and there was little of actual conflict throughout. On the 26th of August there was a sharp engagement, the Afghans being thrown back; on the 31st the British came in sight of Kandahar, where the Afghan leader was strongly posted. They had arrived just in time. To the beleaguered garrison they were like an army dropped from heaven.

On September 1 the action began, and the Seaforths and Gordons were sent forward to expel the enemy from the village in which they were entrenched. A fierce hand-to-hand engagement ensued, and facing the thousands of the enemy Major White shouted to the 92nd: "Highlanders, will you follow me?" "Joyfully and with alacrity the Highlanders responded to the call of their favourite leader, and without pausing to recover breath, drove the enemy from their entrenchments at the point of the bayonet." This was the heaviest piece of hard fighting, and shortly after the enemy wavered and finally broke, being quickly dispersed by the cavalry. An undisciplined army can seldom retire in good order; once broken it is instantly confused, and in a few minutes the Afghan troops were streaming away towards the hills. Roberts, worn out by fever and the anxieties and fatigues of the last few weeks, did not spare himself during that critical day, and when it was over he thanked each regiment personally for their services. Right well had the Highlanders supported him. He had left India for a country seething with revolution, and had carried the Peiwar Kotal. There had followed the murder of Cavagnari, the quick descent upon Kabul, those anxious days when the British forces were besieged outside the city, victory only to be followed by the memorable march to Kandahar, and, last of all, after the frightful fatigues and endurance, this decisive action.

Roberts, in addressing the troops, reminded them of the glory they had won. "You beat them at Kabul," he said, "and you have beaten them at Kandahar, and now as you are about to leave the country you may be assured that the very last troops the Afghans ever want to meet in the field are Scottish Highlanders and Goorkhas."

The Seaforths at Candahar

"Never," he wrote afterwards, "had commander been better served, and I shall never forget the feeling of sadness with which I said good-bye to my men who had done so much for me. I looked upon them all, native as well as British, as my valued friends. Riding through the Bolan Pass, I overtook men of the regiments of the Kabul-Kandahar Field Force, marching towards Sibi, thence to disperse to their respective destinations. As I parted with each corps in turn, its band played 'Auld Lang Syne,' and I have never since heard the memory-stirring air without its bringing before my eye the last view I had of the Kabul-Kandahar Field Force. I fancy myself crossing, and recrossing, the river which winds through the Pass, I hear the martial beat of the drums, and the plaintive music of the pipes; and I see Riflemen and Goorkhas, Highlanders and Sikhs, guns and horses, camels and mules, with all the endless following of an Indian army, winding through the narrow gorges or over the interminable boulders."

It was this vivid picture that came back to the author upon that bleak November day of 1914, when the Indian soldiers, under the grey English heaven, went winding through the rain-driven streets of London. From far away sounded the deep salutation of the guns, the tolling of a bell, the wailing of the pipes. Thirty-four years had passed, and once again "Riflemen and Goorkhas, Highlanders and Sikhs, guns and horses" passed like the ghosts of long ago, or a dream of past achievement and work well done before the falling of the night.

BATTLE HONOURS OF THE SEAFORTH HIGHLANDERS (ROSS-SHIRE BUFFS, THE DUKE OF ALBANY'S).

Carnatic, Mysore, Hindoostan; Cape of Good Hope, 1806; Maida, Java; South Africa, 1835; Sevastopol, Persia, Koosh-ab, Lucknow, Central India, Peiwar Kotal, Charasiah; Kabul, 1879; Kandahar, 1880; Afghanistan, 1878-1880; Egypt, 1882; Tel-el-Kebir, Chitral, Atbara, Khartoum; South Africa, 1899-1902; Paardeberg.

CHAPTER XX
MAJUBA HILL
(1881)

Up beyond the Inyati, where the frontier ranges rise,

Dark and lonely looms the mountain evil-starred;

Staring southward for the column, keeping vigil 'gainst surprise,

Standing grimly like a sentinel on guard.

But at night strange sounds re-echo, and dim phantoms rise from rest,

And the voices of dead captains call again;

Through the winds that wail and whimper round Majuba's haunted crest,

That is peopled by the spirits of the slain.

JOHN SANDES.

It would take too long to deal at all circumspectly with the history of South Africa. It was the Portuguese who originally discovered the Cape of Good Hope, and for long years they were the controllers of the sea and of Africa. Many years later other peoples began to colonise in far-away lands, and Sir Francis Drake ran across the Cape, but as yet there was no interest in the place from a commercial point of view; the coast was merely used as a suitable stopping-place. Later on the Dutch—who were a great sea people then— founded a colony where Cape Town now stands. The French soon followed them, particularly the Huguenots, who had fled from their own country and were glad to settle in Africa. Last of all, the British became very anxious to found a settlement, and in 1795 Cape Colony was added to the British Empire and the rule of the Dutch was ended. The Dutch, who have always proved a courageous and obstinate people, never ready to admit the superiority of anybody else, in due course made their way elsewhere, preferring hardship to dependence.

After the wars of Napoleon the other Powers in Europe recognised that the British were supreme in South Africa, for which acknowledgment the Government paid Holland a large sum of money. From this time onwards troubles came at intervals from the Kaffir wars to the Zulu rising, from Majuba to that greatest of all campaigns in South Africa—the Great Boer War. From the beginning there were difficulties between the natives and the Boers, the Kaffir siding now with the English and now with the Boers, but usually against the latter. In the Kaffir campaigns the Highlanders took part, but they are not of sufficient importance to demand our attention.

There is one expedition, however, that has a memorable place in our history. Some men of the 2nd Battalion of the Black Watch, the 91st Argyllshire Highlanders, and the Highland Light Infantry were, in 1852, shipped for South Africa to take part in the campaign against the Kaffirs. They sailed upon the Birkenhead, and one dark night the ship went to pieces at a place called Danger Point. So swift and sudden was the shock that only a certain number of the boats could be lowered, and had they all been used there was quite an inadequate number for both the troops and the passengers. In perfect order the soldiers formed up in companies, and the women and children were lowered over the side. The horses were loosed and given a last chance for their lives. Then the boats put off and the Birkenhead was left to her fate. As the dawn was breaking, with those silent figures as steady as on parade, the Birkenhead disappeared, and four hundred British soldiers went to their death. That memorable scene has never been forgotten, and should be recalled as one of the most honourable and moving incidents in the history of the Highland regiments.

Subsequent to the melancholy end of the Birkenhead, the Boers had made their Great Trek, and the trouble with Dingaan, the Zulu chief, had resulted in the massacre of their comrades.

With the discovery of gold the whole aspect of South Africa changed. The country was suddenly inundated with all the riff-raff of Europe. The "gold rush" wrought more harm than can ever be fully estimated. Strife and trouble arose on every side. The Boers, who perpetually tyrannised over the natives, also attempted to tyrannise over the British. At last, on the 12th of April 1877, the South African Republic was taken over by the English, and the Union Jack run up at Pretoria. Although the Boers were very much aggrieved, they were quite unable to protect their rights in the matter, as the country was full of British troops.

A Zulu war broke out under Cetewayo, in which the Transvaal Boers would take no part, leaving the British to fend for themselves as best they could. Events followed hard upon each other. The terrible disaster of Isandlwana, where the British forces were cut off and suffered a loss of 800 men, sent a thrill through the whole of South Africa. Within a few hours there followed the heroic defence of Rorke's Drift, when a handful of men kept 3000 Zulus at arm's length for many hours. In 1879 the 91st Highlanders left for Zululand, to take their share in the defeat of the Zulus at the battle of Ulundi and the capture of Cetewayo.

In the meantime the dissatisfaction of the Boers had in no way diminished. Desiring to regain their freedom, they made preparations for doing so.

They elected Kruger, Joubert, and Pretorius as their leaders, and, on the 16th of December 1880, raised the flag of the Republic at Heidelburg, their new capital. War was declared, and in January 1881 the British suffered a reverse at Laing's Nek, where they remained strongly posted. Laing's Nek was very close to a kopje that has passed into our history as Majuba Hill.

We know a great deal more about the Boers now than we did then. We did not realise at that time that they were a clever and courageous foe, linking their intimate knowledge of the country with a sure and deadly marksmanship. The British troops in South Africa were quite inadequate in numbers to deal with such a situation. The 92nd Gordon Highlanders, with their famous march to Kandahar still vivid in the public mind, were hurried to reinforce the troops under General Sir George Colley at Prospect Hill.

General Colley had been instructed by Sir Evelyn Wood that he must not attempt an advance for the present. Despite this order he resolved to occupy Majuba Hill by night, and hold what appeared to be a superior position. Accordingly, at half-past eight on the evening of February 25, the little party, composed of 550 men of the Gordons and a party of the Naval Brigade, carrying 70 rounds of ammunition and three days' rations but no water, began their ascent of Majuba Hill. At the base they left a detachment to guard their lines of communications, thus reducing the force to some 350 men. So far as Colley's plan was concerned it was entirely successful. Just before the dawn broke the British were in possession of the summit, while far beneath them they could see the Boer camp beginning to stir for the day.

General White, V.C., who was then Senior Major of the Gordons, has described the situation in the regimental records. "The approaches," he says, "to the brow below were nearly all concealed from the view of the defenders on the top. The slope of the hill leading up to the brow is broken by natural terraces, which run nearly round the hill, and which afford an enemy, under cover of his firing parties placed for the purpose, an opportunity of collecting in force on any point, and to circuit round the hill without coming under the fire, or even the observation of the defenders."

To put it quite simply, the summit of the hill was like a saucer, while instead of a smooth slope down which the defenders could pick off the ascending foe, the cover was so ample that it was possible for the Boers to shoot the British against the sky-line without exposing themselves.

General Colley had expressed no deeper design than his wish that the men should hold the hill for three days. He made no preparations for the defence, he forbade the troops to entrench themselves, and so the day dawned, and the Boers awakened to the fact that Majuba Hill was occupied by the British. What followed is soon told. A storming party crept up the face of the hill, though quite out of sight of the British, and when Lieutenant Ian Hamilton of the Gordons approached General Colley, begging him to let them entrench themselves or charge, he merely repeated the fateful words, "Hold the place for three days." The Boers, firing against the sky-line, opened the engagement. It was simply a question of time until the little garrison were picked off man by man. Too late was it when Colley, at last thoroughly alive to the danger, running hither and thither, attempted to entrench his men. Still he refused to let the Gordons charge, and the Boers contented themselves for some time in reducing the number of the defenders. At last, growing contemptuous of such warfare, they attempted to finish the business and carry the position by assault. Undaunted, but sick at heart, the Gordons drove them back at the point of the bayonet. The end was near at hand. One hundred and fifty of the Highlanders stood shoulder to shoulder, determined to hold out to the last. Sir George Colley, shot through the head, fell in the hour of his deep humiliation. When at last the belated order was given to retreat, 200 men of that little force of 350 lay dead or wounded, and only 60 or 70 came out of the action. Lieutenant Ian Hamilton, who was later on to uphold the glory of the British arms against the Boers, was so badly wounded that when the enemy came to look at him they said, "You will probably die, you may go."

It had been little less than a massacre. "The top of Majuba," says Colonel M'Bean, "was a horrid sight. The first thing I saw was a long row of dead men—some 40 or 50 of them. There were also numbers of wounded men lying about, most of them frightfully wounded. I went towards the edge of the hill where so many of the 92nd had been killed.... The dead were all shot above the breast, in some men's heads I counted five and six bullet wounds."

It is now admitted that under the circumstances, and under the conditions of the defence, the disaster could not have been prevented. There was only one gleam in the encompassing gloom—to the last the British had fought without quailing.

He knows no tears who in the van

And foremost fight

Met death as should an Englishman

Upon Majuba's Height.

Whether foolishly or not cannot be discussed here, the British Government instructed Sir Evelyn Wood to come to terms at all costs, and the truce that resulted gave the Transvaal into Boer hands, with Mr. Kruger as President. We see now how unwise it was to permit this disgrace and humiliation to the British arms and the British name. Long years of quarrelling between the Boer colonists and those who acknowledged the sovereignty of England, were to make South Africa a place of miserable dissension. The easy success over a few hundred trapped British soldiers was magnified, in the eyes of the more ignorant Boers, into a victory over the whole English race, and until the Great War of 1899-1902 no occasion was ever let slip on which the name of 'Majuba' could be recalled and emphasised.

CHAPTER XXI
WITH THE HIGHLAND BRIGADE AT TEL-EL-KEBIR
(1882)

Where ha'e ye been a' the day,

Bonnie laddie, Highland laddie?

Saw ye him that's far away,

Bonnie laddie, Highland laddie?

On his head a bonnet blue,

Bonnie laddie, Highland laddie;

Tartan plaid and Highland trews,

Bonnie laddie, Highland laddie?

Regimental March.

Previous to 1882 Egypt had for many years been under the control of England and France, but neither of these Powers had actually occupied the country. In 1882, owing to the Nationalist Movement under Arabi Bey, which endangered the lives and property of Europeans, these two Powers decided that some steps must be taken to ensure the security of the white population. Shortly after, France agreed to leave the matter in the hands of the English, and the British fleet bombarded Arabi's position at Alexandria, while the English army under Sir Garnet Wolseley landed upon the coast to crush the Egyptian forces. This action was to end in the English occupation of Egypt, which has lasted until to-day. The principal reason for acting so quickly and with such determination was the danger that would ensue should the control of the Suez Canal fall into the hands of a hostile Power. The Khedive, who was a vassal of the Sultan, possessed at this time a mere shadow of authority, and after the war an English official was appointed to control his policy.

Sir Garnet Wolseley having decided to give the enemy no warning of his advance upon Cairo, planned to descend upon the city from Ismailia, and not from Alexandria as they expected. The position of Tel-el-Kebir was destined to become the scene of the final battle before the march upon Cairo.

The British army included the Grenadiers and Coldstreams, some cavalry and artillery, and the Highland Brigade, formed of the Black Watch, the Camerons, the Gordons, and the Highland Light Infantry. It is also of interest to note that with the force was a major of Egyptian cavalry called Herbert Kitchener.

Following the landing in Egypt, the army marched across the desert in the hope of surprising the enemy. The bombardment of Aboukir took place, and shortly afterwards the enemy were repulsed from Magfar. The British forces now concentrated at Kassassin, where Wolseley decided that the final conflict must be forced. They were now very near to the enemy's position, and on the night of the 12th of September were only some five miles distant from Tel-el-Kebir, where the Egyptians were heavily entrenched.

Sir Garnet Wolseley, having studied the position for several days, learned that the Egyptian pickets did not come beyond their defences at night. This led him to believe that a swift night assault might carry their position without further trouble. There were, however, several considerations that might militate against the success of a night attack. For one thing it was most essential that the enemy should be so thoroughly dispersed that the cavalry could advance without delay upon Cairo. There was also the danger that, in the darkness, the soldiers would fire upon each other, and to prevent such a calamity he placed the infantry at each end of the line and the artillery in the centre.

The troops set out in complete silence, no smoking or even the giving of orders being permitted. It was a moonless night, and, careful as they were, the Highland Brigade at one period lost their direction, and a new formation delayed the advance.

About an hour before sunrise the Highlanders found themselves beneath the parapet of the enemy's position, and the end of the hazardous march was reached. Sir Archibald Alison, who commanded the Highland Brigade, has written: "The Brigade formed for the march in the order in which it was to attack—two lines two deep. The rifles were unloaded, the bayonets unfixed, and the men warned that only two signals would be given—a word to 'Fix bayonets,' a bugle sound of 'To storm.' I never felt anything so solemn as that night march, nor do I believe that any one who was in it will ever forget it. No light but a faint star; no sound but the slow, measured tread of men on the desert sand. Just as the first tinge of light appeared in the east a few rifle shots fired out of the darkness showed that the enemy's outposts were reached. The sharp click of the bayonets then answered the word, 'To fix'—a few minutes more of deep silence, and then a blaze of musketry flashed across our front, and passed far away to each flank, by the light of which we saw the swarthy faces of the Egyptians, surmounted by their red tarbooshes, lining the dark rampart before us. I never felt such a relief in my life. I knew then that Wolseley's star was bright, that the dangerous zone of fire had been passed in the darkness, that all had come now to depend upon a hand-to-hand struggle."

The Highlanders were some hundred and fifty yards from the Egyptian entrenchments, which were 6 feet high and 4 feet deep. Suddenly through the long night silence a bugle rang out, and with a cheer the Highland Brigade broke into a charge. Some 200 men fell before they reached the parapet, the losses being increased before they scaled the entrenchments. Alison had written that he never saw men fight more steadily than the Egyptian soldiers, they rallied every foot of the way. "At this time," he says, "it was a noble sight to see the Gordon and Cameron Highlanders—now mingled together in the confusion of the fight, their young officers leading with waving swords, their pipes screaming, and that proud smile on the lips and that bright gleam in the eyes of the men which you see only in the hour of successful battle."

It is said Donald Cameron of the Camerons was "the first man to mount the trenches, and the second man to fall." A minute, and whole companies of men were swarming and pouring like waves of the sea over the Egyptian defences, and rushing down upon their defenders. Although taken by surprise the enemy made a stubborn fight, but after half an hour's fierce conflict the battle of Tel-el-Kebir was over, and the morning sun rose to pour its rays down upon the flying Egyptian army. Without delay Sir Garnet Wolseley pushed forward the cavalry to advance upon Cairo. Thus Arabi was prevented either from arresting the retreat or sacking the city, and realising that there was no further hope in resistance to the British arms he surrendered his sword, and the rebellion was over.

It had been a swift action, but it would be wrong either to underrate the discipline and bravery of the Egyptian troops or to imagine that it was an easy victory. As General Hamley has written in the Nineteenth Century: "The Scottish people may be satisfied with the bearing of those who represented them in the land of the Pharaohs. No doubt any very good troops, feeling that they were willing, would have accomplished the final advance; but what appear to me exceptional are: First, the order and discipline which marked that march by night through the desert; and, secondly, the readiness with which the men sprang forward to storm the works. The influence of the march had been altogether of a depressing kind—the dead silence, the deep gloom, the funereal pace, the unknown obstacles, and enemy. They did not know what was in front, but neither did they stop to consider. There was not the slightest sign that the enemy was surprised—none of the clamour, shouts, or random firing which would have attended a sudden call to arms. Even very good troops at the end of that march might have paused when suddenly greeted by that burst of fire, and none but exceptionally good ones could have accomplished the feats I have mentioned."

It is worth while repeating these words of General Hamley's, because in a later chapter we shall have to deal with that other memorable night march at Magersfontein. However melancholy the story, it serves to illustrate that when a night attack does not prove a surprise it becomes nothing less than a calamity.

CHAPTER XXII
FROM EL-TEB TO OMDURMAN
(1884-1898)

Vain is the dream! However Hope may rave,

He perished with the folk he could not save.

And though none surely told us he is dead,

And though perchance another in his stead,

Another, not less brave, when all was done,

Had fled unto the southward and the sun,

Had urged a way by force, or won by guile

To streams remotest of the secret Nile,

Had raised an army of the Desert men,

And, waiting for his hour, had turned again

And fallen on that False Prophet, yet we know

Gordon is dead, and these things are not so!

Nay, not for England's cause, nor to restore

Her trampled flag—for he loved Honour more—

Nay, not for Life, Revenge, or Victory,

Would he have fled, whose hour had dawned to die.

The White Pasha, ANDREW LANG.

Considerably before the events of the last chapter, Sir Samuel Baker, the English explorer, had travelled through the unknown regions of the Upper Nile, and found that the country was almost entirely devoted to the slave-trade. An effort was made to improve conditions there. The Khedive for a time asserted his authority over these regions, two Englishmen being appointed in succession as his governors, the first Sir Samuel Baker himself, and the second Charles Gordon. For many years Gordon, who had come fresh from China, struggled to free the natives from the slave-traders, but his labours were rendered useless by the accession of a worthless Khedive. Shortly afterwards he returned to England, and the Soudan relapsed into its old corruption. Then, in 1882, appeared one of those strange dramatic figures that in the East spring into prominence and disappear as abruptly—a fanatic named Mohammed Ahmed, proclaiming himself as Mahdi, and calling to his standard all true Mahommedans.

The Arabs have ever been ready to follow the sword, and very soon 6000 troops under Yusef Pasha were almost annihilated. Swiftly one Egyptian garrison fell after another. The Mahdi advanced towards the north, and cut to pieces an Egyptian army under Colonel Hicks. The word passed from village to village, from mosque to mosque, from one solitary encampment to another that the Mahdi had indeed come at last, and with the defeat of Hicks's army not only was Khartoum in hourly peril, but Cairo itself was threatened.

Fortunately, the Arab—like the Highlander of old—is satisfied with the booty in hand, and very much prefers to see it safely put away before he takes to the field again in search of more. Such practical considerations were a check to the Mahdi's religious zeal, and permitted England to collect her strength—or one should say such strength as lay to her hand; for at this time public interest in Egypt was very luke-warm. The result was the tragic page in history that closed with the death of Gordon in Khartoum. There was one man in Egypt who was later on both to avenge Gordon and to subdue the Soudan, but he as yet was unknown. The name of this young man was Kitchener, and the war correspondent, Mr. John Macdonald, has given the following little sketch of the future victor of Omdurman as he was in the year 1883—the year in which the Mahdi renewed his activities. It is not without interest at the present time.

"Taylor," he writes, "had invited me the night before to accompany him and his friend and witness the operation which they were both to supervise. A tall, slim, thin-faced, slightly stooping figure in long boots, 'cut-away' dark morning-coat and Egyptian fez, somewhat tilted over his eyes—such, as I remember him, was the young soldier who was destined to fulfil Gordon's task of 'smashing the Mahdi.' 'He's quiet,' Taylor whispered to me as we were getting ready; 'that's his way.' And, again, with characteristic jerk of the head, 'He's clever.' And so, in the raw, greyish early morning of January 8, 1883, the three of us drove in our dingy rattle-trap over the white dusty road Nilewards to meet the fellah cavaliers. Taylor did most of the talking. Kitchener expressed himself in an occasional nod or monosyllable.

"At the barracks we found some forty men waiting. I remember Kitchener's gaze at the awkward, slipshod group as he took his position in the centre of a circular space round which the riders were to show their paces. 'We begin with the officers,' said Taylor turning to me; 'we shall train them first, then put them to drill the troopers. We have no troopers just yet, though we have 440 horses ready for them.'

"And now began the selection of the fellah officers. They were to be tested in horsemanship. The first batch were ordered to mount. Round they went, Indian file, Kitchener, like a circus-master standing in the centre. Had he flourished a long whip he might have passed for a show-master at a rehearsal. Neither audible nor visible sign did he give of any feeling roused in him by a performance most disappointing and sometimes ridiculous. His hands buried in his trousers pockets, he quietly watched the emergence of the least unfit. In half an hour or so the first native officers of the fellah cavalry were chosen. It was then that Kitchener made his longest speech, 'We'll have to drive it into those fellows,' he muttered, as if thinking aloud."

The importance of this extract is the glimpse it gives of the material that was the hope of Egypt.

That was the type of man that Kitchener took in hand, and that was the type of man who was to uphold the supremacy of the British arms against the fanatic forces of the Mahdi.

But between 1883 and Omdurman there was more than spade work—there was grim tragedy and humiliating defeat. In August 1883, when the Mahdi was again on the war-path, General Baker despatched native reinforcements from Cairo in the vain hope that they would be able to withstand the advance of the Arabs. On February 4, 1884, Baker's poorly trained Egyptians encountered the Sudanese, and were practically annihilated. This disaster, following so quickly upon the rout of Hicks's troops, awakened the Government at home to the fact that something must be done. Sir Gerald Graham was ordered to proceed with a force of 4000 British troops to Suakin. With his force were the 1st Battalion of the Gordon Highlanders and the Black Watch. On the 29th of February the British troops set out upon the road over which Baker himself had passed, and came in touch with the enemy at El-Teb. The Arabs were defended to some extent with entrenchments, and for an hour maintained a steady fire. Then, having grown confident by their easily-won victories over Egyptian troops, the Sudanese hurled themselves at the Highlanders, shaking their long spears, and shouting their battle-cries. They were met by the solid unbreakable square of the 42nd. Checked and demoralised, their advance was quickly turned into a rout. No sooner did the enemy waver than the cavalry were let loose, and the engagement at El-Teb was turned into a signal success.

On the 13th of March 1884 was fought the battle of Tamai, in which the Black Watch took a leading part. The Highlanders were ordered to charge at the enemy in front, but did not perceive that on their right lay a deep nullah or piece of hidden ground. No sooner was their flank exposed than hosts of the enemy leapt to their feet and broke upon them. The 42nd were caught between two fires and surrounded. The Naval Brigade, forced back, were compelled to surrender their guns. It became a hand-to-hand struggle, each man fighting for himself.

In the words of Kipling:

We took our chanst among the Kyber 'ills,

The Boers knocked us silly at a mile,

The Burman give us Irriwaddy chills,

An' a Zulu impi dished us up in style:

But all we ever got from such as they

Was pop to what the Fuzzy made us swaller;

We 'eld our bloomin' own, the papers say,

But man for man the Fuzzy knocked us 'oller.

Then 'ere's to you, Fuzzy-Wuzzy, an' the missis an' the kid;

Our orders was to break you, an' of course we went an' did.

We sloshed you with Martinis, an' it wasn't 'ardly fair;

But for all the odds again' you, Fuzzy-Wuz, you broke the square.

For a moment it seemed as though Baker's disaster was to be repeated. But the British regulars were very unlike the undisciplined Egyptians. "The spectacle," wrote a war correspondent, "did not so much terrify as exercise a weird, terrible fascination. I do not suppose that either I or any one else who witnessed it will often again see its equal for magnificence. Though retreating, our men literally mowed down their assailants. In the smoke and dust of the battle, amid the bright gleam of their myriad spearheads, the semi-nude, brown-skinned, black, shaggy-haired warriors were falling down in scores. Of all the savage races of the world none are more desperately brave than the Soudan Arabs, who were breaking upon our ranks like a tempestuous sea. At last the pressure of the front upon the rear became so great that those of us who were mounted were for a few moments too tightly wedged together to be able to move; but we felt the collapse was only temporary."

It was touch and go, but the undismayed veterans of the Black Watch and those other troops who formed the British force were bound, sooner or later, to enforce their superiority. Presently, shoulder to shoulder, forming where they could into squares, the 42nd and 65th began to advance. For a moment the conflict was in suspense, then the crisis had passed. The victory was won.

Unhappily, the British Government took no advantage of Graham's successes, and decided upon the evacuation of the Soudan. Under these circumstances the only thing left to do was to ensure the safety of the civilians in the various towns more or less under European control. There was one man above all others who was competent to deal with the exigencies of the situation, and that was General Gordon. He was begged by the Government to leave for Egypt to carry out this mission. We must not overlook, in justice to the Government, that neither they nor probably Gordon himself appreciated the strength of the revolutionary movement in the Soudan, so that when he arrived at Khartoum in February 1884 he was dismayed to find it was exceedingly likely that he would be isolated there, if not actually besieged by the enemy. Accordingly, he advised the Government to make good the advantage gained by Sir Gerald Graham, and ensure a lasting peace in the Soudan. But the Government refused to be interested in the problem. Then Gordon communicated with the country, stating that he had provisions for only five months. Lord Granville, without dealing with the situation in any way, instructed him to leave Khartoum as best he could, and it was not until the end of March that the grave danger to Gordon was realised. Lord Wolseley, voicing the sympathies of the English people, begged the Government to do something to save a man whom they had sent out to represent the country.

Then and only then, Mr. Gladstone, who had placed every possible obstacle in the path of action, permitted the British troops to set out for Egypt, with Wolseley in command. And so there embarked that melancholy expedition, against which time and ill-luck waged a remorseless warfare—an expedition that was to reach Khartoum two days after the murder of Gordon.

Under Major-General Earle the Black Watch came up the Nile, while Sir Charles Wilson was heading for Khartoum. On the 10th of February Earle's columns came into conflict with the enemy at Kirbekan, when, to quote Wolseley's despatch, "The Black Watch advanced over rocks and broken ground upon the koppies, and after having by their fire in the coolest manner driven off a rush of the enemy, stormed the position under a heavy fire."

The Arabs put up, as always, a desperate resistance; they hurled one attack after another upon the guns, but always to be met with a devastating fire. The Black Watch in a later stage in the battle attempted to cut off the retreat of the enemy. Having placed them in an ambuscade, General Earle prepared for a decisive action. "For this assault," says Charles Lowe, "the order was about to be given, when a body of the Arabs, one of whom bore a banner, the rest being armed with swords and spears, boldly rushed down from the heights in front, and charged towards the nearest companies of the Black Watch, under Colonel Green. The Highlanders, though standing in line as at Balaclava, never budged, but met their assailants with such a withering fire that those who were not mown down by the bullets of the Martini-Henrys turned and fled towards the river."

It was the last effort of the Arabs, and a counter-attack now began. With 'The Campbells are comin'' the 42nd rushed up the hill-side, and the battle was soon over. Unfortunately, at the conclusion, General Earle was killed by one of the fugitives.

The Gordons took part in the arduous advance up the Nile to Abu Hamid, and when they reached that place news came of the death of Gordon. The tragic words 'Too late!' echoed throughout Egypt and the world. To those who had strained every nerve to reach him the news was bitter indeed. The expedition had failed, and there was nothing for it but to return. The water in the Nile was falling, and the advance must needs be stopped.

The Government, now roused to action and anxious to satisfy the indignation of the public, decided that the Mahdi must be crushed; but the matter was long delayed, and it was many years before Kitchener came to avenge the murder of a great Scotsman, and one of the most memorable figures of the last century.

The failure of the Gordon Relief Expedition encouraged the Mahdi in the belief that his success was due to the direct guidance of God. In his own mind, at least, he had driven the British home again, and although his death occurred in 1885, it in no way concluded the threatening of Egypt. There were many contests between the Dervishes and the Egyptian troops, who, led by British officers, were now able to hold their own. The labours of Kitchener were already beginning to bear fruit.

In August 1886 he was appointed Governor of Suakin, and instantly set about fortifying the place against the Dervishes. Various engagements followed during the forthcoming years, and the struggle with the Mahdi's forces went on until the campaign opened which was to end in the final and crushing victory of Omdurman. It must not be thought that this success was simply a success of arms; there had been many of those in the past. It was rather the culminating and final achievement in a long and silent campaign extending over many years, opening, as we have seen, with the first rather dismal efforts at training the Egyptians, passing on to that wonderful system of railways which crossed over five hundred miles of bare desert, to reach its appointed end in the fall of Omdurman and Mahdism.

It had taken sixteen years to make the Anglo-Egyptian army, and by the time the battle of Omdurman was fought it numbered 18,000 men, with 140 English officers.

From 1888 to 1892 Kitchener was Adjutant-General of the Egyptian Army; in 1892 he became Sirdar. At last, in 1894, he seized his opportunity. There was at this time a new Khedive—a young man who showed signs of resisting or criticising British rule. Without hesitation the Sirdar showed him very clearly that this would be unwise behaviour. He followed up his action by pushing forward his railways, mile by mile, towards Omdurman, the city of the Khalifa. It was impossible for the latter to surrender the city, for such an action would proclaim throughout the Soudan that the Mahdi was little better than a fugitive. The dawn of peace was already breaking. Omdurman was within striking distance.

The Dongola Expedition took place in 1896, resulting in the capture of Dongola and the dispersal of the Arabs in that quarter. In 1897 the Government at last came to a practical decision, and determined to crush for ever the power of the Khalifa, and for that purpose despatched an army in which were included the Seaforth Highlanders and the Camerons. It was no unexpected event for Kitchener. More truly was it the last mile of the journey. His organisation was complete, his troops were efficient, he could take his own time, and the result was certain.

The Khalifa's army was roughly estimated at 60,000 men, and divided into one division of 40,000 at Omdurman and another of 20,000 at Metammeh. The Sirdar, accompanied by General Gatacre and General Sir Archibald Hunter, was in command of a force of some 12,000 men perfectly equipped, and with some eight squadrons of Egyptian cavalry. The Camerons and Seaforths were brigaded under General Gatacre.

Mahmoud, who commanded the Khalifa's troops at Metammeh, left that place and marched towards the River Atbara, where he settled down in a zeriba, and calmly awaited the British advance. This was a new turn in Dervish tactics; formerly they had been only too ready to rush upon the British bayonet. But Mahmoud had learnt with native shrewdness the foolishness of throwing men upon the British square. He also knew who best could play a waiting game. It was imperative that Kitchener should act, and act quickly, and so, on the night of April 7 he advanced to open the conflict. As the late G. W. Steevens has so graphically written: "All England and all Egypt and the flower of the black lands beyond, Birmingham and the West Highlands, the half-regenerated children of the earth's earliest civilisation, and grinning savages from the uttermost swamps of Equatoria, muscle and machinery, lord and larrikin, Balliol and Board School, the

Sirdar's brain and the camel's back—all welded into one, the awful war machine went forward into action."

The Dervish zeriba lay some twenty miles distant. At about a quarter to four in the morning the advance guard came in sight of the enemy, and instantly the British force halted. It was, indeed, a formidable position that faced them. Mahmoud had studied the lie of the ground very carefully, and sheltered himself from artillery fire by a ridge of rising country. All around his camp was knotted and twisted together an entanglement of desert thorn some 10 feet high, and as much as 20 feet broad in some places. Behind these were trenches and bomb-proof shelters. Without the help of heavy artillery a frontal attack was the only possible way to gain the victory. And so in two ranks the British began their advance on the zeriba, headed by the Camerons and the Seaforth Highlanders. It has been said that General Gatacre was the first man to reach the formidable entanglement of desert thorn. At his heels came the Camerons, who, forcing a way through, managed to enter the zeriba. One of their pipers, standing upon a height of earth, began to play 'The March of the Cameron Men,' and fell almost at once, riddled with bullets. In the fierce conflict that followed none fought more staunchly than Lewis's half brigade of Egyptians. That in itself was worth as much as half a dozen minor victories.

The fire of the Dervishes from their trenches rained thick and fast upon the Highlanders as they came through the break in the hedges, but when they had gained a real foothold inside the zeriba, the Dervishes lost heart, and made away towards the Atbara River. The fine strategy of Kitchener forcing an engagement at this point was now apparent. The enemy were faced with thirty miles of waterless desert, at the end of which it was probable they would encounter the British gunboats. It was more than a victory in arms; it struck the first devastating blow at the power of the Khalifa.

In answer to Kitchener's despatch, Queen Victoria replied: "Anxious to know how the wounded British and Egyptians are going on. Am proud of the gallantry of my soldiers. So glad my Cameron Highlanders should have been amongst them."

A writer in Blackwood's Magazine relates the following striking incident, doubly pregnant with meaning to-day. "After Atbara," he says, "and as we rode through the 'dem,' Lord Cecil joined us, and presently K. pulled up among the charred corpses on the burning ground to make some enquiries. Cecil made a grimace and pointed to the ground; it was strewn with Dervish shells lying about under our horses' hoofs and the hoofs of the chief's horse, with the grass on fire all around them. Neither of us spoke, but Kismet, destiny, or whatever it is that sits behind the crupper, impelled

K. to move on, and a few minutes later a column of smoke shot up into the air—the shells had exploded. But K. had passed on—destiny had need of him still."

In July 1898 began the advance on Omdurman, in which the Camerons and Seaforths took part. The battle was fought on September 2nd. The Khalifa's army numbered some 50,000 men, and the fight that was to end in the utter defeat of Mahdism extended over five hours. The Highlanders did not take as prominent a part here as at Atbara, and the chief battle honours lie with Brigadier-General Hector Macdonald, whose Soudanese troops were handled with much brilliancy, and the 21st Lancers, the glory of whose charge rang throughout England and the Empire.

The Dervishes, trusting to their overwhelming superiority in numbers, advanced in dense hordes against the British lines, and at this point of the engagement the Camerons and Seaforths withstood the fury of the opening attack with magnificent steadiness. The enemy were met with a murderous fire; whole lines and ranks were simply mown down by our shrapnel: attack upon attack was launched with reckless gallantry, always to be repulsed.

In one portion of this campaign it has been related that for two hours a company of the Seaforths were engaged with a great number of the Dervishes, and as their ammunition had run short, they were compelled to use the bayonet. "Not one shot was fired," says an eye-witness, "for two hours, and yet the greatest and most serious losses amongst the enemy occurred during the time when the Seaforths were getting in with the bayonet." At Omdurman, in that great charge of the Dervishes, it became impossible to check them altogether, and so heavy was the fire that the rifles of the Cameron Highlanders became too hot to hold. To avert a repulse the curious spectacle was seen of men carrying and exchanging rifles with the reserve lines behind.

The stand made by the Dervishes has earned the praise of G. W. Steevens, who witnessed it. "Our men," he says, "were perfect, but the Dervishes were superb—beyond perfection. It was their largest, best, and bravest army that ever fought against us for Mahdism, and it died worthily of the huge empire that Mahdism won and kept so long." They lost, roughly, 11,000 men killed with 16,000 wounded; and with the battle of Omdurman came the end of the long struggle in the Soudan, and not only that, but the avenging of the death of Gordon.

The losses amongst the two Highland regiments, and indeed the British force as a whole, were trifling for such a hard-fought action.

Whatever else the Highland regiments may have been asked to face before or since—for whirlwind fury and deathless courage, for wild disturbing swiftness and noisy violence, nothing could surpass a Dervish charge.

Troops that can meet that without wavering—front, rear, and flank—need have no qualms for the future exigencies of war.

CHAPTER XXIII
CHITRAL AND THE GORDONS AT DARGAI
(1895-1898)

Come gather, come gather, ye lads o' the heather,

An' down thro' the glen in the pipers' wake;

Baith gentles and commons, gie heed tae the summons,

An' haste tae the muster make.

Macpherson's comin', Cameron's comin',

Campbell, MacNeill, an' the men o' the island;

An' a' tae enlist in the Gordons, the best,

An' the brawest o' lads in the Highlands.

The Cock o' the North.

We must now return to the year 1895, to follow one of those little wars that flare up intermittently on the frontiers of our vast Empire, and accompany the Gordons through the campaign that is best known for the dramatic moment at Dargai. Minor campaigns such as these are not of the first importance from the military point of view, nor should the name of a great regiment be associated too closely with a single episode, but they have this value, that they have enabled our soldiers to keep in training for great and laborious campaigns such as the Boer War, already looming dark upon the horizon of history.

The initial fighting at Chitral proved to be the beginning of a great deal of guerilla warfare on the North-West frontier of India. Chitral had become united to our Indian Empire in 1848; but the Government took no particular part in controlling the country, the consequence being that when Umra Khan, ruler of Bajour, decided to dispute our suzerainty, war was proclaimed. Umra Khan acted with all promptitude, and at the beginning was rewarded with some success, besieging an English garrison in Fort Chitral in January 1895. On the 1st of April Sir Robert Low, accompanied by a force of 15,000 men, amongst whom were the Gordon Highlanders and the Seaforths, crossed the border country with all speed and rushed the outposts of the enemy on the 3rd of April. It was a hazardous expedition, and the troops in their haste were permitted to carry very few stores or ammunition or tents. Major Bland Strange, in his interesting narrative of the campaign, has written: "The bones of the expedition, like those of the first ill-starred one to Cabul, were also to whiten the passes. The desperate valour of the hillmen, starvation, Afghan guile, and Russian intrigue were to smite us. But the good organisation and reticent generalship of Low, the dash of Kelly, the dogged defence by Robertson, and the steady courage of our troops falsified pessimistic prophecy."

There were two important passes in the enemy's country held by the Pathans, who were in a strong position behind defences along the slopes of the hills some 3000 feet above the advancing troops. In order to carry the position the slope must be rushed under the sniping fire of the enemy.

The Sikhs set out on this perilous business, while the Gordons marched up the centre of the Pass, and then, cutting away to the right, set their faces to the hill-side. They provided an easy mark for the enemy, but the advance was never checked, and when the ridge was reached a hand-to-hand conflict took place. Once on top the Gordons and the Scottish Borderers soon cleared the enemy out of the position. The Gordons and the Gurkhas were then left to defend the famous Malakand Pass, while General Low pushed on after the enemy. By dogged perseverance and the efficiency of the artillery the British were enabled to fight their way through to Chitral, and on April 20 marched into the town. Umra Khan made for Afghanistan, and the campaign was ended. A fort was built in case of further revolution, and that greatest of all factors in civilisation—a road—was constructed to unite India with this outlying post.

Naturally enough, the tribes who were in the neighbourhood of Chitral, and whose country lay between it and India, were by no means pleased by the occupation by British troops, nor did they take very kindly to the road which meant to them their eventual subjection. For a considerable time there were rumours of trouble, and in the end there broke out a sudden rising of the people in the Waziri country. This was in 1897, and so widespread was the trouble that it was not crushed until the Indian Government had put under arms the most formidable force since the Mutiny.

There are several factors in such tribal uprisings that carry with them their ultimate defeat. First of all, there are always rumours of revolt before it actually bursts into flame; secondly, the tribes find it difficult to unite together, or even to rise at the same time—thus a disciplined army can deal with one after another; thirdly, they have no definite system of organisation, and—as in the case of the Afghans—are little better than an army of snipers.

The Waziris rose first, then the Swatis under the Mad Mullah, and so on to the Afridis and the Orakzais. Each of these tribes was capable of putting a great many men in the field. It has been stated that the Afridis alone could provide 30,000 men armed with modern rifles. Sir William Lockhart with 34,000 men, including some 12,000 British troops, amongst whom were the 1st Battalion of the Gordon Highlanders, was sent against these Afridis. In accordance with the native custom of warfare, the enemy took up a position at the summit of the now celebrated ridge of Dargai, and there awaited the arrival of the British. To advance with any safety, this pass must first of all be cleared.

The initial encounter was rather futile. The ridge was carried by storm, and then, as the hillmen were in rapid flight, vacated again. On the return of the British to camp, the Afridis, under the delusion that our troops had taken fright and were in retreat, assembled again in their thousands, and full of elation attacked them in the rear. The task of guarding the safe return of the British troops was entrusted to the Gordon Highlanders, who checked the rush of the enemy with consecutive volleys. The fight went on throughout the night, and so on this day's fighting, though much had been gained, all had been thrown away. Dargai had been taken, only to fall again into the hands of the enemy, and before an advance could be made it must be retaken at the point of the bayonet.

The withdrawal from Dargai has been bitterly blamed by critics, some of them more carping than competent; but one thing is clear enough—the Afridis were so encouraged by regaining the ridge that they were greatly heartened for the next day's fighting, and manned the heights in expectation of victory.

Two days later the engagement was reopened, the British artillery shelling the tribesmen's most prominent defences, but little damage could be done in a country so covered with rocks. The most it could accomplish was to assist the infantry, and under the protection of the guns the Gurkhas began the first assault. They rushed into the bullet-swept zone that lay between the end of the pass and the ascent, to be so harassed by the rain of fire that they were compelled to take cover at the bottom of the slope, and there await support. The Dorsets and the Derbys who gallantly went to their assistance, were also compelled to take cover after a terrible punishing. The zone of fire was concentrated on a narrow stretch of open country, which had to be crossed before the actual ascent of the ridge began. That was the first stage of the attack. Then the stiff climb followed, while at the top of the ridge the Afridis waited under cover. The triumphant shouts of the tribesmen could be heard at the initial success over the British arms, and at this desperate situation, when three battalions were under cover, unable to advance or retreat, the Gordons, with the Sikhs in support, were called forward to carry the position. Colonel Mathias appealed to his famous battalion, "Highlanders," he cried, "the General says the position must be taken at all costs. Men, the Gordons will storm that Pass!" Colonel Gardyne has written that at those words "there was first a tremendous hush—then the answering cheer assured Colonel Mathias that his confidence was not misplaced. The bugle sounds the advance, the pipers play, the officers cry, 'Come!' and a wave of kilted soldiers bursts into the fire-swept open. Almost at once, Major Macbean fell, shot through the thigh.... The gallant young Lamont was killed instantaneously; Lieutenant Dingwall, wounded in four places, was carried out of further danger by Private Lawson. The first division reach the sheltering rocks, panting for breath; they shout, the officers waving their swords to those behind; while Piper Findlater, though wounded and unable to move, still inspires them with his warlike strains. They start again, 'the men cheering like mad,' up the precipitous path leading to the crest where they look for a warm reception. But the top is reached—it forms a succession of ridges along which the Highlanders rush unopposed, and great is the cheering as they realise that the enemy is in full flight."

To put it bluntly, the Afridis had not waited to dispute the position with men who could not be stopped by bullets, and this charge in the face of such a deadly and concentrated fire will be long considered as courageous and splendid a story as anything in the history of the Highland regiments. What followed can be told in very few lines. The war against the Afridis was by no means over, but the eventual issue was already in sight. The advance through the almost impenetrable ravines and over the rugged hills progressed painfully, but with determination. Peace came on April 4, 1898. It had been a memorable campaign, and one that the troops engaged in were naturally proud to commemorate. As Sir William Lockhart said in taking leave of them, "The boast of the tribes was that no foreign army—Moghul, Afghan, Persian, or British—had ever penetrated, or could penetrate their country; but after carrying three strong positions and being for weeks subsequently engaged in daily skirmishes, the troops succeeded in visiting every portion of Tirah, a fact which will be kept alive in the minds of future generations by ruined forts and towers in their remotest valleys."

The Gordons received two Victoria Crosses for gallantry in the action at Dargai, and established themselves, by their exploit, first favourites in the affections of the British people.

CHAPTER XXIV
FROM THE BEGINNING OF THE BOER WAR TO THE BATTLE OF MODDER RIVER
(1899)

"She stands alone: ally nor friend has she,"

Saith Europe of our England—her who bore

Drake, Blake, and Nelson—Warrior-Queen who wore

Light's conquering glaive that strikes the conquered free.

Alone?—From Canada comes o'er the sea,

And from that English coast with coral shore,

The old-world cry Europe hath heard of yore

From Dover cliffs: "Ready, aye ready we!"

"Europe," saith England, "hath forgot my boys!—

Forgot how tall, in yonder golden zone

'Neath Austral skies, my youngest born have grown

(Bearers of bayonets now and swords for toys)—

Forgot 'mid boltless thunder—harmless noise—

The sons with whom old England 'stands alone'!"

THEODORE WATTS-DUNTON.

In an earlier chapter we have seen how the humiliating defeat of Majuba left the Boers in possession of the Transvaal. Since that event many things had happened. The discovery of gold had brought great numbers of people into the Boer territories; the rivalry between the Britisher and the Dutchman grew fiercer and fiercer year by year, till eventually there was this curious situation—that a comparatively small body of Boers ruled with the utmost severity, and taxed with the greatest heaviness a very large population of Englishmen. The Government at Pretoria was as corrupt as a South American Republic; it was determined to embarrass in every way the newcomers who came under its authority, and this constant friction was one of the main causes that were to bring about one of the most critical, most costly, and most humiliating wars in which we have ever taken part.

The troubles of the Uitlanders, as they were called, reached a head when Dr. Jameson, supported by a few hundred men, crossed the Transvaal border on December 29, 1895. It will probably never be known how wide was the conspiracy which inspired this futile raid, but we find it difficult to believe that so small a body of men could have hoped to achieve anything by themselves. In all likelihood the scheme was premature, at any rate Dr. Jameson and his men were rounded up and forced to surrender. The British Government was not in a position to defend Jameson, while Kruger threatened that if the Uitlanders, who, of course, were sympathetic with the raid, rose in rebellion, he would not hesitate to shoot their leader. Instead of doing the Boer Government any damage, the unfortunate Uitlanders had played into Kruger's hands. It was impossible to deny that he had been attacked in an unwarrantable and illegal fashion, but when he acted with apparent leniency he was merely playing a cunning part. He stated—and it sounded quite reasonable under the circumstances—that it would be impossible to give the Uitlanders the vote after such a conspiracy had been on foot.

The raid made things awkward all round. For some time England had learnt with anxiety that arms were being freely imported into the Transvaal. After the raid it was impossible to make any expostulation, and from now onwards until the war the Uitlanders—like the Israelites of old—groaned under Kruger. Their plight was indeed a very hapless one. They had attempted by great patience and industry, and without protesting unduly when the Boers grew rich upon their labours, to win some legal recognition, and had failed. They had then planned for a rising with a view to winning their own freedom by their own arms. This, too, had failed. Finally, they had so embarrassed the mother-country that she could do nothing to help them. At last they decided that they would openly petition the Queen, and in a moment the whole quarrel was lifted from Pretoria to the throne of England. A conference took place between Sir Alfred Milner and President Kruger at Bloemfontein on May 30, 1899. It is doubtful whether the Boer President desired that any agreement should be come to; it is more probable that he was playing for time—at any rate no conclusion was reached, and later on Sir Alfred Milner brought it home, perhaps for the first time, to England that she must take action. "The case for intervention," he said, "is overwhelming, the only attempted answer is that things will right themselves if left alone. But, in fact, the policy of leaving things alone has been tried for years, and it has led to their going from bad to worse. It is not true that this is owing to the raid. They were going from bad to worse before the raid. We were on the verge of war before the raid, and the Transvaal was on the verge of revolution...."[9]

Still, the British Government struggled to maintain peace, and to come to some amicable arrangement. But the Boers, like the Amir of Afghanistan, did not believe England would ever face trouble. They were also contemptuous of the British soldier.

To-day, when the long conspiracy of Prussia is admitted by the most unsuspicious person, it can be recalled that, without question, the Boer Government was in touch with Germany, and that not only cases of rifles passed into Pretoria and Johannesburg, but that Krupp guns, outranging our own artillery, were shortly to create the first of many surprises in that surprising war. The sympathies of Europe were entirely with the Boers, and, doubtless, Kruger had been advised from Berlin. Many Germans took part in the campaign, and it was in certain measure to their expert knowledge that the Boer artillery was so well manned. Beyond that the Boers could fully hold their own. Botha, Joubert, and De Wet were in their several capacities brilliant strategists and resourceful leaders. The burghers were well armed, well mounted, exceedingly courageous, and inspired by the deepest hatred for the British. The British, on the other hand, were very ignorant regarding the Boer, greatly under-estimated the numbers they could put in the field, had no expert knowledge regarding the country or manner of the fighting there, and could not persuade themselves that this was anything but a kind of punitive expedition. By this time, with so many campaigns behind us, some judgment can be formed upon the British Army, not only the Highland regiments with whom we have dealt in particular, but those English Line regiments and cavalry, whose prestige and courage have won a hundred victories. Yet were these to suffer amazing disasters in South Africa. The war was indeed to prove the graveyard of many hopes and many reputations. Looking back at it now, after the interval of many years, and when the greatest war has shown that the British Army is as invincible as ever it was, we can only come to the conclusion that the generalship in South Africa had for a season fallen altogether into decay. The days of the Crimea and the Mutiny were long past; Roberts and Wolseley were old men; Kitchener, the most competent organiser of the younger generation, was still engaged with his great work in Egypt, while a kind of dry-rot seems to have come over the generation that lay between. The ultimate good of the South African War was that it cut this dry-rot clean away; but the story of the war is one of great courage and endurance struggling against the grossest incompetence.

The Boer Government kept the negotiations running until the falling of the rain. With the rain the grass sprouted, the veldt was no longer like a desert, and the days for campaigning were nigh. For many months Kruger had been preparing for the conflict, while the British Government were so deep in the political negotiations that they thought of nothing else. The Boers could place 50,000 burghers, together with their heavy artillery, in the field, while the British forces in South Africa were a mere handful. Troops were despatched from India, including the 2nd Gordon Highlanders, and these arrived at the end of September, bringing the number of the British army in South Africa to 22,000.

On October 9, 1899, President Kruger issued his ultimatum, and within forty-eight hours the Boer War had commenced. On October 12 the Boer forces were on the march, 12,000 of them, with two batteries of eight Krupp guns each, setting out from the north. From the Transvaal came another commando accompanied by a number of Germans, armed with heavy guns, and led by Joubert.

The British forces under the command of Sir George White and General Penn Symons were concentrated at Ladysmith. This position was not a strong one, and should really have been vacated, but it was quite unsuspected that the Boer artillery was as powerful as to include 6-inch Creusot guns. To Ladysmith came the Gordon Highlanders, who eventually were to undergo the famous siege under their old officer. Some 4000 Britishers there were to meet the advancing Boers, who came "winding in and out between the hills as far as eye could reach, the long black string of horsemen stretched like an enormous serpent, with head and tail lost in space." In this manner the Boers entered Natal, and on the 12th of October came into touch with the British under General Penn Symons. General Symons was a man of the greatest courage, and with the utmost confidence and pride in his men. He awaited the arrival of the Boers at Talana Hill, where, with the breaking of the dawn the black figures of the enemy were first seen against the sky-line, and the opening action of the long war commenced.

It was evident at once that the Boer artillery would make our position untenable, and while our guns were endeavouring to gain a mastery over those of the enemy, the infantry were sent up the front of the hill under a very severe fire. General Symons was one of the first to fall. To the last he encouraged his men, and throughout he had refused to take the smallest care for his own safety.

This first conflict, which does not really concern us in this book, was of no strategic value, and resulted in a heavy loss of men, though it was in a sense a success, since the Boers were driven back from Talana Hill. But it was the first indication that in a country like South Africa the storming of one hill in a land of hills without any definite strategic gain is simply bad generalship.

In the meantime, General French, already recognised as our most brilliant cavalry leader, had set out towards Elandslaagte. Coming to the conclusion that the numbers of the enemy were too strong, he communicated with

Ladysmith that he must have reinforcements. In a very short time the Devons, the Lancers, with the Gordons and some artillery united with his forces, and advanced towards the Boer position upon a group of hills overlooking Elandslaagte station. The artillery opened the engagement, and succeeded in silencing the enemy's guns. The Boers, whose memories were fresh with the strange spectacle of an untrenched foe at Majuba, also received a surprise in this war, so full of surprises. To their great dissatisfaction the Manchesters and the Gordons, dressed in undistinguishable khaki, advanced under cover, the only colour visible being the kilt of the Gordons, which they had refused to discard.

The Boer guns, worked by Colonel Schiel, a German, with eighty German gunners under him, opened fire with practised skill and accuracy. The Boer Mausers picked off the advancing British infantry, wounding, amongst others, the Colonel of the Gordons. Suddenly a storm burst over the conflict, a deluge of rain beat upon the faces of the advancing troops, the whistle of bullets sang in their ears, and men were falling rapidly. Having lost their Colonel, the Gordons hesitated when within charging distance of the enemy. At that, Captain Meiklejohn—who was to end his life so heroically in Hyde Park—rushed to the front, calling upon the Highlanders to follow him. For this action Meiklejohn lost one arm, but received the Victoria Cross. The victory was as good as won. "Dark figures sprang up from the rocks in front. Some held up their rifles in token of surrender. Some ran with heads sunk between their shoulders, jumping and ducking among the rocks. The panting, breathless climbers were on the edge of the plateau. There were the two guns which had flashed so brightly, silenced now, with a litter of dead gunners around them, and one wounded officer standing by a trail. It was the famous Schiel, the German artillerist. A small body of the Boers still resisted. Their appearance horrified some of our men. 'They were dressed in black frock-coats, and looked like a lot of rather seedy business men,' said a spectator. 'It seemed like murder to kill them.' Some surrendered, and some fought to the death where they stood."[10]

Hardly had the ridge been taken and the Highlanders had flung themselves down, utterly exhausted, from the long advance and the final charge with the bayonet, when a number of Boers rushed from a place of concealment and opened fire upon the Gordons. It was a moment of dire peril. Men dropped on every side, and things were instantly critical, when Sergeant-Major Robertson rallied the battalion and carried the Boer position, winning the Victoria Cross for his gallantry.

Next day the Gordons returned to Ladysmith, where they were to experience a four months' siege.

Things moved quickly after this. On October 30 was the battle of Nicholson's Nek; on November 2 the last train left Ladysmith. Leaving for a while the battalion of the Gordons to take their part in the defence of Ladysmith, we will follow the Highland Brigade in their advance upon Kimberley.

The opening of the war caused the greatest gratification to all well-wishers of the enemy and a certain amount of despondency at home. On the Continent there was the wildest delight that the Boer army was carrying everything before them. Few nations, apart from America, Italy, Denmark, and Greece, were able to conceal their elation that at last England was likely to pass through her hour of bitter humiliation. After a fortnight, in which five actions had taken place, we had lost a quarter of Natal, a great stretch of railway, and saw our troops besieged or on the eve of being besieged in Ladysmith, Kimberley, and Mafeking. The situation could not be regarded as anything but critical. At the same time reinforcements were being hurried out, and should these various positions resist the Boer attacks there was no reason to suppose that the ultimate victory was far off. On November 12 Lord Methuen had reached the Orange River, and, accompanied by a well-equipped force—though not a large one in number—he set out towards Kimberley, where he found the Boers in possession of Belmont. The first action has been described by Sir Arthur Conan Doyle as "an Alma on a small scale." The British troops took the hill by storm, driving the enemy from their position at the point of the bayonet. But the unfortunate culmination to the majority of these early actions was that the Boers bolted to their ponies and galloped away, and owing to our lack of cavalry it was never possible to turn a retreat into a rout. Lord Methuen repeated this success two days later at Graspan, and on the 28th fought the battle of Modder River, in which the Argyll and Sutherland Highlanders arrived in time to take a part. Having driven the Boer before him on two occasions within four days, Lord Methuen was under the impression that the farmers had lost heart and would no longer put up a formidable resistance.

On the 28th began the advance on Modder River, upon whose banks General Cronje was entrenched. Cronje was a man of considerable strength of character, a skilful general after the Boer tactics, trusted implicitly by his men, and in command of a strong and formidable commando. So far the British had met the enemy entirely in hill country; it had become a kind of dream amongst the British soldiers that if they could only catch the Boer in a plain the effect of discipline and bravery would teach the enemy a severe lesson. There was a certain amount of truth in this belief, and when the Boers did eventually come in sharp contact with the Lancers it was a bitter enough experience for them.

Unhappily no precautions appear to have been taken to ascertain either the strength of the enemy's position or the best mode of attack. For some reason or another, probably owing to an under-estimation of Cronje's position, the men were not even permitted to breakfast before the march began, and so on a beautiful morning they set out towards the undulating plain that lay upon the other side of the river.

Cronje had laid his plans with the utmost care and assurance, placing his men on both sides of the river, entrenching them upon the sloping ground, and concealing his artillery. The question has been raised—and Sir Arthur Conan Doyle raised it again—Why the river should have been crossed at that particular point; also why the British forces should have been led over an open plain without any attempt at reconnaissance? Such problems as these, however, might be multiplied to little purpose throughout the earlier part of the South African campaign. Perhaps the briefest answer to them would be that it was just because of such incidents as these that the country was eventually to plead with its oldest soldier to take over the command. Now that we have tested the lessons that South Africa taught us, the humiliation has passed into thankfulness that they came in time.

Cronje simply waited until the British were within range of his fire, and then very suddenly opened a tornado of bullet and shell fire at a range of seven hundred and fifty yards. One moment, and in front of them had lain an apparently peaceful landscape, a few houses and farms sleeping under the morning sun; the next, and the whole horizon was blazing with death. It was fatal to advance; the cavalry could do nothing, while the infantry were dependent upon the guns to gain the superiority. At this critical moment one of the most dramatic incidents in the war occurred. Out of the unknown, with staggering horses and guns caked with mud, lumbered up the 62nd Field Battery, which had covered thirty-two miles in less than twenty-four hours. It was a providential piece of good fortune.

Throughout the long day the infantry lay under the broiling sun, just as the remnants of the Highland Brigade were to endure it not very long after. The artillery engagement wore on, the heat passed, and as night came the British were gaining the advantage. All day they had been without food. At last, in the late afternoon, the North Lancashires managed to get across the river and take up a position on the extreme left, where they were joined by the Coldstreams and the Argyll and Sutherlands. The action was turning against the Boers. With this desperate little force on their flank, and the artillery shattering their guns on the front, they took advantage of the night to evacuate their trenches and retreat. It had indeed been a costly action, and might have been a humiliating defeat. What perhaps it was more than anything else was a proof of British bravery under the most dismal conditions.

Lord Methuen remained upon the Modder River until he was joined by the Highland Brigade, composed of the 2nd Seaforths, the Highland Light Infantry, the 1st Gordons fresh from Dargai, and the 2nd Black Watch, with whom was Major-General Andrew Wauchope. Wauchope had seen service in the Soudan, and was one of the best-beloved officers in the history of the Highland regiments.

A spectator has written: "Watching the arrival of the Highland Brigade, very magnificent they looked as they swung into camp, pipers strutting before them, kilts swish-swishing, all in perfect order and perfect step—the finest troops in the world."

The Boers, having fallen back from the Modder River, halted at Magersfontein, a circle of hills which Cronje endeavoured—with what success we shall see—to render impregnable. It was the next step towards Kimberley, and on Saturday, December 9, Lord Methuen despatched one of the most critical and forlorn expeditions in our history, and the most tragic in the story of the Highland regiments.

CHAPTER XXV
WITH THE HIGHLAND BRIGADE AT MAGERSFONTEIN
(December 11, 1899)

I've heard them lilting at the ewe-milking,

Lasses a' lilting before dawn o' day;

But now they are moaning on ilka green loaning,

The flowers o' the forest are a' wede away.

Highland Funeral March.

Confronting the British troops lay a circle of hills which might or might not be tenanted by the enemy. Lord Methuen followed the established military course of shelling these hills from a long range, preparatory to an advance. Unfortunately it served no purpose, for the enemy retired temporarily, only to return when the bombardment was over, knowing that after the artillery had concluded their futile expenditure of shells, the British infantry would, in the course of things, advance. It was on Sunday, December 10, that the Highland Brigade set off early in the afternoon under a deluge of rain. When they came within a few miles of the Boers they halted, and darkness began to fall.

At this point Lord Methuen communicated to the Brigade commanders his plan for carrying the enemy's position. The attack would be launched by the Highlanders at break of dawn.

At midnight, under a lowering sky, and in the black darkness of an African night, the Highland Brigade set out upon its tragic march. The men were drenched to the skin, carried no food, and were formed in quarter column. On the right the Black Watch, then the Seaforths, the Argyll and Sutherlands next, and in reserve the Highland Light Infantry. The Gordons, who had only arrived before the march began, remained in camp. It is important to follow out the plan of attack as indicated by Lord Methuen in his despatch.

"The night march was ordered for 12.30 A.M., the bearings and distance having been ascertained at great personal risk by Major Benson, Royal Artillery, my Deputy-Assistant-Adjutant-General. The distance is two and a half miles, and daybreak was due at 3.25 A.M. I may remark that two rifles went off by accident before the march commenced, and it is pretty clear flashes from a lantern gave the enemy timely notice of the march. Before moving off, Major-General Wauchope explained all he intended to do, and the particular part each battalion of his brigade was to play in the scheme, namely, that he intended to march direct on the south-west spur of the kopje, and on arrival near the objective before daybreak the Black Watch were to move to the east of the kopje, where he believed the enemy to be posted under shelter, whilst the Seaforth Highlanders were to march straight to the south-east point of the kopje, with the Argyll and Sutherland Highlanders prolonging the line to the left, the Highland Infantry to be in reserve until the action was developed. The Brigade was to march in mass of quarter column, the four battalions keeping touch, and if necessary ropes were to be used for the left guides. These ropes were taken, but, I believe, used by only two battalions. The three battalions were to extend just before daybreak—two companies in firing line, two companies in support, and four companies in reserve—all at five paces interval between them."

It is not our business to criticise the scheme of attack, but only to deplore the fact that so many brave men should lose their lives in such an abortive attempt. It would have been impossible to reach the Boer lines in anything but disorder had the Highland Brigade not advanced in close column: the blunder appears to have been that they maintained close formation too long. Long before, in the year 1746, the Highlanders, who might be expected to have an intimate knowledge of the country through which they were passing, set out upon a similar night attack, only to find themselves hopelessly lost—and that not so very far from Inverness. At Magersfontein the distance was a short one, but the difficulty of ascertaining how far the Boer trenches were from the foremost columns led to chaos. No one has described the situation more graphically than Sir Arthur Conan Doyle in The Great Boer War. "With many a trip and stumble," he writes, "the ill-fated detachment wandered on, uncertain where they were going and uncertain what it was they were meant to do. Not only among the rank and file, but among the principal officers there was the same absolute ignorance. Brigadier Wauchope knew, no doubt, but his voice was soon to be stilled in death. The others were aware, of course, that they were advancing either to turn the enemy's trenches or to attack them, but they may well have argued from their own formation that they could not be near the riflemen yet. Why they should be still advancing in that dense clump we do not now know, nor can we surmise what thoughts were passing through the mind of the gallant and experienced chieftain who walked beside them.... Out there, close beside him, stretched the long trench, fringed with its line of fierce, staring, eager faces, and its bristle of gun-barrels. They knew he was coming. They were ready. They were waiting. But still, with the dull murmur of many feet, the dense column, nearly four thousand strong, wandered onwards through the rain and the darkness, death and mutilation crouching upon their path."

The end came quickly enough. Within a few hundred yards the Boer rifles opened fire upon the massed columns of the Highlanders. They fell in solid ranks and companies. The destruction inside a few moments has been rightly enough compared to the fall of corn before the reaper. Out of the darkness there was one single lurid blaze of light, a prolonged roar of musketry, and the Highland Brigade was decimated as it stood.

Just as the fire opened, the order had been given for the men to deploy, but the extension never took place. Wauchope was one of the first to fall. As his biographer has finely said: "General Wauchope fought and fell as a man and as a soldier, carrying out his orders loyally to the end. He died where he would have wished to die—at the head of his gallant Highlanders, with his face to the foe."

It was impossible for the Highland Brigade to advance in any order: their officers were killed, their ranks were broken, they were confronted by barbed wire and strong entrenchments, and yet it came hardly on them that they should have to retreat. F. G. Tait, the famous Scottish golfer, who was destined to fall at the Modder River, remarked in a letter home: "General Wauchope and our Colonel, and Captain Bruce and young Edmonds were all killed, with the lot of men that I accompanied. General Wauchope is in no way responsible for the fearful loss of life amongst the Highland Brigade: he got his orders, and had to carry them out, and he was killed in front of his brigade. I feel certain that if we had been led up in line we should have rushed the position with probably a quarter of the loss that we actually suffered. As it was, we arrived rather late, and in mass of quarter column.... You might imagine the effect of a tremendously hot rifle fire into that compact body."[11]

According to F. G. Tait the first orders that emerged from the chaos and noise and the groans of the wounded were those of, 'Lie down, fix bayonets, and prepare to charge.' This, unhappily, led very little farther. Tait writes as follows: "We got along a hundred yards or so when we got into the dreadful flanking as well as frontal firing, and lost very heavily. I could now see that the enemy were in trenches about 200-250 yards off. We managed to get 50 yards nearer, losing heavily all the time, and there we lay down (what was left of the lot with me) and began firing. I was about 15 or 20 yards in front, and had just got up to get back in line when I got a bullet through my left thigh. I was able to turn over on my stomach and fire at the Boers. A quarter of an hour later it was quite light, and then we began to get it properly. The men on each side of me were hit straight away, and in a few minutes very few were left unhit. It was quite impossible for any ambulance or doctor to advance, so all our wounded lay within 200 yards or so of the Boer trenches all day in a broiling sun, being shot at whenever they moved until seven o'clock at night, most of them without a drop of water."

And yet out of this dismal event, despite their terrible position, the Highland Brigade did not lose their prestige. Trapped, bewildered, unable either to advance or retreat, they held their ground and died without fear. Many, indeed, perceiving that no officers were left to lead them, advanced on their own initiative through the hail of fire, and were discovered in the morning suspended on the barbed wire before the Boer trenches. A section of the Black Watch, it is recorded, refused to retire, and entrenching themselves as far as they could, carried on the combat throughout the long terrible day, until when night fell there was not one single survivor left. All through that desperate day the Highlanders lay exposed to the Boer fire, refusing to surrender, without food or water, wounded and unwounded together, awaiting the support from the artillery and the reserves, which was so difficult to give. It has been recorded of the Argyll and Sutherlands that their claim to the pledge, "We die, but we do not surrender," was most nobly earned that day. At Magersfontein the regiment that had provided the 'thin red line' at Balaclava remained steady under the terrific fire, and it was owing in a large degree to the 93rd and to the Coldstream Guards that their unfortunate comrades, who had led the advance and suffered more terribly, were enabled to hold out during the day.

To return to the actual conflict. It is stated that within a few moments of the opening of the Boer fire at least 600 men were out of action. Less courageous or disciplined soldiers would have broken and scattered wildly to the rear, and none could have called them cowards; but the Highland Brigade, assembling as far as was possible within their own units, had by the break of day made some attempt at following up the belated attack. Unfortunately the Boers were so securely entrenched that it was a very one-sided affair. The rising sun brought the Horse Artillery up at the gallop, and under cover of their fire the Highland Brigade were enabled to get some respite from the deadly Boer marksmanship. As day advanced reinforcements were hurried up, the Gordons coming with the 1st and 2nd Battalions of the Coldstreams, and the gallant Yorkshire Light Infantry to protect the flank. In the afternoon the Highland Brigade—who had tasted neither food nor water for twenty-four hours—made a pitiful effort to charge the Boer position. The fire that was opened upon them was, at so short a range, almost annihilating. It was inevitable that they must remain out of action until they could fall back and reassemble. The Gordons, who came fresh into action, did what was possible to distract the Boer fire from their unhappy comrades, and when the evening came the merciful darkness enabled the wreckage of the Highland Brigade to creep back to the rear.

The bitterest day in the story of the Highland regiments was, at last, at an end. The disaster at Magersfontein brought with it a loss of nearly 1000 men; out of the Highland Brigade 57 officers had fallen, and in the Black Watch alone 19 officers and over 300 men. Never in the annals of that regiment had there been such a loss since the action at Ticonderoga in 1757.

In his report of the action, Lord Methuen sums it up as follows: "The attack failed. The inclement weather was against success. The men in the Highland Brigade were ready enough to rally, but the paucity of officers and non-commissioned officers rendered this no easy matter. I attach no blame to this splendid brigade. Nothing could exceed the conduct of the troops from the time of the failure of the attack at daybreak. There was not the slightest confusion, though the fight was carried on under as hard conditions as one can imagine, for the men had been on the move from midnight, and were suffering terribly from thirst."

The next morning the Boers awaited a British attack, which never came. It was evident from the disaster that had overtaken the Highland Brigade that it would be almost impossible to storm the Boer position by a frontal assault. Lord Methuen, feeling that he could not carry out a flanking movement without reinforcements, decided he would rest his troops, and postpone for the present the advance on Kimberley.

CHAPTER XXVI
PAARDEBERG AND LADYSMITH

Pibroch of Donuil Dhu, Pibroch of Donuil,

Wake thy wild voice anew, summon Clan Conuil.

Come away, come away, hark to the summons!

Come in your war array, gentles and commons!

Regimental March.

In the meantime various engagements had taken place elsewhere, and a curious condition of stalemate was gradually setting in, during which the British troops kept in touch with large bodies of Boers, but were in most cases quite unable to advance and relieve the beleaguered townships of Ladysmith, Mafeking, and Kimberley. The whole situation gradually formed itself for the long-awaited advance of Sir Redvers Buller, with all its unfortunate contingencies. But we must first deal with the engagement at Stormberg. It has been narrated, in a former chapter, how General Gatacre—or General 'Backacher,' as he was called in the Service—was the first to reach the thorny entanglements of the Dervish camp at the Atbara. He was a man of the greatest bravery, but by no means a skilful general, relying solely upon the courage of the British soldier. In a country like South Africa, where a pound of personal bravery was not always as fruitful as an ounce of strategy, optimism of this kind was only overloading a willing horse. It was magnificent, but it could not stop a rifle bullet at a thousand yards. Unfortunately, too, the forces under General Gatacre had been largely drawn upon for the assistance of Lord Methuen and Buller. On the night of December 9 he discovered that the Boers were in position at Stormberg, and with his little force of 3000 men set out for a night march, intending to storm the Boer trenches at dawn. The whole scheme of attack, on a lesser scale, was painfully similar to that at Magersfontein. It was so splendidly obvious.

By the time the men had come within reach of the Boer position they were so tired they could hardly drag their feet along. To Gatacre fatigue was nothing. At the break of the dawn he alone was full of zeal and courage, and spurred on by dread of a reverse to storm the position. Unfortunately it was the Boers who opened fire on the British, when a deadlock instantly ensued. It was difficult to carry the hill under such conditions; for on such occasions, when aeroplanes did not guide artillery fire, our own guns played as much havoc among our own infantry as among the Boers.

In a similar plight at Dargai the Gordons carried the position and enabled their comrades to move; but here it was impossible to extricate the men, and this led to a miserable surrender of a good many and the forlorn retreat of the rest.

Gatacre fell back after the action, and was shortly reinforced, but the incident had in no way improved matters for the prestige of the British arms. Within a week Methuen had suffered a crushing reverse at Magersfontein while Gatacre had been again beaten.

Fortunately by this time great numbers of troops were arriving in South Africa, and soon after Sir Redvers Buller prepared for the crossing of the Tugela River. On Friday, December 15, he advanced from Chieveley Camp to storm the Boer position. It was the first step towards Ladysmith. As none of the Highland regiments took part in this action, it is merely necessary to record that the battle of Colenso took place, and despite the heroism of the British soldiers, and in particular the Irish Brigade, the action was lost, and our troops, after a loss of 600, fell back on Chieveley Camp.

The first advance to the relief of Ladysmith had been severely and ignominiously checked.

The Christmas of 1899 was as black as any through which our nation has passed. The repeated defeats of the British forces flung a gloom over the country that for a moment almost paralysed it. More and more troops had been despatched to South Africa, and numbers only seemed to magnify our disasters. At such a moment Britain turned to her sons in this country and throughout the Empire.

But it was necessary to do more than raise new armies: the whole country required reassurance, and the name of one man instantly rose before the public mind. When Lord Roberts was asked to take supreme command in South Africa, with Kitchener as his Chief of Staff, he accepted with the same readiness that Sir Colin Campbell displayed at the time of the Indian Mutiny. "It is God's will," said Roberts, now heartbroken at the death of his son, and two days before Christmas he left London for the front.

His very name was half the battle, for, to recall the familiar lines:

There is something that's audacious

In the very name of 'Bobs,'

There's a dare and dash about it

Makes you sort of want to shout it,

So that all the world can hear it

As you cheer.

On January 10, 1900, he landed at Cape Town, and appreciated at once the extreme gravity of the situation. The successes of the Boers were encouraging signs of revolt amongst the Cape Colonists, and to crush these symptoms at once Roberts set out towards the Orange Free State, anxious at the same time to distract the pressure upon Kimberley and Ladysmith. But there were many other things to do. In such a country as South Africa great numbers of mounted troops were a necessity. No attempt had been made so far to work upon the material that was already to hand. Regiments were formed of South African colonists, and mounted forces such as the Yeomanry and the Australian and Canadian Horse were to prove one of the most potent influences in the later stages of the campaign.

In the meantime there was continued bad news from the seat of war. Again Buller had attempted to cross the Tugela River, and had met with utter defeat. The forlorn capture of Spion Kop, with a loss of men amounting to forty per cent, had only proved a futile engagement and a barren victory.

Buller, who was courageous as a lion, admitted that his heart failed him after Spion Kop, and that he feared the relief of Ladysmith had become an impossibility. But Roberts telegraphed to him that whatever the cost might be, Ladysmith must be relieved. In the meantime Roberts set out upon the road to Bloemfontein with the hope of relieving Kimberley by the end of February. On February 8 he reached Methuen's camp on the Modder River, and knowing so well how sore the Highland Brigade must feel over the disaster at Magersfontein, he made them a little speech stating that he had never campaigned without Highlanders, and hoped he would never do so, and it was the Highlanders in India and Afghanistan who had brought him his success. He then wired to Kimberley the three words that were to mean so much, "We are coming."

It was all like a rushing of clean wind in a parched land. Now for the first time the Boers found themselves baffled as to the intentions and plans of a British leader. They had hitherto taken it for granted—and rightly so—that they would be forewarned of every move that was to take place, and had acted accordingly. Lord Roberts gave them the impression that Bloemfontein was his objective. Instead, on February 12 he instructed General French to make a dash on Kimberley, while he would follow with the infantry. French, the only general to make his reputation in South Africa, and almost the only one who did not lose it, set out with his cavalry, made his way round the Boer position, and pierced the Boer lines. Then, hastening on, he broke through the enemy, and that same evening entered Kimberley.

The genius of French was even more apparent at Koodoostrand Drift, where he cut off Cronje's retreat toward Bloemfontein. It was a piece of military daring as great as the sudden appearance of Montrose at Inverlochy, or Jackson at Manasses Junction. Speedily Cronje entrenched his men, but the arrival of the infantry rendered his ultimate surrender inevitable.

Inside the laager Cronje, despite the bitter recriminations of the Boers, did his best to put up a stout resistance, while outside our troops crept nearer night by night, until on February 27—the anniversary of Majuba—the Gordon Highlanders, to whom such a task was naturally very acceptable, advanced upon the Boer trenches under a heavy fire, and won a position controlling the inside of the laager. Cronje, realising that further resistance was impracticable, sent in a notice of his surrender to Lord Roberts. The meeting of the Boer commander and the hero of Kandahar must have been one of the most graphic incidents in the war. An eye-witness has narrated: "Presently the body of horsemen came past the hospital tents into the camp. A heavy bundle of a man was lumped atop of a wretched bony little Boer pony. Was this the terrible Cronje? Was it possible that this was the man who had held back the British army at Magersfontein?... Lord Roberts stepped forward, saluted, shook hands, and handed his fallen enemy a chair: 'You have made a gallant defence, sir; I am glad to meet so brave a foe,' was his greeting."

Thus within a brief fortnight Roberts had entirely altered the whole aspect of the war. He had inflicted a heavy defeat upon the Boers, relieved Kimberley, and captured Cronje, together with 4000 men. From now onwards his swift advance, his unerring judgment, and the services of his mounted troops not merely gave fresh heart to the Empire, but broke the confidence of the enemy.

We must now return to Ladysmith. It was on October 30, 1899, after the humiliating disaster at Nicholson's Nek—a disaster that can be compared to the surrender of the Duke of York's troops in Flanders in the eighteenth century, that Sir George White made what preparations he could to defend the town of Ladysmith. On November 2 the last train had left, and the long siege commenced.

White had some 10,000 men under his command, and although the Boer commandos numbered a very large force, the defenders managed to give throughout the siege of four months an exceedingly good account of themselves. Ladysmith was a place of considerable military importance, and it would have been a signal disaster if it had fallen into the Boer hands with so large a number of men. At the same time it was a very difficult position to hold, being commanded from every side by kopjes, and lying, as it were, in a saucer. The Gordon Highlanders, who were the only representatives of the Highland Brigade to serve in the siege, were old comrades-in-arms to White. He had led them in the advance upon Kabul and Kandahar. With him was Sir Ian Hamilton, who had been with the 92nd at Majuba.

From November 3 onwards the progress of the siege was marked by daily fighting and increasingly short rations. Each regiment was given a certain section of the circumference to defend. Time dragged on, until by the beginning of December, news came that Buller had reached Frere Camp, while, in the far distance, could be heard the booming of his guns. Later, it was borne in upon the garrison that the British force must have suffered a reverse, and that relief was probably farther away than ever.

Enteric and typhoid were thinning out the ranks, food was running short, and things began to look very hopeless when, in the first gleam of light on January 6, 1900, the enemy launched a formidable attack. The defeat of Buller had enabled the Boers to send reinforcements from Colenso. They were full of confidence, and at the initial assault carried everything before them. It very soon became a case of hand-to-hand fighting, in which the Gordons were called up with Ian Hamilton in command. The Boers were determined to capture Ladysmith, knowing the great moral effect that would be produced following upon their victory at Colenso. The Manchesters, nearly overcome at Caesar's Camp, put up a magnificent resistance, until the Gordons came up. It was in this advance that Colonel Dick-Cunyngham was killed.

The British were determined that their positions should never be taken by the enemy while they survived, and in one place defended by sixteen of the Manchesters, at the end of the day fourteen lay killed, the remaining two out of action. Throughout that day this fierce fighting continued, until at last the Devons, with the Gordons and the Rifles, cleared the ridge of the enemy. It had been touch and go, but at the last extremity the Boers could not face the gleaming steel of the bayonet, and a few minutes later were falling back from their trenches. A fight lasting for twenty-six hours was over at last. "But the end," says Sir Arthur Conan Doyle, "was not yet. The Boer had taken a risk over this venture, and now he had to pay the stakes. Down the hill he passed, crouching, darting, but the spruits behind him were turned into swirling streams, and as he hesitated for an instant upon the brink, the relentless sleet of bullets came from behind. Many were swept away down the gorges and into the Klip River, never again to be accounted for in the lists of their field cornet. The majority splashed through, found their horses in their shelter, and galloped off across the great Bulwana Plain, as fairly beaten in as fair a fight as ever brave men were yet."

This was the final attempt to take Ladysmith by storm, and it cost the British 13 officers and 135 men killed, with 28 officers and 244 men wounded.

Meanwhile it had been rumoured that Ladysmith was on the point of surrender, but the famous heliograph had bravely answered, "We have not come to that yet," and, indeed, rather than hand over their arms the garrison would have fought their way towards the Tugela. Each day found things more desperate, and relief came only in time. Buller drove his way to within a few miles of the town, and in the heart of the battle sent his message, "Doing well." It was in the night of February 28 that the Boers could be heard saddling up and leaving Pieter's Hill, and just before dawn Lord Dundonald, accompanied by some cavalry, reached the British lines.

"Halt! Who goes there?" rang out the familiar challenge, at which the dramatic and long-prayed-for answer was returned, "The Ladysmith Relief Column." Quickly the news spread through the town, the good tidings that after all they had passed through, their defence had not been in vain.

The sentiment that was uppermost both in the minds of the garrison and throughout the Empire was best expressed by Sir George White himself. "I thank God we have kept the flag flying," he said in his address to the soldiers; and it is recorded that an old Kaffir woman remarked as she watched the troops entering Ladysmith, "These English can conquer all things but death."

After the siege 2000 of the garrison, refusing to take a well-deserved and altogether necessary rest, set out upon the tracks of the retreating Boers, surely one of the most pitiful spectacles in history. "It is God's mercy," wrote Sir Arthur Conan Doyle, "that they failed to overtake them."

Mafeking and Bloemfontein were the only towns still to be relieved, and the former suffered from no shortage of food.

To return to the Highland Brigade, we have not dealt with the part that they took in the advance upon Kimberley. With the hope that he would distract the Boers, Roberts despatched the Black Watch, the Argyll and Sutherlands, the Seaforths, and the Highland Light Infantry, with Hector Macdonald, popularly known as 'Fighting Mac,' at their head. Macdonald crossed the Modder River, seized Koodoosberg, and sustained an attack from the Boers the next day. For a long time it fell to the Black Watch to resist the furious onslaught of the enemy, who were by no means satisfied to leave the situation undisputed. It was here that Lieutenant Tait—one of the most popular men in Scotland—was mortally wounded. There is an interesting letter that not only records his death, but also shows how the Highland soldiers had fallen into the manner of Boer fighting. A private writes: "I got down beside our officer, Lieutenant Tait, on his right hand. He said, 'Now, men, we will fight them at their own game.' That meant that each man was to get behind a rock and just pop up to fire and then down again. And we found it a good way, for we were just as good as they were at it, and we did not forget to let them know it either, for whenever one showed himself, down he went with half a dozen bullets through him. After firing for about half an hour the Boers stopped, and the order was given not to waste our shot. Lieutenant Tait's servant came up with his dinner, and he asked me if I would like a bit, and I said I would, and thanked him very much. He gave me and another man half of his dinner between us.... Just as we finished he said, 'I think we will advance another fifty yards, and perhaps we will see them better and be able to give it them hot.' We all got ready again, and Lieutenant Tait shouted, 'Now, boys! We were after him like hares. The Boers had seen us, and they gave us a hot time of it. But on we went. Just as our officer shouted to get down he was shot."

Lieutenant Tait was one of the most beloved men in Scotland. Thousands had seen him upon the green, and few in Scotland could read of his death without a sense of personal bereavement. In the middle of June 1915 another eminent golfer of equal fame and no less popularity, Captain John Graham, of the Liverpool Scottish, was fated to give his life for his country. No two finer men and finer sportsmen ever brought fairer honour to the name of Scotland in peace and war.

The action continued all day, and eventually, on the approach of the 9th Lancers, the Boers fell back and the Highland Brigade returned to the Modder River, having lost some fifty men. There followed afterwards the relief of Kimberley, and from thence onwards to the end of the war the part taken by the Highlanders was peculiarly arduous and without many distinguished features. Month after month they were employed in hard marching, holding positions that the mounted troops had carried, uncomplaining as always, and winning back here and there some of the losses that they had suffered at the hands of the enemy at Magersfontein. We have seen how the Gordons were instrumental in the capture of Cronje, despite the heavy fire with which they were met from the Boer trenches, and it is a notable fact that the Highland Brigade, for all their handling at Magersfontein, appear to have suffered in no way in prestige, and were only too anxious to make good. "On the 18th," says General Colville, speaking of the end of Cronje, "the courage and determination shown by the Highland Brigade in their advance over some fifteen hundred yards of perfectly open plain, and their passage of the river, both under heavy fire, are beyond all praise."

CHAPTER XXVII
WITH SIR IAN HAMILTON TO PRETORIA
(1900)

To you who know the face of war,

You, that for England wander far,

You that have seen the Ghazis fly

From English lads not sworn to die,

You that have lain, where, deadly chill,

The mist crept o'er the Shameful Hill,

You that have conquered, mile by mile,

The currents of unfriendly Nile,

And cheered the march, and eased the strain

When Politics made valour vain,

Ian, to you from banks of Ken,

We send our lays of Englishmen!

ANDREW LANG.

It was during the halt at Bloemfontein that the Highland Brigade received reinforcements from home, and no praise could be too high for the volunteers who formed additional companies to the regiments of the regular forces. To-day, when thousands and hundreds of thousands are trained soldiers who a year ago had never held a rifle in their hands, it would be futile to belaud the qualities of the amateur soldier. But until the Boer War no one had taken unprofessional soldiers very seriously. Just as the Territorials won the esteem of the Regulars in Flanders, so the companies of Volunteers earned the admiration and gratitude of the country in the Boer War.

The great need at this time was still for mounted troops and more mounted troops, and it is interesting to note that the Gordons were to a large extent mounted to prove more effective. Our soldiers have always been able to fit themselves for whatever was required of them. The infantry were mounted in the South African War, and the cavalry in the German War were placed in the trenches.

It was on May 3 that the British Army left Bloemfontein and set out upon the road to Pretoria. De Wet, who was now to take the ascendance in Boer generalship, and to lead the British troops in wearisome pursuit for many months, was in command of a mobile force moving swiftly across country, gathering food where it could. With the utmost patience our Highlanders covered over twenty miles a day, "winning their way," as some one has said, "at the expense of their boots and not of their lives."

Lord Roberts was in command of the main division and General Ian Hamilton was over the right column. With him were the Highland Brigade, including the Camerons, new come from Egypt. The Brigade, as a body, never reached Pretoria, though the Gordons and the Seaforths entered the Boer capital. It is the march on Pretoria with General Hamilton that we must first follow.

The Commander of the Highland Brigade was an old Gordon officer, by training and heredity a soldier. Born in 1853, he first saw service in the Afghan War. He was wounded at Majuba, losing the use of one hand. He received the D.S.O. for gallantry in the Soudan, fought in the Chitral and Tirah campaigns; and in this chapter we will accompany him on the march to Pretoria, in which he covered four hundred miles, fought ten engagements, and took five towns. After the Boer War he accompanied the Japanese army to Manchuria, and upon his return was made General Officer Commanding-in-Chief Mediterranean and Inspector-General Overseas Forces in 1910.

No finer, more experienced, more brilliant soldier could have been placed in command of our forces in the Dardanelles.

It was at Thabanchu Mountain that the Gordons brought additional distinction to their name, linked with that of Captain Towse. The British troops were having it all their own way when the Boers were reinforced by a party of the foreign legion commanded by a Russian, the majority of them being Germans. The situation was a very curious one. The German troops advanced in their customary close formation, and with their usual deliberateness, and for some time it was not realised that they were part of the enemy's forces. At the same time Captain Towse, with a party of the Gordon Highlanders, was moving in their direction, but concealed from view behind the shoulder of the hill. The Gordons could not see the enemy any more than the enemy could see the Gordons, and it was seen that the two forces would confront each other at the brow of the hill. "At last," says Winston Churchill, "with suddenness, both parties came face to face at fifty yards' distance. The Germans, who had already made six prisoners, called loudly on Captain Towse and his little band to surrender. What verbal answer was returned is not recorded, but a furious splutter of musketry broke out at once, and in less than a minute the long lines of the enemy recoiled in confusion, and the top of the hill was secured to the British."

Unhappily, however, a chance shot deprived the gallant Captain Towse of the sight of both his eyes. For this action he received the Victoria Cross he so richly deserved.

The advance now proceeded on the road to Pretoria. The town was stated to be heavily defended, and regarded as practically impregnable. President Kruger had established himself there, and it was thought that a very long siege would await the British. On May 29 the Gordons encountered the Boers at Crow's Nest Hill, very close to the place where the Jameson raiders had surrendered to Cronje, and here the Gordon Volunteers had their chance. The Highlanders, "in perfect discipline and with disdainful silence," drove the Boers out of their position, and it is worth while recording, in the words of an eye-witness, the manner of the attack. "It was not without a thrill that I watched this famous regiment move against the enemy. Their extension and advance was conducted with machine regularity. The officers explained what was required to the men. They were to advance rapidly until under rifle fire, and then to push or not as they might be instructed. With impassive unconcern the veterans of Chitral, Dargai, the Bara Valley, Magersfontein, Paardeberg, and Houtnek walked leisurely forward."

At eight hundred yards they came in for a heavy fire from the Boer rifles. "But the advance neither checked nor quickened. With remorseless stride, undisturbed by peril or enthusiasm, the Gordons swept steadily onward."

The Boers were never able to tolerate that kind of advance, and finding that rifles would not stop the Highlanders, they hastily retreated, and soon afterwards General Ian Hamilton rode over to congratulate the battalion on their exploit. Lord Roberts was not long in sending his praise. "Tell the Gordons," he wrote, "that I am proud to think that I have a Highlander as one of the supporters of my coat-of-arms."

During this action the fourth Victoria Cross was given to the Gordons, being awarded to Corporal Mackay, who "repeatedly rushed forward under a withering fire at short range to attend to wounded comrades, dressing the wounds, while he himself was without shelter, and in one instance carrying a wounded man from the open under a heavy fire to the shelter of a boulder."

On May 31 the Union Jack flew over Johannesburg. At this point General French arrived, and as senior officer took command. General Sir Ian Hamilton then thanked the Gordons, "the, regiment my father commanded and I was born in," for their support. On June 3 the army set out for

Pretoria, when suddenly the whole contemplated resistance of the Boers faded away like smoke. President Kruger, not forgetting two millions of money, but leaving his wife instead, hurried to Delagoa Bay, and with his departure came the unconditional surrender of Pretoria. It had been a long and arduous march, covering forty-five days and some four hundred miles of country. The Highlanders engaged in nine actions, and occupied five towns. It must have been a dramatic and inspiring spectacle to see the Gordons and the Camerons, gaunt and lean with all the fatigue through which they had passed, in tattered clothes and soleless boots, marching into the Boer capital. It might have been thought that the fall of Pretoria would have brought with it the conclusion of the Boer War. But the fall of Pretoria held no special significance to the Boers. Many of them had probably never seen the town, and took no interest in it. They resorted to a manner of warfare peculiarly suited to their habits of life, and which, developing over an extensive country, threatened a hopeless stalemate. They hoped by a guerilla warfare to weary the British forces into a favourable peace. From this point to the end of the war that agile leader De Wet was to make his name familiar as a kind of military will-o'-the-wisp.

Every week brought with it news of some minor engagement in some isolated part of the country. Here a position had been attacked or there a convoy had been seized. Often it was a raid on the long line of railway running from Capetown to Pretoria, but always De Wet, despite the efforts of the British, would manage to elude capture and fling his burghers upon another part of our lines.

On July 11, 1900, the Gordons won their fifth Victoria Cross, and established a record in the history of the Army. An officer who was present has recorded the incident. "The enemy's position," he says, "consisted of two long hills, with a 'nek' between them about five hundred yards long. In front of, and about six hundred yards away from the nek were two small kopjes. The guns galloped up between these kopjes, which were one hundred and fifty yards apart, and opened fire on the big hill on the right. The Gordons were advancing behind the guns in open order. The guns fired a few shots, and then suddenly the enemy opened fire from the hill on the left, which was only eight hundred and fifty yards away. Very soon fifteen out of the seventeen British gunners were wounded, so that the guns could no longer be worked. The Gordons by this time had reached the kopjes, and were about one hundred yards from the guns, the intervening space being in the enemy's line of fire. At this moment orders were signalled by the General in the rear, from Lord Roberts at Pretoria, telling General Smith-Dorrien to retire. The Colonel of the Gordons, reluctant to leave the guns to fall into the enemy's hands, sent up the teams of horses to fetch them, but the Boer bullets were raining around, and two of the horses were shot. Colonel Macbean then shouted for volunteers to fetch in the guns. Captains Younger, Gordon the Adjutant, and Allan called on the few men around. They ran out under heavy fire, and with the greatest difficulty they dragged back the gun along seventy yards of the way, but it would not even then have been saved if three more men had not run out and helped for the remaining thirty yards to the kopje. As it was, one of the men was hit only ten yards from the kopje, but he was got in all right. Captain Allan was now ordered away with his company to the left flank, where they were kept for the rest of the day, but Captain Younger, with several men, ran out to try and save the second gun. It was got in, but not before Captain Younger was shot dead."[12]

This incident is interesting, not only as a record of a gallant feat of arms, but also because this Captain Gordon who won the Victoria Cross was later on to command the Gordons in the present war, and unhappily to fall a prisoner with many of his men.

At the end of August Lord Roberts met Buller and French at Belfast. Botha, a very able general, and the future conqueror of German South-West Africa, was beaten at Middelburg, and this defeat added the Transvaal to the British Empire. The news that Kruger had fled to the Portuguese was another disappointment to the enemy, but their determination to resist the British was so strong that they refused to surrender, for a long time carrying on the unequal contest.

To return to the history of the Gordons in South Africa, the Volunteer companies assisted Buller against the Boers in Natal, and came into action against Botha. Throughout their engagements they acted up to the highest traditions of the Highland regiments. Early in September there was a dramatic and picturesque scene, when the two battalions of the Gordons came face to face. "The old 75th, with their Dargai laurels scarcely faded, were meeting the 92nd on a scene of victory amid mountains such as rear their heads in Aberdeen. For a few moments discipline was thrown to the winds, and questions were eagerly asked."

In due course the Highlanders were placed in block-houses throughout the country, and the pursuit of the Boers was mainly carried on by the mounted troops.

We must now turn very briefly to the fortunes of the other regiments of the Highland Brigade who, while the Gordons were at Thabanchu and elsewhere, were under the command of General Macdonald, and employed in driving the Boers out of the Orange River Colony. The months that followed were marked by ceaseless marching, interrupted by occasional conflict. De Wet was a constant menace, convoys must be escorted, bodies of Boers must be kept on the move, and occasionally—as on June 3, 1900, when De Wet captured 150 of the Black Watch—minor disasters occurred. At the same time, though their work was inglorious, it was invaluable, and every now and then some incident, such as the capture of Prinsloo with 5000 men and 5 guns, would break the monotony of their heavy tramping. "With half rations," says Cromb, "and muddy water as food and drink, they marched and fought and fought and marched through scorching hot days and bitter cold nights."

The concluding features of the war lay in the hands of Lord Kitchener, who, with his genius for organisation, set about building block-houses to link up great sections of the country and co-operate with the work of his mounted troops.

At last, in the beginning of June 1902, the long-looked-for peace came to Britain and Boer in South Africa. The Highland regiments had one and all suffered very hardly during the campaign, while none in the whole army had given more lavishly than the Gordons, who both in losses and honours attained a distinction as sad as it was honourable. They received five Victoria Crosses, losing 141 killed, 431 wounded, 12 captured, and 101 dead from disease.

It should be unnecessary, after a narrative recording the actions in which the Highland Brigade took part, to emphasise their gallantry and their untarnished prestige, but if any support for such a statement were required it would be in the tribute of Lord Roberts: "No words of mine can adequately describe their magnificent conduct during this long and trying campaign. We have only to look at the gallantry displayed by the Gordons at Elandslaagte, at the unflinching bravery of the Highland Brigade at Magersfontein, and at Paardeberg, to realise that the traditions of these regiments are nobly maintained."

CHAPTER XXVIII
THE GREATEST WAR
(1914-)

Thus only should it come, if come it must;

Not with a riot of flags or a mob-born cry,

But with a noble faith, a conscience high

And pure and proud as heaven, wherein we trust,

We who have fought for peace, have dared the thrust

Of calumny for peace, and watched her die,

Her scutcheons rent from sky to outraged sky

By felon hands, and trampled into the dust.

We fought for peace, and we have seen the law

Cancelled, not once, nor twice, by felon hands,

But shattered, again, again, and yet again.

We fought for peace. Now, in God's name, we draw

The sword, not with a riot of flags and bands,

But silence, and a mustering of men.

ALFRED NOYES.

Some day when the smoke has lifted from the battlefields of Europe and the tramp of feet has died away down the avenues of Time—when even such a war as this is falling into perspective, and order is disentangled from chaos—then will the story of the Highland regiments be told, and the great part they played in the cause of freedom and liberty become an inspiration for the years to come.

It would be a commonplace to repeat that there is something new and terrible about this conflict—that it resembles in no way the struggles of our earlier chapters. It is not merely the greatest war—the war of nations instead of armies,—it is the most inhuman war. In it none of the laws of the game have been practised. From the sack of Louvain to the wreck of the Lusitania the policy that has controlled the army and navy of the enemy has bowed neither to pity nor to good faith. In this colossal war, regiments, brigades, armies, even nations have been swallowed up into the dense confusion of ceaseless battle. Upon every frontier, every mountain pass, upon the water, under the water, and in the pure air of heaven the grim struggle is waged night and day. When great peoples sway to and fro in their millions the time has passed for speaking of individual battalions.

We have followed the fortunes of the Highland regiments in the days when war was the profession of soldiers. We have recorded the brilliant deeds of one regiment or another, or, on occasions, of one man. But all that has gone. Each regiment has taken to its colours a dozen or two dozen comrade regiments bearing its ancient name, and carrying on, unseen, its proud prestige. To-day the soldier belongs to no particular calling. From the clerk to the dock-labourer—all have become soldiers pro bono publico and pro patria. Every day, in some part of the far-flung battle line, deeds are being performed that we would have proudly recorded in those earlier chapters; day by day, death has been met by amateur soldiers with the unbroken steadiness of veteran troops.

All this is familiar. I only mention it to clear the way for what I am about to say. It is not yet possible to write in any detail concerning the Highland regiments, but at the same time, through the night of conflict some ray of light occasionally pierces—some incident, some letter, some fallen word, or act of bravery so splendid, shows like the faint tracing of feet upon the sand, the way that the Army has passed.

Never in the history of our nation has war been declared with such unanimity of opinion and such absence of idle demonstration. The honour of England was at stake. The neutrality of Belgium had been violated, and her people looked to England, whose word has ever been her bond. War was never less welcome, never less foreseen, but in a moment, once the inevitable burden was accepted, England laid down the things of peace to take up the business of war.

And in that hour of suspense a remarkable thing happened.

In the bitter humiliation of the South African War the Empire had not deserted the Motherland, but all had not been satisfied that the cause was good; in the grave struggle that was about to be opened with the greatest military tyranny in history, every freeman became a bondman in chains of patriotism to an ideal.

From Canada, Australia, New Zealand, India, South Africa, and the most isolated outposts of our great Empire, arose like the vast stirring of a sea, the salutation of the Colonies and Dependencies. Germany had relied upon conspiracy in India, instead of which the Princes and Chiefs were amongst the first to offer their services and their wealth. The following remarkable letter, written by an old Indian soldier to a young soldier at the front, was published in an English newspaper: "Praise be to the Guru. Your father Sundar Singh here writes a word to his dear son Sampuran Singh. It is meet for a young man to be in the battle, and on this account I am not taking thought. I am well and happy, and I pray to the Guru for your welfare and happiness. When you receive this letter answer it and relate to me the full conditions of the war.... Take no thought for your life in the battle, for it is right to fight for the King, and great glory will come to Hindustan, and the Sikhs, and fame to the regiment."

Germany had valued at nothing our amateur Colonial soldiery until their baffled forces reeled back before the charge of the Canadians at Ypres. In our own country, impoverished though many districts have been by emigration, the answer to Britain's summons was epic. In our Highlands and to those who know their history, it was such as to bring a lump to the throat. Long ago Sir Walter Scott wrote: "In too many instances the Highlands have been drained, not of their superfluity of population, but of the whole mass of the inhabitants, dispossessed by an unrelenting avarice which will one day be found to have been as short-sighted as it is selfish and unjust. Meantime, the Highlands may become the fairy ground for romance and poetry, or the subject of experiment for the professors of speculation, historical and economical. But, if the hour of need should come, the pibroch may sound through the deserted region, but the summons will remain unanswered."

The summons has not remained unanswered. The Highland regiments have been doubled and quadrupled, while from over the seas the Highlanders have come back under Canadian Colours. There is not a man with the old Celtic fire who has not, if he were able, delivered a blow for the sake of the women and children of Belgium. Why did they come? "Me no muckle to fight for?" said Edie Ochiltree, the old beggar. "Isna there the country to fight for, and the burn-sides that I gang daundering beside, and the hearths o' the gudewives that gie me my bit bread, and the bits o' weans that come toddling to play wi' me when I come about a landward town?"

The swift progress of the German advance guard upon Belgium, the fall of Liége and Namur, and the horrors that befell the Belgian peasantry, brought one thing home to us very painfully, and that was the need for a large army. What was done was done quickly. Lord Kitchener was given a free hand to raise new armies, and until these should be trained he relied upon our Regulars, Territorials, and the drafts of troops from Canada and India to withstand the German arms. It was more than a handful of men should have been asked to do. What concerns us is how they did it. The German advance came on swiftly, relentlessly; and in the darkness of a summer night, without confusion, without a qualm, our little advance guard crossed the Channel.

It is certain that amongst the first to cross to France were the Argyll and Sutherland Highlanders, the Black Watch, the Camerons, the Seaforths, and the Gordons. An eye-witness of those early days has written: "Hurrying into Boulogne, I was in time to see the Argyll and Sutherlands marching through the streets of the town to the camps which had been prepared for them upon the neighbouring hills. The population of Boulogne rushed to the unaccustomed sound of the bagpipes, and it was through lines of the old Boulonnais fishwives, who had that morning bade tearful farewell to their fisher-sons off to the depot, that our men stepped gaily along, with a cheery grin and a smile for the words of welcome shouted out to them."[13]

The Highland regiments took part in the retreat from Mons, the most terrible in history, and throughout that awful action, when officers could not ride their horses for fear of sleeping and falling to the ground, when fighting never ceased for days on end, and our soldiers held at bay a German force many times their superior in numbers—the Highlanders fought sternly, heroically, giving way with an utter disdain for their own safety, and a longing for the day when the retreat would end.

The unconquerable British Infantry have never displayed the qualities of dogged endurance so finely as in that eventful rearguard action. The Germans could neither outflank, pierce, nor crush the thin khaki line. It was the supreme test of a veteran regular army. It is of interest to recall that, on his return from the march to Kandahar, Lord Roberts, at the Mansion House, stated that he would never have undertaken the risk of covering 300 miles of country unless he had been accompanied by veteran troops. "The characteristics of young soldiers," he said, "are to win a winning game; to attack with dash where success seems probable; or even to stand up to superior forces where courage has not been damped by previous reverses and faith in their leader remains unimpaired. Under such conditions they may even surpass their older comrades. But in times of danger and panic, when the bugle sounds the Retire, when everything seems to be going against us, and when danger can only be avoided by order and presence of mind; then it is that the old soldier element becomes of incalculable value; without it a commander would indeed be badly off."

The Argyll and Sutherlands Entering Boulogne August 1914

During the retreat from Mons the Highland regiments lost very heavily in officers and men, and amongst them there fell the Master of Burleigh, a very gallant and popular officer in the Argyll and Sutherlands. "He was too brave for anything," related a Highlander, "he simply wanted to be at 'em, and at 'em he went. I don't know where his sword was, but he hadn't it when I saw him—he had a rifle with the bayonet fixed, just like the rest of us. I saw him at the time he was wounded, and he just fought on gamely till he and his party of brave fellows were cut off and surrounded."

We learn that the Camerons were in close touch with the Black Watch at Mons, and at one point in the retreat when the 42nd were in danger of being surrounded, the 17th Battery R.F.A. and the Camerons staved off an outflanking movement of the Germans.

The 1st battalion of the Gordons were practically annihilated in their first battle. For long they had the melancholy reputation of being the most badly hit regiment in the Army, until Neuve Chapelle and the losses of the Cameronians and the Seaforths, while in the first week in February 1915 the Black Watch fared no better.

The battle of the Aisne inflicted heavy casualties on the Highlanders, particularly the Black Watch, losses which after the battle of the Marne brought the following unforgettable tribute from Sir John French: "The Black Watch—a name we know so well—have always played a distinguished part in the battles of our country. You have many well-known honours on your colours, of which you are naturally proud, but you will feel as proud of the honours which will be added to your colours after this campaign. At the battle of the Marne you distinguished yourselves. They say that the Jaegers of the German Guard ceased to exist after that battle. I expect they did. You have followed your officers, and stuck to the line against treble your numbers in a manner deserving the highest praise. I, as Commander-in-Chief of this Force, thank you, but that is a small matter—your country thanks you and is proud of you. The Russians have won great victories, but you, by holding back the Germans, have won great victories as well, as if you had not done this the Russians could not have achieved their successes. I am very glad of this opportunity of addressing you, and thanking you personally for your splendid work."

One member of the battalion has written: "We lost heavily in taking up position, and the men were saddened by the loss of so many officers.... Then later, the men had to deplore the loss of their commanding officer, Colonel Grant Duff—one of the bravest and best officers the regiment ever had. He died bravely. He was hard pressed, and doing execution with one of his men's rifles when he fell with a mortal wound."

The melancholy fate of one battalion of the Gordons has yet to be revealed, but from various accounts there is little doubt that in the confusion of the swift retreat, and the overwhelming force of the Germans, the message for a withdrawal did not reach them, and acting up to the gallantry of their records, they and their distinguished Colonel remained at their posts until surrender was the only course left to them.

The battles of the Marne and the Aisne were the turning of the scales before the German retirement. On September 13 Colonel Bradford of the Seaforths was killed. One account of his end runs: "It was in the battle of the Aisne, when the Seaforths had taken up a position near a wood, that the Germans began a heavy fire. The Colonel was standing with two other officers surveying the field of operations, when he was struck by a shell and killed instantly."

Another affecting passage runs: "We laid him with two other officers to rest on their field of honour, on a hill-side overlooking a valley of the river. It was a sad but glorious moment for us to stand and hear the padre tell us that they had not shrunk from their duty, and had fallen for the sake of their comrades. The next day I found some Scotch thistles growing close by, and I plucked the blooms to form a cross over the dead chieftain's grave."

A doctor who was appointed to the Seaforths has recorded: "At present (on the Aisne) we are entrenched. Our first day in this place, where we have been for five days, was awful, for we were under fire the whole of the day, with practically no protection, and our total of killed and wounded amounted to seventy. The men never wavered, and gaps were always filled. Grand are the Highland men, and grander still will be the account they will render; I am lucky to be with such men."

What simple words, and yet what a tale of sacrifice and heroism lies behind them. Well might General Sir H. Smith-Dorrien write from the front to the Soldiers' and Sailors' Families Association: "Never has an army been called on to engage in such desperate fighting as is of daily occurrence in the present war, and never have any troops behaved so magnificently as our soldiers in this war. The stories of the battle of Mons and Le Cateau are only beginning to be known, but at them a British force not only held its own against a German army four times its own size, but it hit the enemy so hard that never were they able to do more than follow it up. Of course our troops had to fall back before them, an operation which would demoralise most armies. Not so with ours, however; though they naturally did not like retiring for twelve successive days, they merely fell sullenly back, striking hard whenever attacked, and the moment the order came to go forward there were smiling faces everywhere. Then followed the battles of the Marne and the Aisne. Tell the women that all these great battles have, day by day, witnessed countless feats of heroism and brave fighting. Large numbers will be given Victoria Crosses and Distinguished Conduct Medals, but many more have earned them, for it has been impossible to bring every case to notice. Tell the women that proud as I am to have such soldiers under my command, they should be prouder still to be near and dear relations to such men."

About this time the 2nd Highland Light Infantry lost a gallant young officer in Sir Archibald Gibson-Craig. He bravely offered to lead his platoon against a German machine gun that was doing considerable damage amongst our men. At the head of his Highlanders he fell, but the gun was taken, and another hero added to the long list of those who counted death less than life. Upon the same day Private Wilson of the same battalion won the V.C. for capturing, single-handed, a German machine gun and killing six of the enemy. Very fortunate have the 2nd H.L.I. been, and very richly have they deserved such honours. Upon November 11, for relieving a dangerous situation, Captain Brodie of the same regiment was awarded the V.C.

In October Lieutenant Brooke of the 2nd Gordon Highlanders was awarded the Victoria Cross for gallantry, and Drummer Kenny of the 2nd Gordons the V.C. for rescuing wounded men under fire.

Sir Arthur Conan Doyle has truly said that "from October 25 to the second week in November Sir John French and Sir Douglas Haig were like engineers holding up a dam of water visibly giving way." The great German advance towards Calais established the most critical situation of the war, and the ultimate success of our troops at the battle of Ypres, when 150,000 British and Indians withstood 600,000 Germans, will some day be proclaimed as the most brilliant achievement in our military history.

In the first great battle at Ypres the Highland regiments were supported by their comrade battalions of the Territorials. In this desperate rush for Calais, when the Germans came flocking onwards like ants upon the side of a hill, when opposed to them was an army vastly inferior in numbers, things looked desperate indeed. The headquarters of General Haig were blown up, and when General French reached the British lines a retirement of four miles had taken place. He motored from one spot to another, propping up, as it were, this heroic handful of men. The British fought doggedly, watching their regiments rent to tatters, calling up every man, even the cooks, to take a hand. Cavalry and infantry, officers and men fought till they could fight no more. But the tide was turning, and when night fell upon the 31st of October the grand attack was beaten off. Of the losses of our soldiers and our brave Highlanders some estimate may be made by the casualties of individual regiments, one of which entered the battle with 1100 men and came out with only 73, and another which numbered 1350 returned only 300 strong.

On November 15 the Prussian Guard, the finest body of men in the German army, advanced under the eyes of the Kaiser to wrench the road to Calais from the British. They were met by the English Guards, by the hard-fighting Highlanders, by the English fine regiments, by Irishmen, Welshmen, and our gallant Indian soldiers—and they were held until their dead lay eight deep.

These actions at Ypres were costly in casualties—50,000 out of 120,000; they were beyond all price in glory and honour.

The coming of winter, and the construction of trenches, brought with it a state of stalemate that was to last without a decisive offensive until the spring of 1915.

During those long dreary months we were not idle. Our new armies were in hard training, our war manufactories were making equipment, but unfortunately not enough shells, and our Navy was carrying on its imperishable vigil upon the sea, and under the sea, without which our Empire would cease to exist and our Army would be cut off by twenty miles of water.

The Highland regiments settled down with their customary fortitude to the weary months of trench warfare, months that brought daily losses in officers and men, bitter cold, and ceaseless rain, while overhead screamed and broke the German shell fire.

Never have troops been called upon to endure such a prolonged strain. On land and on sea, in patience and good temper, our soldiers and sailors held on without a murmur.

Of the actual fighting there is little to tell, for little is known. The monotony of trench warfare was broken by occasional frays and night attacks. A Seaforth writes on October 20: "We were digging trenches when we heard a volley of rifle fire come right over us, and we got the order to stand to arms and advance. Their trenches were situated in a row on a rise in a field, and we could not get our range on them. In a minute the signal to charge went, and we all scrambled up the hill to get at them. The first to get up was one company officer, and he was hit. We all dived into their trenches at the point of their rifles, shooting and stabbing, and then came the onslaught. Some of them were too terrified to get out, whilst others rushed out and were shot down, and the remainder sought refuge in a house.... About fifty surrendered. I am proud to say that we were only one company. I shall never forget that charge as long as I live. The General said, 'Bravo, Seaforths! It was a grand charge.'"

A Frenchman has recorded his impressions of a Highland regiment taking part in an advance. "Resolutely," he writes, "they crossed what had seemed impossible ground. They seemed to do it, too, without sustaining very much loss, and fixing bayonets, they made straight for the German gunners. They charged to the shrill sound of the bagpipes. They charged like heroes of Walter Scott, with their ribboned bonnets and their dancers' skirts. Neither ditch nor barbed wire could stop them. Their dash carried them right into the midst of the Prussian batteries. Shooting the gunners at their posts, they rendered the guns unserviceable, and having completed their daring mission, prepared to retire."

The French Nord de la France is no less emphatic in its praise. "The British soldier," it says, speaking of an advance of the Highlanders under a murderous fire, "is wonderful. He is a slave to duty. For him to retreat he must be ordered to do so, and these Scotsmen were prepared to give their lives to the last man."

Speaking of a charge in December a Gordon Highlander has written: "I reckon it was one of the fiercest fights that the 'Gay Gordons' took part in, and as usual the good old regiment covered itself with glory. A certain General and officers who had witnessed the famous Dargai charge told us it was ridiculous compared with that of December 14."

From January 25 to February 7 the actions at Givenchy and La Bassée took place, and were followed by a brief lull, with an outbreak of fighting at Ypres upon February 14.

On March 10 the operations that were to develop into the battle of Neuve Chapelle and St. Eloi commenced. It was the beginning of the great offensive, which, so long looked for, was to fail so dismally owing to the need for shells, and the German use of poisonous gases. It resulted in the taking of two miles of German trenches, and the killing and capture of 8000 of the enemy. In this action our soldiers drove the enemy from their trenches, and after heavy losses resisted all attempts to evict them.

All through the preceding night our troops had marched to their positions, and with the breaking of day our artillery began to bombard the German trenches. A hundred heavy guns spoke with one prolonged roar, the field guns joined in, the whole British artillery was concentrated upon the enemy. No trenches could stand such a destructive fire.

Forty minutes later the advance began and the village of Neuve Chapelle was carried at the point of the bayonet.

It was in the rush upon the trenches that the Middlesex, faced by unbroken barbed wire, were mown down in scores and hundreds. Helplessly they tore at the entanglement—in silence they died rather than retreat.

Following that came the attack upon the German position, and in this advance were the 2nd Gordon Highlanders and their Territorial battalion the 6th. It was in this action that Lieutenant-Colonel Maclean of the 6th Gordons lost his life. To a subaltern who went to his assistance he said, "Thank you, and now, my boy, your place is not here. Go about your duty."

The battle of Neuve Chapelle was finely conceived, and more finely carried out. Most unfortunately, owing to the lack of reserves at the height of the engagement, the full force of the attack was spent too soon.

The story of how the Canadians fought and died at the second battle of Ypres upon April 22, and how the comrade regiment of the Royal Highlanders brought immortal honour to the North, is a tale of four days' heroism against unnatural and horrible odds.

Mr. J. Huntley Skrine has written somewhere:

Sons in my gates of the West,

Where the long tides foam in the dark of the pine,

And the cornlands crowd to the dim sky-line,

And wide as the air are the meadows of kine,

What cheer from my gates of the West?

What indeed! Nothing less than death rather than defeat. Whatever the Canadians might be, they were not veteran soldiers. The Canadian Division numbered doctors, lawyers, farmers, with a sprinkling of men who had seen service in the South African War. Let us see how they faced the German onslaught.

The use of asphyxiating gas compelled the French, who held the left of the Canadians, to retire. In consequence of this the Canadian left flank was moved southward. During the night the Canadians carried a wood in the teeth of heavy machine-gun fire, continuing the conflict till dawn. In the morning, to relieve their left they launched a counter attack upon the German trenches. Over the open space the Canadian battalions rushed. Colonel Burchill, the commanding officer, fell at the head of his men, and with a shout of rage they reached the trenches, and drove the enemy out. Our Colonials had not merely preserved their left—they had pierced the German line.

Upon the same day a new cloud of gas reached the Canadian Highlanders. It is recorded that they remained unshaken. But their very bravery sealed their fate. The Germans slipped across their left and isolated the wood from St. Julien. In this wood the remnants of the Canadian battalions, disdaining surrender, fought to the last round and the last man. The gallantry of the officers of the Royal Highlanders of Montreal was wonderful—so magnificent as to call forth the highest praise. The name of Canada rang throughout the Empire. In a moment of awful peril she had sacrificed her bravest for the sake of Britain.

In the Canadian retreat not a gun was lost.

Upon May 9 it is recorded that the 1st Black Watch got the order to advance upon the German trenches. Already several attempts to carry them had failed. The English soldiers helped them upon the parapets of our trenches and wished them good luck. Bayonets were already fixed, the pipers struck up the famous tune, 'Highland Laddie.' That was the first time in the war in which the 42nd had charged with their pipes. There was only 300 yards to go, but it is said that ere that distance was covered the sound of the pipes was hushed in death. The grand old regiment cleared the Germans out of their trenches, and held them for long in the face of a heavy artillery attack, only withdrawing upon an order from the General. The following extracts are taken from the enemy's Press: The Frankfurter Zeitung, after describing the French attack on May 9, says: "Then the British came into action with tremendous fierceness. They would break through, cost what it might. They attacked in three lines. The front regiment was mowed down by our fearful fire, and the following regiment, under a terrible hail from the guns, was unable to advance. Then the British sent one of their best Highland regiments to the front, the best they have anywhere. The Black Watch advanced. The gallant Scots came on, but even their really heroic bravery was in vain, for they were not able to turn the fate of the day."

The Deutsche Tageszeitung says: "The British advanced with extraordinary force. They had in action about a division, and called upon them to advance in three lines. After the first line had been thrown back with fearful losses, the second line could not advance. The élite regiment, the Scottish Black Watch, was called forward, and bled to death without having obtained anything. Two men actually reached our breastworks, and had to lie in front of them from five in the evening until six the next morning before we could look after them."

Between May and July there was no sustained activity upon the Western Front, but on many other parts of the Allies' vast campaign the ceaseless struggle proceeded. Italy was pressing onwards towards the Austrian line while Sir Ian Hamilton was endeavouring to retrieve the initial blunder at the Dardanelles. Russia was fighting tooth and nail her amazing rearguard action, retreating victoriously, relinquishing at a terrible cost territory already stripped and barren. It was the beginning of the great retreat. Warsaw fell upon August 5, and a month later the Czar took over the supreme command, and the Grand Duke Nicholas left for the Caucasus.

In July came the news of our first great British victory, a victory the more welcome as it was won by General Botha, whose strategical skill and courage we had learned to admire in the Boer War. Despite the plotting of De Wet and Beyers, Kemp and Maritz, Botha had overcome disloyalty amongst the dissatisfied burghers, and followed it up by the complete rout of the Germans in South-West Africa.

With the month of August one year of bloodshed was reached, and looking over the wide field of hostilities there were those who asked what had been accomplished in return for precious lives lost upon a hundred fields of strife. Our casualties numbered 330,000, while the loss of life amongst our brave Allies had been enormous. Russia was no nearer Berlin than at the commencement of the war, France was no nearer the frontier of Belgium, England had not stormed the Dardanelles.

On the other hand, the Allied Armies were growing stronger, and the German armies weaker; the scales were turning. Time was upon the side of the Allies, and the greatest victory of the past year was won by no array of arms, but by the sleepless vigilance of the British Navy. It was a struggle between an invincible Army and an invincible Navy, and unless some unforeseen catastrophe overwhelmed the Allied Armies the issue lay in the hands of Great Britain.

To return to the Highland regiments, there were many individual acts of heroism during those summer months that should be recorded.

On May 9 the Black Watch won two V.C.'s for magnificent bravery under fire—Private John Lynn working a machine gun until he was overcome by gas poisoning, to which he fell a victim, and Corporal John Bridley leading a few Highlanders against the enemy's trenches, and maintaining his position.

Upon June 12 at Givenchy, Lance-Corporal William Angus of the Highland Light Infantry won the V.C. for rescuing a wounded officer under heavy fire, sustaining some forty wounds from bombs.

In the middle of June at Hooge, the Liverpool Scottish, a Territorial battalion second to none, advanced against the German trenches, supported by the H.A.C. The plan of attack was that the Scottish should take the first line of German trenches, and leaving the H.A.C. to hold them should advance upon the second line. Following the cannonade of our guns, the Scottish leapt over the parapets and charged into the curtain of smoke. The first trench was carried without a halt, the second fell immediately after, and pausing to take a breath the battalion captured the third after severe fighting, and faced the fourth. This, too, was carried. What need for comment when words are blinded by achievement!

Many gallant men fell, including Captain Graham, the great amateur golfer. Unhappily a sorrowful toll of lives must ever be the fruit of bravery and self-sacrifice.

It is difficult where heroism has become a commonplace, and courage inseparable from the nature of the task that lies behind us and in the future, to conclude this chapter and this book upon a note at once comprehensive and mature, a note that will not sound dim when other tales are told, nor sufficiently local to be overshadowed by some vast offensive.

With the battle of Festubert certainly one, and perhaps two stories of Scottish heroism will, in my opinion, be for ever sacred in Scottish hearts.

Nothing could be more forlorn, more Celtic in tragedy than the tale of the 4th Cameron Highlanders, whose night attack was checked by a deep ditch full of water. Some swam across, many sank never to rise again, but the battalion passed on. In the black darkness they struggled on, undaunted. A desolating fire raked their ranks. One company was annihilated, another was hopelessly lost, a third took a German trench. But the battalion was cut off. No machine guns could cross the stream to their support, and in the grey dawn the situation for the Gaelic remnant grew intolerable. The company in the German trench were forced to retire under a heavy fire. Colonel Fraser and twelve other officers had fallen. But that single company of Camerons were unbroken. Sergeant-Major Ross it was who gathered the remnants to him and brought them safely across the zone of fire. Never has a more hopeless withdrawal faced a British force. Never has a finer fortitude awaited it.

Again, in the British advance a detachment of the Scots Guards lost touch with the main body, and were surrounded. Admirably has Mr. John Buchan spoken of their end. "For them," he says, "as for the steel circle around the King at Flodden, there could be no retreat. When, some days later, we took the place we found the Guards lying on the field of honour with swaths of the enemy's dead around them. The history of war can show no more noble ending."

It is with such pictures as these that I would close this chapter, pictures of courage and self-sacrifice unsurpassed in the story of our regiments. Whatever the future may hold, one thing is certain—victory must always greet men inspired by a cause that is at once noble and just.

For while the tired waves, vainly breaking,

Seem here no painful inch to gain,

Far back, through creeks and inlets making,

Comes silent, flooding in, the main.

And not by eastern windows only,

When daylight comes, comes in the light;

In front the sun climbs slow, how slowly!

But westward, look the land is bright.